HEALING IS A
CHOICE

Other Books by Stephen Arterburn

Every Man's Battle

Every Young Woman's Battle

The God of Second Chances

Avoiding Mr. Wrong

Finding Mr. Right

Lose It for Life

Feeding Your Appetites

Every Man, God's Man

Flashpoints

The Seven Keys to Spiritual Renewal

Boiling Point

Can't Live With 'Em, Can't Live Without 'Em

The Secrets Men Keep

Walking Into Walls

The Encounter

Is This the One?

The Exceptional Life

HEALING IS A
CHOICE

Ten Decisions That Will Transform Your Life
& Ten Lies That Can Prevent You From Making Them

Revised and Updated

Stephen Arterburn, M. Ed.

Healing Is a Choice Workbook

Stephen Arterburn, M. Ed.
with Bill Martin

THOMAS NELSON
Since 1798

NASHVILLE   DALLAS   MEXICO CITY   RIO DE JANEIRO

Published in Nashville, Tennessee, by Thomas Nelson, Inc.

Thomas Nelson, Inc. books may be purchased in bulk for educational, business, fund-raising, or sales promotional use. For information, please e-mail SpecialMarkets@ ThomasNelson.com.

Scripture quotations noted MSG are from *The Message* by Eugene H. Peterson. © 1993, 1994, 1995, 1996, 2000. Used by permission of NavPress Publishing Group. All rights reserved.

Scripture quotations noted NLT are from the *Holy Bible*, NEW LIVING TRANSLATION, © 1996, 2004, 2007. Used by permission of Tyndale House Publishers, Inc., Wheaton, Illinois 60189. All rights reserved.

Scripture quotations marked NKJV are taken from the NEW KING JAMES VERSION®. © 1982 by Thomas Nelson, Inc. Used by permission. All rights reserved.

Scripture quotations marked NIV are taken from the Holy Bible, New International Version®, NIV®. © 1973, 1978, 1984 by Biblica, Inc.™ Used by permission of Zondervan. All rights reserved worldwide. www.zondervan.com

The "NIV" and "New International Version" trademarks are registered in the United States Patent and Trademark Office by International Bible Society. Use of either trademark requires the permission of International Bible Society.

Scripture quotations noted NASB are taken from THE NEW AMERICAN STANDARD BIBLE®, © The Lockman Foundation 1960, 1962, 1963, 1968, 1971, 1972, 1973, 1975, 1977, 1995. Used by permission. (www.Lockman.org)

Scripture quotations noted KJV are taken from the King James Version. Public domain.

ISBN 978-0-7852-3243-8 (revised)

Library of Congress Cataloging-in-Publication Data

Arterburn, Stephen, 1953–
    Healing is a choice : ten decisions that will transform your life & ten lies that can prevent you from making them / Stephen Arterburn.
        p. cm.
    ISBN 978-0-7852-1226-3 (hardcover)
    ISBN 978-0-7852-8846-6 (tradepaper)
    ISBN 0-7852-8351-X (ie)
    1. Spiritual healing. 2. Decision-making—Religious aspects—Christianity.
    3. Errors, Popular. I. Title.
BT732.5.A76 2005
248.8'6—dc22   2005007059

Printed in the United States of America

HB 04.30.2021

To Aunt Mary and Uncle Charles

This book is dedicated to two of the most wonderful people on this planet, my Aunt Mary and Uncle Charles. Mary is a healer of wounds and a lifter of spirits. She always has a kind word that I believe in many cases comes directly from the Lord. I admired her when I was young because of her beauty and her amazing ability to defeat the toughest of opponents in tennis. As I grew older she stayed connected to me, congratulating me on accomplishments and consoling me in the midst of tragedy. At the height of my young rebellion, she never let go, always spurring me on to good things. She has become a legend in the world of Women of Faith and New Life Live. When I mention her name, the most devoted know exactly who I am talking about.

Aunt Mary is married to one of the finest, most honorable men I have ever known, Uncle Charles. He has used his wisdom in the world of business and numbers to help my mother after the death of my dad. But more than that, he has poured out his kindness and love in quiet and gentle ways, never seeking to be the center of attention or to call attention to himself at all. The world needs more people like Uncle Charles.

Together they have blessed me and our family with kindness, wisdom, and guidance. We watched as they raised two remarkable women, Patty and Lynn, who are both shining results of quality parents and smart decisions.

The dedication of this book to you is a small nod compared to the large contribution you have made to my life. Thank you for being who you are and sharing all that you are with me and our family.

Contents

Preface

THIS BOOK WAS ORIGINALLY PUBLISHED IN 2005, AND THERE have been many changes, developments, and new insights since its publication. Before I wrote *Healing Is a Choice* I was a strong advocate for marriage, and I believed that no matter what, the first response to marital problems and even betrayal needs to be steps toward reconciliation and saving the marriage. I am more convinced than ever that even in the case of betrayal, reconciliation needs to be the first focus when a marriage is broken apart.

I knew God hated divorce, but I did not fully understand many of the reasons until I went through it myself. The pain of it all is more intense than I ever imagined, and that pain lasts much longer than I had expected. It is not totally out of my system yet, even years later. It lingers deep in my heart, and no matter how effectively I grieve, I suspect that there will be some painful residue for the rest of my life.

My pain is probably nothing compared to what my daughter Madeline has gone through over these past ten years. She has handled it better than most could. She graduated from high school having never experimented with alcohol and drugs and without succumbing to other temptations or possible rebellions. Her soccer coaches awarded her the Coach's Award for her character. They hailed her as a role model on the field and off. I could not be more proud of how she has chosen to live her life. She made it onto the soccer team at Azusa Pacific University, where she is currently a sophomore. She has not played as much as she did in high school, but her coach has also used her as an example of someone with an amazing work ethic and who does not give up. She not only works hard on the soccer field but makes As and Bs as a result of her disciplined study habits. I don't know how she does it, but no matter what the adversity she finds a way to adjust to it and excel in some way.

I went from having one daughter at the time of this book's first release to now being the father of five. In addition to Madeline I have two "bonus boys," James and Carter, who were my wife Misty's boys before we married. They are great blessings to me, and I love our relationships and look forward to the years ahead with them. They are bright, handsome, and equipped with great senses of humor.

We then added a son, Solomon Russell, who is four and a half, bright and fun, and fascinating to parent. And Solomon has a sister, two-year-old Amelia Pearl, who is sweet and gentle but equipped with an inner truck driver who knows what she does or does not want. All of these children are unique blessings to me and proof that there is life after divorce.

I have found peace with my past and have found happiness in my marriage to Misty and as a father of five, but none of this has changed my view of divorce. It is horrible and should be avoided if at all possible. Stay together for the sake of the kids, or the dogs, or God, or whatever you can use as an excuse to stay together and work on a new relationship.

While I have a new life and a rewarding life, it has been forever changed by divorce. The divorce stole a decade of my life. It was a decade of pain, insecurity, and loss. The money paid to attorneys and accountants was necessary but wiped out almost all of my savings and investments—and those costs are still mounting.

I have borne other losses and adjustments, but one thing that has not changed is God's presence, unconditional love, and provision in my life. I have healed and recovered and now enjoy helping others pick up the pieces of their lives, no matter what they have lost or been through.

My pain led to this book, and this book has produced study groups literally around the world. I've received e-mails and letters from those who have thanked me for a path to healing and have told me of their own restoration. What a privilege to be part of their stories. Just two days ago, a woman told me of being in a *Healing Is a Choice* group where thirteen years of lost memories of abuse seemed to return to her. She and her husband are now successfully dealing with those memories, and the healing continues. Others have found hope for a future they had lost hope for. I am so grateful I did not hide this embarrassing and humiliating part of my life.

———

At the end of this book is an affirmation. I challenge readers to read it every day for forty days and let me know the results. So far the results have been sensational. It is not a cure-all—people still need to connect, grieve, and forgive—but the affirmation points them toward priorities and realities and away from trivialities and fears that incapacitate them. I hope you will take the forty-day challenge when you finish this book.

There is a fine line in finding a future after divorce and divorcing to find a future. I had no choice in my divorce, but I have found a future beyond it. You can find a future beyond whatever pain—of any kind—that you're experiencing too. I remain on a mission of loving and helping people transform their lives from emptiness and despair to fulfillment and hope. I hope that is what you will find by reading this book. Healing is a choice, or it is many tough choices, and the results are worth the pain.

Thank you for picking up this new edition with the workbook included. I pray that you will experience a major change in your life and that you will experience God's presence in the midst of the transformation.

INTRODUCTION

The Choice to Heal Your Life

AT ONE TIME OR ANOTHER, EVERY HUMAN BEING NEEDS healing. The type of healing needed will differ depending on who the person is, and his or her circumstances. In every instance, healing is a choice in which God and man are involved. Healing is a choice; it is God's choice. Also, there is a human side to the matter—there are choices we can make to ensure we experience whatever healing God, in His eternal purpose, has for us. Ultimately, however, we must remember the Creator of the universe is also the Healer of His universe. He is the ultimate decision maker as to how, when, and from whom we receive healing.

Surely God must love healing since He allows so much of it to occur every day. He created our bodies with healing properties within us. A cut finger, in most cases, heals itself. There has to be something severely wrong with a person for a cut not to heal on its own. A broken limb has the ability to fuse back together. The cold virus is defeated and destroyed by the healing ability within our own bodies. Healing goes on all around us and within us. It is a miraculous ability that every person possesses to some degree or another. Although God has given us healing abilities, we can impair that process. Sadly, the ability to heal emotionally, spiritually, or physically has been destroyed or weakened for some. A physical wound must be cleaned and medicated rather than ignored. Emotional and spiritual wounds also need attention. They don't just simply fade away.

Disrupted Healing

When my brother, Jerry, contracted AIDS, I was an eyewitness to what happens when a body's ability to heal is weakened. As Jerry's body grew weaker from the disease, his immune system could not ward off the attacks by numerous viruses and germs. The inner lining of his esophagus became full of infection. His mouth and throat swarmed with organisms that most of our bodies are able to destroy. His skin was marked by rashes and lesions resulting from an almost-daily new infection moving in.

Each new day could bring a surprise disease that none of us had heard of before. As my family watched disease upon disease riddle his body, we marveled at just how hard our bodies must be working to protect us, and how strong they are to push back so many diseases that could destroy us. We mourned as we watched Jerry withering away to nothing because he no longer had the ability to heal from within. With the miracle of healing completely destroyed, my handsome and talented brother died at the age of thirty-three. God chose not to heal him physically, but emotionally and spiritually his last days were some of his healthiest times on earth.

Jerry could not make the decision to heal the AIDS virus. He decided to take the best medications available, but they were not perfected, and most people taking them did not live too long. He changed his diet to give himself the best possible chance of a physical healing. He also went to a healing service. Nothing stopped the disease from destroying his physical body, but there was a healing within his soul. The angry and defiant brother I had known found peace with God and peace with this world.

It was a miraculous transformation. My brother chose to heal; the sicker his physical body became, the more he chose to heal spiritually. He even reached out to others who were struggling alone with no visitors. He served up his affliction to help others, and when he died, he died a fulfilled man. He realized that from his book, *How Will I Tell My Mother?*, and television appearances he had reached more people, touched more lives, and made a bigger difference than if he had lived out a normal life span. He saw the affliction as a gift and experienced healing of the soul.

My brother chose to heal; the sicker his physical body became, the more he chose to heal spiritually.

BEYOND PHYSICAL HEALING

The properties of healing are not found just within our bodies. They are also present in our minds and souls. God provided us with the ability to heal from emotional trauma and tragedy. When we lose someone we love, we are devastated; we mourn and grieve while wondering if our days will ever be full of light again. Our souls are sick from the loss of the love and from the pain that at times seems too much to endure.

As our grieving progresses, we start to have a portion of a good day, and then a whole day or two good days come together. We start to sense a change from our constant agony and know that at some level, healing is taking place. In a year or two, if all goes well, we look back and see just how far we have come; just how much healing has taken place. God built that emotional and spiritual healing ability into most of us. If the ability to heal were not there, loss after loss, piling pain on top of pain, would so overwhelm us that we could not continue. We would lose our minds and could not go on. Almost everyone is fortunate to have the ability within to heal from hurts, rather than to be destroyed by them.

A few years ago I discovered just how fortunate I was that this ability to heal was available to me.

THE BEGINNING OF THE END

Everything in my world changed while waiting to board a flight to Colorado Springs for a dinner with a wonderful ministry couple, John and Lisa Bevere. Lisa, author of such books as *Kissed the Girls and Made Them Cry*, was a writer who had helped women—young and old—with her authentic style and deep wisdom. John had written a book that I found to be remarkable and that had caused me to make a reservation for dinner with strangers. So I was on my way to Colorado Springs to meet with the Beveres.

I was one of the last to board the plane. As I stood on the ramp, just about to walk through the curved doorway into the plane, my phone rang. I flipped it open, put it to my ear, said hello, and after a short conversation said good-bye to the life I had known. My life completely changed in an instant—nothing would ever be the same again. I will sum it up by saying it was during that call that I discovered my wife, Sandy, and I were going to be divorced. Although this book is not about my divorce and subsequent recovery, I can't write about suffering and healing without telling about a portion of my journey back from the depths of despair.

People often say they felt numb at difficult times in their lives. There was nothing numb about this experience. My stomach began to ache; my face flushed as a thick, dark curtain seemed to close inside my mind. I was dizzy and nauseated as I fell into my seat. The plane's door slammed shut behind me, and I began to breathe heavily to keep myself calm. I once had experienced a panic attack and feared the embarrassment of another attack. I did what I could to keep it together. I began to repeat what I did not believe yet: "You're going to be okay. You're going to be okay. You're going to be okay."

Tears began to tumble into my lap as I turned toward the window to prevent anyone from seeing me—I was a mess. I felt trapped and wanted to run, but it was too late. We were already taxiing out to the runway. I needed to talk to someone, but I was shut off from everyone. Anger, dread, fear, and disgust swept through me as never before.

The ugly reality of divorce began to sink in as I imagined the catastrophe of the outcome. I hurt for our daughter, Madeline, and how this would cause her unimaginable pain. I was certain I had written my last book and that everything else I loved doing was over. It was the most painful plane ride of my life; I have never felt so alone in such close proximity to so many people. As I sat there, alone and terrified, I began to think back over the twenty years of marriage that had culminated in this horrific moment.

HISTORY OF PAIN

Not all of our marriage was miserable. There were some very good times, great adventures, and a few sweet moments, such as our adoption of Madeline. None of the good, however, pushed away the growing darkness. We each had our problems, and our conflicts were never resolved, mistakes were never forgiven, and hurts were relived day after day. Small cuts and scrapes in our relationship did not heal as they seemed to in others' relationships, but became infected and ravaged our lives. Almost every day was full of dread and of dodging conflict.

Numerous marriage counselors did little or nothing for us—each experience was more frustrating than the previous one. I was a broken man, but I did what I knew to keep the marriage going. I was far from perfect, made many mistakes, but was willing to do anything I could to have a marriage we both could enjoy and to have the family our daughter needed and deserved. The last marriage counselor had seen some hope. Just a few days before, she had told me that she thought Sandy had finally made peace with our marriage. The counselor felt we would be able to have an enjoyable marriage that would last, even though it would most likely not ever be a great marriage. She could not have been more wrong.

I was about to become a divorced writer who wrote about relationships; a divorced radio talk show host whose show dealt with marriage, relationships, and all sorts of other issues that did not just hit close to home—they were my home. I was about to become a divorced speaker and preacher who attempted to inspire people to hold on to hope, but sitting in that plane seat, I doubted I would ever feel hope again. I was about to have a public divorce, and I knew the humiliation and embarrassment would be intense. I was not wrong.

All of these dismal thoughts were flickering before me as the peaks and valleys opened up thirty thousand feet below. The snow-capped mountain peaks were a reminder that within a very short length of time I would be meeting two strangers for dinner approximately two hours after my life had taken a sharp and painful turn. Showing up for that dinner with the Beveres would be the first little miracle I would experience on my journey toward healing.

AN EVENING DESIGNED BY GOD

We landed, and it took everything within me to keep from flipping the phone back open and canceling dinner. But it had taken months for us to schedule, so I proceeded with the evening. The Beveres picked me up at Glen Eyrie, a castle turned into a ministry-run hotel. I instantly felt safe with them. I listened to their stories about serving God, personal struggles, and growing intimacy with each other.

Over dinner we talked about their books and how to start a movement among young people being raised in homes where all the gifts of the spirit were experienced. I did my best to focus, but it was obvious to them something else was very heavy on my heart. There wasn't an elephant in the living room that no one was talking about—the elephant was sitting at our table. I just did not know how to bring it up.

Someone might call what happened next a coincidence, but I do not see it that way. Victor Oliver would have been at the top of my list of people I would have placed in the restaurant that night who could have helped and comforted me. Victor is a remarkable man with a deep faith and rich relationship with God. He has the inner strength of a giant, combined with a gentle spirit and sensitivity matched by none. He published my first book in 1984. He introduced us to Madeline's birth parents and facilitated her adoption. He is a great man, and for some strange reason he was in Colorado

Springs rather than back home in Georgia, and for some reason he was in the restaurant that night.

I saw Victor walk by, excused myself from the table, and told him about the events of the past few weeks and about the phone call. He comforted me, assured me God was there for me, and said he would help walk through this with me. He hugged me and gave me the courage to go back to the table and share what was going on with my life. This man of prayer said I would be at the top of his list. No shame or rejection came from him. As always, he was a powerful healing force in my life.

Victor left, and I sat back down and shared my heart. The Beveres were shocked but seemed as if they had been prepared for the evening. Lisa had a dream about our dinner and knew that something would not be right. We talked for a while, and then they took me back to the hotel to pray for me. I think they must have been there for about an hour, praying with me and praying for me.

They specifically prayed that I would not be bitter. They prayed for forgiveness, whether reconciliation was a possibility or not. They prayed I would forgive everyone involved so that I would not be bound to this horrible moment for life. It was a supernatural intervention, and from that time forward I have had a forgiving heart that I cannot explain. I was able to express anger and to experience the depths of despair, but it was on top of a forgiving heart. With the Beveres' help I made my first healing choice—the choice to forgive.

YOUR JOURNEY OF HEALING

That was the beginning of many choices I had to make to experience healing from my divorce. I am still having to make those choices today, and will make them each and every day of my future. Throughout this book I will share those with you. I have not always made the best choices. I have stumbled along through this just as I have stumbled through the rest of my life, but God has been with me through it—watching over me and bringing hope and healing where there was none.

This book is about so much more than just my divorce. It is about your divorce or your loss or your abuse or your abandonment. It is about the disgust you have felt at whatever cruelty has been thrust upon you. It is about the isolation you have felt from abandonment by people who looked nice to the outside world but who were monsters to you at home. It is also about the abuse or neglect you have given others. It is about the shattered dreams and lost hopes that you are living with right now. This book is about your healing and the choices you have to make to experience the healing God has for you.

You may have picked up this book at the beginning of your healing journey. I am thrilled if you have, because you are seeking healing earlier than most. I am hoping this will usher you through the process with wisdom you may not have previously experienced. I pray that even though I have not lived my life perfectly, as I share it I hope it will give you some definite direction and point you to directions that will help. Unlike some counseling sessions, during which you have to guess at what is important to deal with, I want to help you address the priorities for healing.

You may be years into your healing journey. In fact, you may be further from healing today than when you started years ago. If that is the case, I want to help you redirect your life. I am going to confront some of the lies you are telling yourself and using to stay in a state of pain and sadness. I am going to use ten choices to help you pull out of the rut where you are living a life much different from the life God has called you to live. They are not all easy choices, but they all will move you along and help you experience whatever healing God allows for your life.

THE CHOICE ALMOST EVERYONE MAKES

I was speaking on these choices to a group of women who were all struggling with some area of pain or suffering. I laid out all of the available choices, hoping to inspire them to take at least a small step beyond where they were on that day. I wanted them to ask God to give them anything and everything He had available for them. When it was over, a lovely young woman came up to me and told me of the depressing news that she had MS. She was still grieving her limitations and the impact the disease would have on her family and her. She then told me something that made her the exception to what most people do when they are in the midst of disease and despair. She told me she had never asked God to heal her; she had never fallen to her knees and asked God to take the disease away— for her sake or for her family's sake.

It was hard for me to believe, because this is the one choice that almost everyone makes. In fact, this is the only choice that many people make, but she just could not do it. Why? Because she could not handle rejection. She had experienced rejection by her earthly father and could not endure the thought of experiencing rejection by her heavenly Father if she asked to be healed and was denied. She really was the exception to almost everyone I have met. I encouraged her to do what almost everyone does: to at least ask God to heal, but I did not want her to stop with that request. There was a good chance she would never experience healing. If that was the case, I did not want it to be the end of the healing process for her—it has been for many.

I work with men who are sex addicts and who struggle with lust, and I hear the lamest excuses for why they continue to struggle. Most often it is because they have done only one thing to heal their empty souls. The only thing they have done is ask God to take the problem away. I hear how every day they feel the same urge, and they plead with God and sometimes cry out to God to take away the pain and remove the desires. In the absence of God's intervening in history and miraculously undoing what has been in process for years, they do nothing else. They believe that asking God to take it away is enough, or they use it as an excuse to do nothing else.

You may have found yourself doing the same thing. You may have begged God to fix your weight, remove your cravings, change your husband, transform your wife, repair your kids, ease your pain, or anything else that has been troubling you. There is nothing wrong with asking God. In fact, God told us that often we don't have something because we have not asked for it. If you are still stuck on only asking God to heal you or take away the struggle, then I have a question to ask you that Jesus asked a man about two thousand years ago.

A Man, a Mat, and a Matter of Choice

I love Bible stories that have a twist or a hidden message that, when uncovered, sheds new light on my own life. One of my favorites is found in the fifth chapter of the book of John. It is the story of Jesus visiting a place where people, hundreds of people, were sick, blind, crippled, and paralyzed. They were at Bethesda, a pool in Jerusalem near what was known as the Sheep Gate. These people lay all around in the alcoves, hoping to experience healing. Supposedly, the water would stir and the first one to enter the pool would be healed.

One of the things I love about this story is that Jesus was quite a phenomenon at the time. He was known for His miracles, healings, and radical teaching. He could have been anywhere talking with anyone on the planet because of His fame and the fact that He was God in human form. He had total access to the powerful and mighty, but rather than be with those at the top, He was there at the pool with the down-and-outers who had nothing better to do but lie around and wait to catch a healing wave.

I can only imagine the sight of all those desperate people with oozing wounds and withering bodies. The sounds of those groaning in pain and screaming in agony must have made it one of the worst places to go. The smell of rotting flesh and rampant disease probably brought on a gag reflex for most people, but Jesus chose to be there. I love that about Jesus.

The smell of rotting flesh and rampant disease probably brought on a gag reflex for most people, but Jesus chose to be there. I love that about Jesus.

Jesus approached one of the sick who were stretched out by the pool that day. This was not a man who had heard about the healing pool and traveled from a distant city for a shot at instant healing. This man was a permanent resident of the poolside community; he had been there thirty-eight years. Can you imagine the despair of a life unlived, spent lying by a pool that never brought healing? Thirty-eight wasted years seeking something that never happened as he tried the same thing over and over again with absolutely no results.

Then, on that fateful day, Jesus walked right over to his mat and asked him an amazing question that I want to ask you. Jesus did not just heal him. He did not assume that the man wanted to be healed after thirty-eight years spent as an invalid. Instead, Jesus asked him, "Do you want to get well?" (John 5:5–6 NIV).

The man had a choice to be healed or not. There had to be a "want to" in his will. He could have decided to stay unhealed forever, and there could have been some reasons to do so. He may have wanted to remain unhealed so he could just lie around, or he may have grown accustomed to begging and knew begging was easier if he had a severe health problem. He may have become comfortable in his role as an outcast. He may have used his illness to disconnect from the world and the other pressures of life. There are many reasons that he may not have wanted to be healed, even though Jesus was offering to heal him. Jesus took the time to ask if he wanted to be healed, rather than just barge in and heal him on the spot.

Asking a man who has been ill for thirty-eight years if he wants to be healed is not a bizarre question. I have worked with many people through the years who could have experienced healing but refused it. If Jesus had asked if they wanted to be healed, they might have said no. Some of them continued to stay overweight because it had some benefits they did not want to give up. They chose obesity over health because they liked the invisibility—no one paid attention to them as fat people. No one spoke to them or showed interest in them, and that made them feel comfortable and secure.

Others chose to stay heavy because it protected them. They had been abused earlier in life, and the fat kept them from becoming an object of desire for anyone. Or in the absence of the strength to set boundaries, their weight provided a portable boundary that few would want to cross. Actually their weight was not a boundary; it had become a protective wall, so they chose to stay fat. The benefits for them were too many to choose the path of healing.

I know sex addicts who have refused healing. They knew they were sick. They knew they had destroyed their character, respect, marriages, jobs, relationships with God, and even their health. They knew all of that, but they chose to stick with being sick. They refused to make the choices that recovering sex addicts make when they decide they want to be healed and be well. The intensity and disconnection of the addiction remained a stronger lure than the hope of authentic intimacy and a loving relationship, so they chose to stay sick.

I have talked with alcoholics' sick wives who refused to get well. The women structured their lives around their husbands' alcoholism and lived in reaction to what they did and how bad they were. They had no lives of their own, just the lives of enabling and covering up for their sick men. These well-meaning martyrs kept the alcoholics in the booze and kept themselves on the sidelines of life as they tried to control the uncontrollable. They lost themselves and refused to make some healing choices that could have led them back to the life God intended for them. They chose to remain the same. They chose to stay on their codependent mats, wallow in the pool of self-pity, and wade through their shame rather than to get up and walk the path of healing.

I know women who were cruelly abused as young children. I know women who were repeatedly raped by their fathers and kept silent about it for years. The abuse was horrific, and their anger and bitterness were justified. They did not want to let go of their feelings, and no one could blame them, but they were still being affected by the abuse years later.

They were unwilling to go through the healing steps so that the abuse would become just a part of their lives, not the controlling factor. They chose to remain stuck in the bitterness and refused to heal, so the abuser continued to influence them and keep them stuck. Even though it seemed impossible, they could have found healing.

You may be one of those who have chosen to stay stuck rather than be healed. But now you are reading a book about ten choices that could take you down a different path. Today is different for you—you are finally interested in risking to live a different life. You want to know what to do and how to do it, or at least you are curious if someone might have some hope to offer you.

I don't know how long you have struggled, but I know this: it is time to pick up your mat and walk.

I am thrilled that you are finally at that place and have chosen this book as a step toward healing. I am confident that if that is what you desire, you are going to experience some level of healing from the choices offered here. Your healing may be physical or it may be emotional, and it could be spiritual. I don't know what God has for you. I am confident, however, that if you make the healing choices presented here and counter the lies you need to stop living, you will experience some level of healing to a new degree.

When Jesus met the man at the pool of Bethesda, He asked if he wanted to be well. Fortunately, the man did want to be well, and when Jesus told him to pick up his mat and walk, he did. He was healed after thirty-eight years. How long has it been for you?

I don't know how long you have struggled, but I know this: it is time to pick up your mat and walk, or pick up your mat and cry, or pick up your mat and drive to a meeting, or pick up your mat and take your medicine, or pick up your mat and help someone else, or pick up your mat and utter a simple prayer of surrender to taking the path toward healing. It is time to pick up your life and experience all that God has for you. In order to do that, you may have to do some things that will take you out of your comfort zone and push you into places you don't really want to be.

STRANGE STEPS TOWARD HEALING

I don't know of anyone who would not prefer his or her healing to be instant and easy. All of us like the quick fix and instant solution. We live in a fast-paced world, and we want the pace of transformation to keep up. We would like God to pronounce us healed so we can just get on with our lives. We say to God and ourselves that if this one problem would just go away, we could change the world or change our family or at least change our attitudes. If that is what you are waiting for, you are probably wasting your time. All of us want it that way, but it seldom happens that way.

God's ways are not our ways. His ways transcend human reasoning, and we will not know why God chose certain things to happen the way they happened until we land in heaven—if we land there. We come to believe that God wants us to be healed instantly, and sometimes we demand it, but that is usually not the case. God rarely provides an instant fix to our problems, because it does little to change our hearts or grow our characters. As a result, we either stay stuck in our difficult lives or finally decide to do things God's way—or we at least come to believe that our own way may not be the best way. The sick man waiting thirty-eight years by the pool wasted much of his life. But waiting may not have just wasted his life. It may have wasted yours. Perhaps you are thinking it is time for you to pick up your mat and walk and begin to live again. There is evidence in Scripture that God sometimes offers a strange path toward healing that is easy to resist or reject outright. The story of Naaman—found in 2 Kings, chapter 5—is an example of how easy it is to doubt that God's way is the best. Naaman was a highly respected general who had led King Aram's army to victory. Actually, God had given him the victory. Naaman had an embarrassing problem—he was a leper. Luke 4:27 tells us that not one person in that day had been healed of leprosy. Naaman wanted to be the exception.

Fortunately for Naaman, his wife's maid knew of the prophet Elisha of Samaria and knew he could heal Naaman. When Naaman heard about Elisha, he went to the king and asked if he could pay a visit to the healer. The king agreed and wrote a letter to the king of Israel. Naaman set out with the letter, 750 pounds of silver, and 150 pounds of gold to meet Elisha. He must have been a bit discouraged when the king of Israel read his letter and was angry because he thought it was some kind of trick. Elisha heard about Naaman and the letter and asked the king to send Naaman to him.

Naaman showed up in grand style, expecting to meet face-to-face with the great prophet, only to be greeted by a mere servant who told him to go wash himself in the muddy Jordan River seven times if he wanted to be healed. Naaman, rather than excited to have a plan, was mad as a hornet. He thought he would get the quick fix and, with the wave of a hand, be made well. Seven baths in a dirty river was just too much to handle. Can you believe it? No one had ever been healed of leprosy, and rather than being grateful for a plan, he refused to follow it. At least he refused until his friends convinced him to give it a try.

Are you like Naaman? Are you unwilling to try what God has laid out for you as the path toward healing? Do you think you deserve a better plan? Do you have a plan of your own that you wish God would adopt? If Naaman had continued to demand his own way and refused to try God's way, he would have missed the healing God had for him. It was for him to choose or refuse.

You are in the exact same spot right now: you can choose to follow God's plan, or you can refuse and continue to follow your own path. It is in your hands. Naaman turned away from his own desires and gave God's way a chance. It probably was not so much fun getting in and out of the water. It most likely made no sense to him, but he did it, and his skin was as good as new—just like the skin of a baby. Because Naaman did what God wanted him to do, he was the only person of his day in his land to be healed of leprosy.

God could instantly heal you, just as He could have instantly healed Naaman, but perhaps that is not the path God has chosen, and that is why you are reading this book. Don't be discouraged. Don't lose hope. God has not given up on you, so don't give up on God or His plan. Remember, God gave Naaman military victory; God favored Naaman. God gave Naaman healing, just not the way Naaman imagined it would be.

I don't know you, but I know God has given you favor. God loves you so much He wants the best for you. He also wants to know if you want what is best for you. Do you want the best so much that you are willing to give up what is comfortable and predictable but is anything other than God's best? In some strange way God stands before you or within you asking if you want to be well. He asks if you are willing to give up your old ways for His ways. I hope your answer is going to be yes. If it is, I believe there are ten choices God wants all of us who desire healing to make.

None of these choices is easy, but all of them can be life changing. I have been inviting fellow strugglers to make them for the past twenty years. I hope you will choose to make them. If you do, they will lead you down the path toward the healing God has for you. If you are struggling with a physical ailment, I hope these choices lead you to healing. If God does not provide physical healing, I know there are new levels of emotional, relational, and spiritual healing available to you. My prayer for you right now is that whatever level or area of healing God has for you, you will make the courageous decisions you need to make to experience all of what He has for you.

Healing is a choice. It is God's choice, but there are choices that each of us must make if we are to experience whatever healing God has for us. I hope and pray this book will provide you with life-changing choices. I hope this is the beginning of healing, transformation, and a new life for you. I am pulling for you, praying for you, and asking you to join me on the journey of a lifetime. I am hoping that one day you will look back and say that it all began right here on page 19, when you became willing to make the choices you needed to make to be healed.

Do you want to be healed? Say yes and read on!

Some Questions You May Have About the Workbook Sections at the End of Each Chapter

What will the *Healing Is a Choice* workbook sections do for me? The workbook sections will guide you through a study of the ten important choices that contribute to healing, and the ten lies that work against people in the healing process. It will challenge you to engage in introspection concerning the need for healing and to develop a proactive approach to becoming well.

The lessons look long. Do I need to work through everything in each one? *Healing Is a Choice* begins with an important premise and builds upon it throughout the text. Reading from the beginning to the end provides a thorough understanding of the subject and its applications. You need it all to receive the most benefit. The workbook portion is intended to reinforce the truths in the book and guide the reader toward application. If you neglect selected passages, you may experience some loss in application. Choose carefully.

How do I bring together a small group to go through the workbook portion? There is no greater learning environment than an interactive small group. If you share this book with friends and colleagues, you will probably discover a keen interest among them. The fact is that many people are in need of healing, or they certainly know people who are. Gathering some of them into a small group to study this book might be just the prescription that will change their lives.

How should I use the workbook sections? We will consider one chapter at a time. Reading it will give you the basic information. Using the workbook portion will provide reinforcement of the book's content through a variety of questions, exercises, and devotionals.

Take time to complete them. Following this method will provide the greatest impact.

What is the structure of the book and workbook? *Healing Is a Choice* identifies and explains ten important healing choices that people can make as they seek healing. In contrast, it identifies ten big lies that hinder and derail healing. This contrasting style encourages an emphasis on the healing choices, while making us aware of the lies that would dissuade us from making choices that heal. In every case, healing is a choice in which God and man are involved. Healing is God's choice. Man's choice is to reject the lies that work against healing.

I

THE FIRST CHOICE:
The Choice to Connect Your Life

THE FIRST BIG LIE:
"All I need to heal is just God and me."

RACHAEL'S STORY

The following story is true, down to the last detail. It is from a woman who asked that her name be changed only so that those involved would not know her story was in this book. She is an amazing example of someone who made the healing choice of connection. I will call her Rachael. An adolescent extended family member sexually abused Rachael when she was around seven years old. She believes the abuse occurred multiple times throughout the course of a year. When the abuse eventually ended, some of the memories and most of the guilt remained. She blamed herself and was too afraid to tell anyone, so she lived alone with the mounds of guilt and shame that had been inflicted upon her.

Rachael was never able to fully forget, but she was able to disconnect from many of the raw emotions that she had never dealt with. This helped her survive when the abuser would show up and interact with her at family gatherings. During these times, she would tell herself that it was over and she did not need to think about it anymore. The more the time passed, the more Rachael tried to tell herself that nothing needed to be done because it had happened so long ago.

Thoughts and memories continued to come up often, but she became skilled at pushing the thoughts away from the forefront and focusing on other things. She also focused more on "cracking the whip" inside her mind so that the shame of "the secret" would not be exposed and the bad things that had happened would never happen again. If she did her best, she thought she could protect herself from further pain. She shoved the memories, thoughts, and feelings further and further inside her. Her body did not carry the burden of her secret well. As a very young girl, extreme stomach pains became her constant companion.

MAKING THE CHOICE TO CONNECT

Roughly six years of silence and secrecy passed. Finally, she was able to open up to a very close girlfriend who was the same age. Rachael made her friend promise not to tell anyone, and she never did. Rachael said it felt good to be able to talk to someone about what happened, and even though she knew she was not entirely to blame, she did not take any further steps toward healing at that time. After all of those long years in isolation, she had finally made a choice to heal. She had made the choice to connect with another person and share the secret. It was a start.

When Rachael was sixteen, she made another bold choice to heal. She did something she swore she would never do. She told her mom what had happened. When pressed by her mom for details, she acted as if they were hazier than they were. She couldn't say to her mom specifically what the boy had made her do. Her mom was very disturbed and upset by the information Rachael gave her, but she tried to avoid dealing with the reality of it all and wrote it off as something that had happened long ago. Later Rachael learned that her mother had wondered if the whole incident had been made up because Rachael was a creative child.

Rachael's mother also made another mistake. She reasoned that it either had never happened or had not been very damaging, because Rachael seemed so happy and healthy. The minimization of the incident did not help the healing process for Rachael, but that did not stop Rachael from continuing to make the healing choice to connect.

OPENING THE DOOR TO PROFESSIONAL HELP

A couple of years later, Rachael graduated from high school and attended a local Christian college. During a challenging summer job following her freshman year, she shared her past with another good friend she worked with. This time Rachael's choice to connect struck gold. The friend told her she knew others who had been abused. She told her that counseling had helped them immensely, so Rachael began to think about getting some counseling and shared the idea with her mother.

Her mother had a negative bent toward counseling. She doubted that it would help or was even necessary. She also did not like the idea of not knowing what a counselor might want Rachael to do. Overall, Mom stuck with her "don't rock the boat" approach and deterred her from pursuing it any further. Although her mother once again tried to move Rachael off the path toward healing, Rachael's choice to connect and heal did not end there.

A good friend at school became Rachael's boyfriend at the end of her freshman year in college. In the fall of her sophomore year, they e-mailed each other regularly. Although they saw each other every day, they were constantly e-mailing each other as well, which allowed them to grow deeper in their knowledge of each other.

While writing an e-mail one day, Rachael opened a deeper part of her heart just a crack and shared how she really did not love herself. She sent the e-mail and walked across campus realizing with each step just how true those words had been. Thoughts of the past abuse came into her mind, and she tried to convince herself, as she had so many times before, that "it happened a long time ago—why even think about it now?" The problem was that this time it did not work.

Rachael kept attempting to push the thoughts and memories into the back of her mind, but it did not work. The harder she tried, the more intense the thoughts and emotions grew. She had homework to take care of and exams to study for, but she could not focus on anything except the abuse. She said her mind became like a frozen computer screen, and she could not shut it down. The rest of the day became a time full of mental torment that God would use for her good.

That evening, Rachael was so full of pain and turmoil that she was willing to do just about anything. She had gone to a friend's dorm room to talk, only to find the room empty. She waited for a few minutes, and as she was about to leave, her friend returned from her part-time job. Rachael shared the story of her awful day and her pain-filled past. Her friend listened and then gave her some wise advice. She told Rachael about a Christian counselor who regularly visited the campus. The counselor had a sliding scale for fees, and the school would even help pay for the sessions.

Rachael took the name and the phone number and left a confidential voice mail with the counselor. She was very nervous about the first session, but with God's help and prompting decided to take the risk and chose—for the first time—to connect with a professional who could help.

RELEASING THE EMOTIONAL FLOOD

To Rachael's surprise, the words almost came out by themselves. She said she experienced at least one moment where she seemed separated from herself—almost as an observer—and watched with amazement at the intensity and range of emotions that seemed to pour out from her. After a powerful hour of self-revelation, Rachael still needed to ask the woman if she thought there was a need for counseling. The counselor replied, "What do you think?" A second later Rachael nodded her head yes, and thanked her. That became the first of many regular sessions in what Rachael called giving the healing process "her best shot."

Much healing and good came into Rachael's life as the connection between counselor and client grew deeper through the next two years. It felt so good to be making progress in an area of her life that had been primarily closed to the world, although it was challenging for her to work through her buried emotions. The counseling and healing process was a major test in her dating relationship, but it was also a blessing. She shared the story of her past with her boyfriend, the first male she had ever talked with about the abuse. He had never dealt with that kind of experience before. Rachael saw his true colors with the test of time, and he was a faithful friend through it all. He did not always know what to say, but he was a good listener and cared about her healing. Both of them learned a lot through the process.

CONNECTING THROUGH CONFRONTATION

Now Rachael talks of her deep gratitude to God and to all those who poured their lives and hearts into hers. As her peace and contentment grew, so did her courage. During the second semester of her junior year, she was actually at a place in the process where she was able to confront the family member who had sexually abused her. The meeting was scheduled with her counselor, her boyfriend, and the friend she had first shared her story with. It was a powerful meeting that produced another level of healing.

Today Rachael knows there are still many areas God wants her to work on and grow in. She is always willing to get more counseling when needed. Even her mother is supportive of her and now praises her courage to make healthy choices. Her boyfriend attended some of the counseling sessions with her, and eventually they went to see the same premarital counselor. They have been married for more than five years.

Rachael said God knew what He was doing when He prompted her so strongly to seek help and healing. She cannot imagine how her relationship with her husband would be if she had not been open with him about the abuse and not been open to counseling and healing. Well, I can imagine what it would be like. I am so glad Rachael chose to connect and chose to heal.

FACING THE BIG LIE

Healing is a choice. It was God's choice for Rachael, but for that healing to come, Rachael had to choose to make a connection through the abuse rather than isolate and hide because of it. Just consider for a moment if she had listened to some of the lies that prevent healing: "It happened a long time ago." "You are doing fine; why get help?" There are many more, but the most common of all the lies that prevent people from connecting with others or allow them to stay disconnected is the lie, "All I need is God and no one else." If Rachael had played out her life based on that lie, there would have been a very different outcome. How do I know? I talk to people encased in this belief almost every day.

The "only God" lie is actually a form of denial. It is a lighter layer of denial. The heavier layer only lasts for a while. You can only convince yourself and others that there is no problem for so long, and then reality seeps in and people see your situation for what it is. Outright denial just looks foolish, and you have to retreat. So you give some ground, admit that life has not been perfect, and acknowledge that some of that might have spilled over into adulthood.

You are willing to acknowledge that there is something that needs attention. You admit there is smoke but balk at the notion of fire. You admit to something but deny that it needs attention from others. Rather than just stay isolated inside your own solitary cave, you hole up in there with God, expecting God to meet every need and heal every pain. It does not happen, because that is not God's plan. God's plan is for us to connect with each other to facilitate healing in our lives.

If you are like me, you don't really want this to be true. I wanted to make it on my own; I did not want to be open and honest. I was afraid of further rejection when I shared the news of being rejected. I just wanted to be left alone to grieve and whine and whatever else I wanted to do as I limped through this new dark reality that had come upon me. But the faithful efforts of others kept dragging me out of that dark pit and meeting with me face-to-face.

The uncomfortable connection with others became the healing connection for me, and it will be the same for you. You may have some pretty good excuses to not connect with others, but God has some pretty good reasons that will overpower your excuses if you will allow them to. You cannot read what God has to say about connecting with each other and be convinced that He wants us to face our pain with just Him and Him alone.

You cannot read what God has to say about connecting
with each other and be convinced that He wants us
to face our pain with just Him and Him alone.

GOD'S TRUTH FOR EACH OTHER

I invite you to pull out a Bible and take a moment to let God's Word sink in. Here are some convincing scriptures that God's way is for us to work with one another and be there for one another—connected—as we seek healing. Look at God's truth:

- Romans 12:5 tells us to depend on each other as one body in Christ.

- Romans 12:15 tells us to weep with each other, when we often just want to weep alone.
- Romans 15:14 tells us to counsel and teach each other, when we want to just wait and hear from God.
- 1 Corinthians 12:25 tells us to care for each other.
- 1 Thessalonians 5:11 tells us to encourage and build each other up.
- Ephesians 4:2 tells us to uphold each other, when we try to act like we don't need anyone.
- Ephesians 5:21 tells us to submit to each other, meaning you are to do more than just submit to God.
- Hebrews 10:24 tells us to stir up love in each other and share it.
- 1 Peter 4:10 tells us to minister to each other, so God's generosity is shared.
- James 5:16 tells us to tell each other what we have done wrong—then we can experience healing.
- Galatians 6:2 tells us to bear each other's burdens, when all we want to do is take them to God.

Over and over we see the Scripture pushing us back toward each other. Look at all of the healing actions encouraged by God. Look how God directs us back to one another when we want to hide. It encourages us to deepen our connection with others by love, devotion, confession, honor, encouragement, prayer, hospitality, submission, kindness, forgiveness, service, counsel, acceptance, and fellowship. We were born for connection—it sustains us and heals us. Isolation is the way of the fool. Connection is the way of God.

MAKING THE CONNECTION

Have you made the healing choice to connect? Could the lack of connection or the superficiality of your connection be keeping you from the healing God has in store for you? If so, there is so much hope for you. I have met many desperate singles who were desperate and single because they had never made the effort to learn to connect, and many who had learned to connect, but only sexually. I have worked with many stable and satisfied married couples who did not know what they were missing. Their marriages were stable, convenient, and functional, but there was no rich intimacy because there was no deep connection. Connection is the first choice to make in the healing process.

I have worked with many who looked connected and healthy, but in reality they were lonely and isolated and just struggling to get by. Hamilton was one of those who looked good on the outside but was deeply disconnected to everyone around him. As a college student, he finally realized that for most of his life he had suffered in isolation. He told me that in high school he was involved in nearly every activity imaginable: football, band, speech, drama, student council, quiz bowl, key club, academics—you name it and he was in it. People always looked up to him for leadership, voting him student body president, band president, Thespian Society president, and class president. They spoke frequently of what a good Christian he was and how pure he was. They thought he had it together, but it was all an act.

Hamilton had been addicted to pornography since he was eleven, and the shame he felt because people thought he was a good and godly person just drove him deeper into his world of fantasy and lust. He said, "For the record, I usually was a good person, always nice to people and trying to be the good Samaritan." He had never had a physical relationship with a girl. He felt absolutely alone. He had millions of "friends" (he said "acquaintances" would be a better term), but he had no best friend to help him through his problem.

The result was a deeper attachment to pornography and masturbation. They became his "closest friends" because they were the only things that made him feel intimate. After graduation, he was utterly alone in his thoughts, even though he attended college in the same town as his high school. He saw dozens of his former classmates every day, but he was still alone. His shame, habits, and secrecy walled him off from others who could have helped in his healing.

Hamilton wrote to me weeks after he read *Every Man's Battle*. He wrote because he stopped using pornography and masturbating. He stopped, and with the end of his shame he opened the door to others. He began to connect as he had never connected before. In the past, he had begged that God would help him and heal him, but healing came when he stopped the source of disconnection and started risking connection with others. I don't think Hamilton would have experienced healing if he had not found a way to make the first choice of healing, the choice to connect.

The reason that the choice to connect is the first choice is because God wants people in your life to bring about the benefits of the other choices. The other choices do no good for the hermit. You need others, and the alienation you experience in your pain blocks them off from you. So you must take a step away from your comfortable surroundings and allow others to minister to you and nurture you—no matter how difficult it is.

THE DIFFICULTY WITH CONNECTION

Connection was always difficult for me. The reason was simply inexperience—I was not raised around it. I was talking with my mom the other day about how hard it was for my father to connect with his three sons. His father was about the least connected or connecting person I have known. My father was not raised around connection, and neither was I. I was never attracted to anyone who was connected either. I went for the tough and rugged isolated persons who looked and acted as if they did not need anyone. Their eventual rejection of me was proof that they did not need me—at least it felt that way to me. I was attracted to them because I was inexperienced with people who were connecting.

As I healed, I found myself doing a one-eighty on the connection front. Now I am married to not only a connected person but the most connected person I have ever known in my life. Misty is deeply connected to her family and loves her friends dearly. They speak of her ministry to them, and she speaks of how they have walked the tough paths with her. It is fascinating and inviting to me to see such a great connection between her and her family, friends, and church. Her church is a valued part of her life because of the abundant connections she has there. On our honeymoon, we ended up in a room next to a smelly compost heap, but she did not want to move because she had developed a connection with Taru, the lady who took care of our room. This level of connection was not something I was used to, but once I realized how much I needed it, I was drawn to it.

Inexperience is the problem for some like me. Experience is the problem for others. You may have experienced connection and felt very uncomfortable. Perhaps in the most connected of relationships you were betrayed or disappointed. Someone you loved may have turned on you, and you made a choice to protect yourself from a repeat offender. The experience can also be horrific if you are connected to a smotherer who only wants you for his or her own comfort and security.

There are many unhealthy forms of connection such as clinging or controlling connections. Anyone who has experienced them quickly learns to run from moving deeper into relationships. You may fear the unknown or being controlled and losing yourself again. Fear can become the biggest blockade to moving closer and connecting. Many people become isolated because of their fear of connection with others.

THE PROTECTIVE WALL OF WEIGHT

In working with mildly overweight and morbidly obese clients, I have seen the heartache of what fear of connection can do. Often people have been damaged early in life. They don't feel secure and competent to take care of themselves. They don't trust themselves or believe in themselves, and they fear all others because of the abuse of one person. So gradually they build a wall of weight that becomes their defense against the world.

They find invisibility in being large. People don't talk to them, don't seem to notice them, or don't want to connect with them when they are big. They find comfort in how they feel as a heavy person, although they hate the way they look. The weight stays on until they can make the bold move out of defensive isolation and back to healthy connection.

There is another big motivation for disconnection—shame. People living in shame do not want to be known. The unforgiven and unresolved sins of the past keep them in hiding. They fear that if they are found out, they will be thrown out. Through the years, the magnitude of their sins and wrongs grow beyond reason. Often when they finally do open up, the very thing that separated them from others becomes an excuse to connect. They find other strugglers who work with them to rid them of their shame. Shame falls away in the loving embrace of accepting connection.

If you are living in isolation because of shame, I want you to know that God wants you out of hiding and into the arms of a healing community. God can and will forgive your past, and there are places where people will accept your past, no matter what. You can call 1-800-New-Life, and we will help you find one of those healing communities.

---

*If you are living in isolation because of shame,
I want you to know that God wants you out of hiding
and into the arms of a healing community.*

TOUGH REQUIREMENTS OF CONNECTION

The requirements of connection are very tough for many of us. Not impossible, just tough. They require us to grieve the loss of some dreams, accept the reality of what is, and move toward others in spite of our pain and disappointment. I think of the pain and heartache that parents of young prisoners must experience as they make the drive on a Sunday to visit their child who has done nothing but disappoint and come up short of the least of expectations. To make that trip and connect and nurture that child and try to build a relationship is not an easy duty. It is the toughest of assignments, but it is a requirement if there is to be hope for that child once on the outside.

I grieve for parents who wanted the best for their children and had images of a whole and healthy family, only to end up with shattered hopes and seemingly unbearable pain. Parents have a huge choice to make when a child gets into trouble. They can either feel sorry for themselves or make some choices to heal the family and build a relationship that might be real and authentic for the first time. I worked with a woman who found herself in that exact situation. I will refer to her as Dana.

Dana had a special daughter whom she loved dearly. Dana and her husband were fairly well off and dreamed of a special wedding day for their daughter, with men in tuxes, a wedding cake covered in marzipan, and dancing on into the night. They had high hopes for their darling girl after she graduated from college, but before she was out of high school, she was raped. Railing at God for allowing it to happen became a daily ritual for Dana. She shook her fist and her whole body at God. She was so angry she could barely comfort her daughter. Dana instantly saw a change coming over her child. She became hard, rebellious, and disconnected from the family. Dana's pain intensified.

Just when she thought it could not get worse, her daughter informed her that she was pregnant by her new boyfriend. Remnants of any kind of dream went down in ashes with that revelation. The daughter had the baby, and they all lived together—baby, mother, grandmother, and grandfather. Dana tried to make the best of it all while she cried in secret almost every day.

The problem came when the father of the baby wanted to come around. He was young, immature, and ill mannered. All Dana wanted was for him to pick up his plate and take it into the kitchen. She resented this boy, the dream killer. And the least he could do was clean up after himself. She wanted advice on how to deal with a boy who was not a very good member of the family. He was not carrying his weight, and she wanted to correct that.

I told Dana that she had a great opportunity for connection. One night over dinner, her husband could stand up and look at the boy and say, "Hey, pick up the dishes with me and let's wash these for the women." Then Dad and boyfriend could talk about what makes women tick and what makes them ticked—two entirely different things. They could begin to establish a relationship that would reinforce the boy's desire to be part of his new baby's life.

I encouraged Dana to make a connection, rather than a correction. First she was going to have to give up on the dream that would never be. She was going to have to grieve the life of her daughter as she had planned it and accept the reality before her. Once Dana did that, she would be able to create a new family and a new dream with many moments of fulfillment and happiness—but only if she stopped hanging on to what would never be.

As in the instance above, connection does not only heal you; it will also heal your family. Healing sprouts up all around you when you change your way of operating from protecting your rights or correcting others to connecting with others. You model it for kids, and then they spread the connection virus to others. It becomes a way of life that promotes healing versus the old way of disconnection that robs your soul of the nurture from others that is so needed for healing.

For this family to experience healing, this mother had to meet some tough requirements. First she had to get out of her pride and humble herself for the sake of her family. Dana could continue to have prideful entitlement to how her family ought to be, or she could humbly forget about herself and accept her family's reality. She also had to have courage to try to interact with this young man in a different way. She had to have courage to face her friends and be open and honest with them even though they might reject her because she had not created the ideal family. She also needed perseverance. She needed to persevere when it did not magically work out the first time she tried to connect. She needed to persevere when other problems surfaced in the future.

Connection also requires some selfless love: loving God even though He did not prevent pain and tragedy; loving others as God would love you; and loving yourself because you are a valuable creation of God's. This kind of love heals broken families. It lays a foundation for connection and nurtures whatever connection is there. This kind of love also motivates you to surrender to the reality that is before you. Surrendering to God and allowing God to take over is never easy, but it allows God's infinite healing power to provide the path to healing, rather than our finite and futile attempts at control and manipulation. Healing is a choice, and it begins with a choice to surrender to God's way rather than to our own. So before we march forward on a healing path, we must be sure that we really want God's way, not our own.

WISDOM OF A THIRTEEN-YEAR-OLD

I am often amazed at what my daughter Madeline has picked up from listening to the radio show or hearing me talk to others on the phone or watching me just be a dad. When she turned thirteen, I threw her a bowling party. While Madeline and her friends waited their turns to bowl, I turned on the video camera and asked them each to tell Madeline what they liked best about her. I am so glad I did that for Madeline and me.

The girls consistently came up with three things. They said Madeline was a good friend—I loved that. They also said she had a great sense of humor—I knew that. Then they said something that meant a lot to me. They said she gave good advice. I was surprised and really moved.

Back home after the party, I told Madeline what her friends had shared with me. I told her how much I loved that she gave good advice, and then I posed a question for her: "What would you tell one of your friends who had a mom who was hard to get along with and kind of into her own world and not really into the stuff young girls are into?" She said these exact words: "I would tell them to go ahead and find a way to connect with her anyway." I burst out: "Madeline, that is just amazing advice! That is the kind of stuff we say on the radio. You are so wise; no wonder your friends say you are good at giving advice. Why don't you come on the radio with me and give advice to young people?" She looked up at me, pursed her lips, and shut me down with a long, drawn-out, "Dad!"

Okay, so I got carried away with her answer. I was astounded that she understood one of life's greatest truths. We must connect with people even though they give us many excuses not to. We have to find the cracks in their walls of defense and pry them open with an honest desire for connection. That is a lesson I wish I had learned when I was much younger. It is a lesson I hope we all learn. We must make connections if we are to live a lifestyle of healing.

boundary or an unhealthy wall. Does it lead to healthier connection or prevent connection from taking place? If it is the latter, the first task of healing is to tear down that wall. Remove the barriers between you and others, and then engage in a relationship that may indeed hurt you or neglect you but won't allow you to exist in a semicomatose state. To clarify, I am not asking you to go into a relationship that is sick, but all relationships require risk. You may get hurt. You may be neglected. But if you are well connected to others who are helping you decide about life, love, and relationships, the likelihood of a bad outcome is greatly diminished. So tear down the walls and build up the connections.

There are many ways we live out the lie that we must protect ourselves at all costs from all people so that we don't get hurt again. One way is to lead others while we keep our distance. Or we cling to others so they fight to keep their distance from us. (I call this dominance or dependency dilemma.) Or we spew out an exhibitionist confession that pushes people back and away from us. All of these are connection killers when what we need is real and true and deep connection. We find this type of connection in mutuality by sharing ourselves and wanting to share the experience of others.

We must listen, receive, and have empathy while at the same time giving, contributing, and reaching for the hearts of others. When we do, life opens up before us in ways we never knew possible. If single, we learn that we can connect without sex, and that sex prevents us from experiencing God's plan for connection and love. If we are married, stable, and set, but disconnected, we can step into a new level of intimacy with our spouses when we go to work on our connection. Wherever we are in life, we can move closer to others as we move closer to God.

THE REWARDS OF CONNECTION

There is a sense of safety and control in isolation and disconnection, but it is a false sense of safety. In fact, living lonely is anything but safe. It is a dangerous way to live, because it allows you to miss real life and real people and all of the benefits and rewards that go with growing relationships. You can begin to experience the many rewards of connection by taking a small, courageous step out of isolation.

When you decide to connect, you decide to live life as God intended it. His very existence, the Trinity, is a model of relationship. He designed the family, which is a collection of relationships. His church exists and builds His kingdom while in relationship. He ordained marriage as the ultimate relationship between a man and a woman. So when the barriers come down and you reach for connection, you start to experience life as God intended. Although you might be uncomfortable, you start to come alive as you seek deeper levels of connection with those around you.

You also experience God's love. God loves us through others. People become expressions of His love, with skin on. And you experience His tempering of us. He uses others to mold us into the people He wants us to be. In isolation, our character has little chance to grow. But connection offers us the opportunity to put ourselves aside for someone else and grow closer to the image of God.

Connection allows us to feel accepted. We fear rejection, and we might experience it, but if we continue to risk in our connections, we will one day find acceptance and validation. This is healing to the soul in a way we would never know if we stayed alone. There is relief when we connect. It fills in the gaps and provides the missing pieces, because our makeup is aligned toward connection with others. We need connection, and it heals us; it allows us to move to the heights of emotions—feeling love, joy, and hope.

Whatever you can do to connect, do it. Face-to-face connection is the richest form of connection, but if the only way you can get outside of your house is the Internet, then find some safe groups to connect with. If you are a missionary in the most remote part of the planet and cannot connect deeply with those you serve, writing and receiving letters may be your only way to connect. If so, do it intimately. Don't let any limitation be an excuse not to connect. Attempt to build a community with different levels of connection. At one end of the connection spectrum is mere support, where you can count on others to be there for you when you need them. They encourage and comfort in times of need. At the other end of the spectrum is true intimacy, where there is the sharing of the deepest parts of who you are. In this intimacy, you feel a bond, an inseverable link that strengthens with time; as you grow, you develop many levels of intimacy through humor, history, shared dreams, and common joys. This level of communication provides the richest life possible.

FROM CONNECTION TO COMMUNITY

Connections come in many forms. You need a growing connection with God, but you know you need more than just God to experience connection. You need many people in your life with varying levels of connection and intimacy. When you experience connection with many different types of people, you experience collective connection, which is most commonly called *community*. Living in community means that you are part of something bigger than yourself. You are a vital, contributing, and receiving member of a group of people with common interests and mutual goals. Search the world over to find a place where you can experience connection in community. You may find it in a church, some places of work, a small town, or a neighborhood. Community can be found, if you search for it.

A few years ago, I opened up my house for our community to tour. The house was built in 1928 and has a beautiful old garden and a view of the ocean. It is on the inside of a loop, and many people walk or jog by the old place and wave. After the tour, I decided to invite the neighbors over for a little music and a time of getting to know each other. It turned out to be a great success. People were there who had been feuding for years, and they talked and made up and healed their relationships.

People spoke of that gathering for months, wanting to get together more often and volunteering to host a gathering at their place next time. It was a simple affair, but it was a huge success because people felt part of our community. A connection was made that had never been made before. We have repeated the event with the same results.

I believe there are people in your area who want to connect with each other and with you. You might be residing in an assisted-living facility, and you could become the connecting point and establish community for others around you. You might be living in a nursing home, and you could be the one to ensure that it is a healing community. At work, you might start a lunchtime discussion group on a certain day of the week. That meeting could be the beginning of turning your workplace into a community of healthy connections. Wherever you are, you might be the catalyst for connection and community. In choosing to do that, you will experience a new level of healing and lay a strong foundation for more of the same.

CONCLUDING THOUGHTS ON CONNECTIONS

The choice to heal through connections starts with our connection with God. We begin by acknowledging that He exists and that we want a new or renewed relationship with Him. We build this connection through the study of God's Word, meditation, and prayer. In studying God's Word, we can revitalize our connection every day. In prayer, we can sustain that connection. We learn about Him, spend time with Him, and then modify our behavior to please Him. Changing our behavior, doing the next right thing, and choosing to do what is right are ways we can strengthen our connection to God.

As we live more for Him and live more to please Him, we experience a growing awareness of His presence and an intimate connection that takes us through the toughest of times with hope and the best of times with divine joy. Make certain your connection to God is properly in place before you make any other choices to heal. When it is, the other choices are easier and more fulfilling.

If you are tired of running your own life, running from God, and running from others, consider what God promises when you connect with Him and trust in Him. Jesus asked some questions and provided a life-changing answer:

Are you tired? Worn out? Burned out on religion? Come to me. Get away with me and you'll recover your life. I'll show you how to take a real rest. Walk with me and work with me—watch how I do it. Learn the unforced rhythms of grace. I won't lay anything heavy or ill-fitting on you. Keep company with me and you'll learn to live freely and lightly. (Matthew 11:28–30 MSG)

Keeping company with God is a great way to live. It is a way that brings comfort and rest and the path to living free.

Connection with God is vital to our healing, but it is not enough. We must branch out from a "God only" mentality and reach out to others. In humility, we can begin a new level of connection with others that is essential to the healing process. We can connect with individuals and connect in community. Healing communities such as healthy churches, support groups, and recovery programs become the healing foundation upon which all other choices are made and played out. Go no further before you stop and choose to connect with God. Then take a healing risk and connect with others who can help you heal and experience life to the fullest.

Healing is a choice. It is the choice to connect.

CHAPTER 1 WORKBOOK QUESTIONS

THE FIRST CHOICE:
The Choice to Connect Your Life

THE FIRST BIG LIE:
"All I need to heal is just God and me."

IF WE SENSE THAT WE ARE NOT WELL AND REALLY WANT TO recover, it is important that we connect with others. Whether it is a physician, a health practitioner, a counselor, or a trusted friend, the need to connect during the healing process is profound. A physician has the expertise to diagnose and prescribe medicine. A counselor can help us examine the emotional pain we often have and guide us toward the means of dealing with it, so that healing occurs. A friend stands solidly with us during illness—supporting, praying, helping, and most of all, caring.

In fact, connecting with friends in our time of illness or crisis is one way to fulfill God's purpose in relationships.

THE FIRST CHOICE:

The Important Choice to Connect Our Lives with Others

Key Scripture: *Carry each other's burdens, and in this way you will fulfill the law of Christ.*

—GALATIANS 6:2 NIV

The introduction to *Healing Is a Choice* makes the point: "At one time or another, every human being needs healing" (Introduction, page 1). It is a rare person who marches through life without being ill. Such folks are fortunate, because the more common human condition is that people get sick from time to time.

Typically, our illnesses are physical. We catch a cold, have a headache, or are down with the flu. Other illnesses, like high blood pressure and diabetes, do their damage "silently" without visible symptoms.

We can usually find effective medications and treatments to manage most of our physical illnesses. Medical treatment often speeds our healing. Frankly, we should be very thankful to live in a society where good medical service is available.

THINK ABOUT IT!

Medicine cannot benefit us unless we are willing to take it. The doctor can only prescribe the medicines we need. It is our choice to take them and to experience the healing that results. In fact, every illness provides a number of choices for people. Most people feel just the opposite. They have a sense of being out of control during illness, but that is rarely the case. Rather, an ill person usually has many choices to make.

Exercise #1: So Many Choices

Remember a time when you were ill. (If you've never been ill, think of a friend or a family member.) Try to remember how the illness began, what visits to the doctor were like, and what was required for you to ultimately be well. Can you recall how many choices you had—such as doctors, treatments, drugs, or doing nothing—during the entire experience of the illness?

List the decisions below, no matter how important or insignificant they seem.

Seven spaces have been provided, but you may add more.

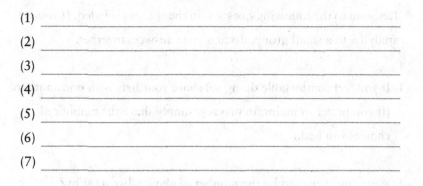

(1) _____

(2) _____

(3) _____

(4) _____

(5) _____

(6) _____

(7) _____

CHOICES, CHOICES, CHOICES!

Were you surprised by the number of choices you had? Thinking it through usually reveals that we had far more choices than we imagined during the illness. An individual must choose whether to see a doctor or consult a different kind of medical expert. In most of the United States, people can select the doctor they will see. When physicians diagnose a problem and suggest treatment options, the patient is usually part of the discussion and can make choices regarding various treatment plans. He or she must decide whether to rest and recover or continue to work. As mentioned earlier, the doctor may prescribe medicine, but the ill person must make a conscious choice to take it responsibly. He or she may choose to utilize therapy and rehab. A critical choice people face is the decision to be optimistic and hopeful or to sink into dark depression.

Every illness provides us with choices. In the context of healing, the greatest choice is the decision to pursue healing! When people make that choice, they typically improve.

Exercise #2: Thinking About Choices

Respond to the following question in the spaces provided. If you are studying in a small group, discuss your answers together.

1. If you feel comfortable doing so, share your lists with one another. (If you prefer to maintain privacy, simply share the number of choices you had.)

2. Were you surprised by the number of choices listed? Why?

_____

_____

3. How did it feel to have choices during your illness? Elaborate.

_____

_____

4. How might it have felt if you had been denied choices? Why?

_____

_____

THE POWER OF CHOICES

It is vitally important to realize that you have choices to make when illness strikes. You are not left alone at the mercy of circumstances or the medical community. The truth is that you are the most important part of the process!

As we've just discussed, you will have more choices than you previously thought. It is vitally important to make your choices, because doing so is personally empowering. Making choices builds spiritual, emotional, and physical strength, which is necessary to fight illness.

When ill people are denied choices, they often suffer from depression and regression, which negatively impacts the healing process. Thus, the choices we face during illness are powerful!

A DIFFERENT KIND OF PAIN

To this point, the focus has been on making choices in regard to physical illnesses. However, *Healing Is a Choice* begins with Rachael's story. Her illness did not derive from organic causes. It was not the pain of disease. Her pain was emotional, spiritual, and psychological, and it was the result of physical, sexual abuse. Rachael's pain was incessant; the pain of traumatic memories that won't go away, regardless of how hard one tries to forget.

Rachael's healing required a unique approach very different from treating the flu or setting a broken limb. She needed a treatment plan that would heal the painful emotional and psychological pain that felt so debilitating.

Sadly, healing the pain we carry in our minds is often much more challenging than taking medicine. Our physical bodies tend to respond quickly and positively to good medicines and treatments. So, when we get sick, we can take a few pills and know that, typically, we'll be better in a few days.

However, the emotional, spiritual, and psychological ills we suffer rarely respond to needles and pills. A different approach is required. The most powerful medicine for this pain includes God's Holy Spirit, pastors, counselors, trained therapists, loving families, and prayer and Scripture, just to mention a few.

So healing is available to those battling physical ailments, and it is equally available to those battling emotional, spiritual, and psychological ailments. God cares about all forms of illness and how He can heal them.

VERY IMPORTANT

Though we acknowledge that there are many ways to be healed, the choice to heal, whether it is physical, spiritual, or psychological, is a personal choice each person must make. Healing is a choice!

Exercise #3: Rachael's Story

If you are doing the study alone, reread Rachael's story on your own.

If you are studying in a small group, ask a volunteer to read the story.

To help us understand Rachael's story more clearly, so that we might use it in a study exercise, let's outline it:

Rachael's Story

I. As a youngster, Rachael was sexually abused by an older adolescent relative.

    A. The abuse ended, but she was left with painful memories, guilt, and shame.

    B. She blamed herself and was afraid to tell anyone.

    C. She was unable to forget what happened, so she engaged in denial.

    D. When memories recurred, she pushed them deeper and deeper inside.

    E. She told herself there was no need to tell anyone.

    F. She experienced extreme and constant stomach pains.

II. After six years of silence and secrecy, Rachael shared her dark secret with a girlfriend. This was an important step for her, but she took no further steps toward healing for almost ten years.

    A. At sixteen years old, she made a brave decision to tell her mother, something she thought she'd never do.

    B. Her mother pressed for more details, but Rachael could not bring herself to describe them. She pretended not to remember. (Rachael learned later that her mother questioned the whole incident, wondering if Rachael had made it up.)

    C. Because Rachael seemed happy and healthy most of the time, her mother believed the abuse, if there was any, had not been damaging.

III. After high school, Rachael enrolled in a Christian college.

A. Still troubled by her past, she told her story to another good friend. It was an important healing choice for Rachael, because it connected her to someone who was able to help her significantly.

B. Her friend told Rachael she knew other people who had been abused and noted that counseling had helped them. She encouraged Rachael to seek Christian counseling.

C. At first, Rachael was reluctant. She just wanted to forget her past, but she couldn't. Her mother, who took a dim view of counseling, adopted a "don't rock the boat" attitude.

IV. Following her freshman year, Rachael found a boyfriend. For the first time, she confided in a man about her abuse. She added that she had difficulty loving herself. She was still denying her pain, and pushing the abuse into the past.

A. This time it did not work. The more she tried to push it away, the more it was on her mind. She had trouble focusing.

B. Encouraged by a close friend, Rachael made an appointment with the counselor.

C. She poured out her story, her pain, and her pent-up emotions.

D. With the help of her counselor, she gave the healing process "her best shot."

E. It was painful at times, but she made continuous progress.

V. Through it all, her boyfriend continued to be a good listener and a loyal friend.

VI. The relative who abused Rachael eventually confessed. As a result, Rachael's mom had a change of opinion and praised her daughter for her courage as she pursued counseling and healing.

A. Today, Rachael is deeply committed to God and appreciative to all those who poured their lives into her and supported her.

B. Rachael's healing continues, and the boyfriend who stood with her became her husband. They have been married for some time.

1. Using a pencil or pen, refer to the outline above and circle each opportunity Rachael had to make a healing choice. If you are studying in a small group, compare and discuss your responses.

2. Again, using the outline above, underline each person or event in which Rachael made the choice to connect with others. Remember, *Healing Is a Choice* teaches us that the first choice is the important choice to connect our lives with others.

In your small group, compare and discuss your responses.

Do You Want to Get Well?

In John 5:1–8 (NLT) we read about a man known only as "one of the men lying there . . ." at the pool of Bethesda, where the disabled people gathered. He had been an invalid for thirty-eight years. Jesus went directly to him and asked, "Would you like to get well?"

That might be one of the most important questions in Scripture. To some extent, spiritually or physically, we all must face that question. Do we want to get spiritually well? Do we want to be physically healed?

Though racked by emotional pain most of her life, Rachael pushed through it. When Rachael faced the question "Do I want to get well?" her answer was, "Yes! I want to be healed!"

So with God's help, she began to reach out and connect to people who could help her. Rachael began to heal, because she connected with people who could facilitate her healing. Without those friends, she might still be suffering in her pain. Because of them, she is becoming the person God planned her to be.

Exercise #4: Rachael's Healing

If you are doing a personal study, answer the following questions.

If you are studying in a small group, discuss the questions together.

1. When did Rachael realize she had a choice in her healing?

_____

2. Does pain ever serve a positive purpose?

_____

3. Why is it important to share our pain with other people?

_____

4. Why is it often necessary to seek professional help?

_____

5. What was the benefit for Rachael in confronting her abuse?

_____

6. How did God demonstrate His love and faithfulness to Rachael?

_____

7. How did Rachael's positive choices impact her healing?

_____

8. Could Rachael have recovered apart from the healing choices she made?

_____

GOD'S ACTION ON RACHAEL'S BEHALF

What choices did God make that led to Rachael's healing? Clearly, He was at work. For example, He provided:

- a personal sense of His presence in her life;
- courage to tell others what happened;
- friends who were caring, active listeners;
- professionals who could help her process her pain;
- redemption to help her reinterpret the abuse in her past;
- a loving husband; and
- continuing healing.

GETTING THE POINT

Isn't it wonderful to realize that God is at work in our lives in so many ways, guiding us toward the people who can help us, and moving us closer and closer to healing? Stories like Rachael's remind us that:

- people who've suffered great pain can be healed;
- God is faithful;
- we need friends and loved ones who love, support, and listen; and
- the body of Christ is an important source of "connecting" when we need healing. In fact, the clearest lesson in Rachael's story is the value of connecting with others who can help us make healing choices.

So many things separate us from others. It's a long list of destructive habits, addictions, excessive work, lack of or failure in relationships, seeking fame and fortune, and more. Such things are diversions that disconnect us from what matters most: good friends and companionship. Without connection to others, we become self-centered and selfish, isolated and alone, often unaware of our own pain.

That leads us to the first big lie described in *Healing Is a Choice.*

THE FIRST BIG LIE:
"All I need to heal is just God and me!"

On the surface, this sounds great! What could be better than God and me? It's an unbeatable combination. However, rather than being truly spiritual, that statement is sanctimonious. It's a brag.

All we're really doing is hiding behind God and excluding from our lives the very people He has ordained to help us. This first big lie boxes God in, rather than clearing a path for Him to work in us. It is false pride and smacks of arrogance ("healing is just God and me").

In truth, this notion is a psychological ploy, a defense mechanism to keep us separated from others.

A CHRISTIAN PRINCIPLE

In Galatians 6:2, Paul issued one of the fundamental principles of Christian human relations. He said, "Share each other's burdens, and in this way obey the law of Christ" (NLT).

Notice that Paul describes the mutual bearing of one another's burdens as a law! Clearly, he does not intend this to be optional. To some degree, God intends for all His children to be healing agents. We should be available to one another and ready to respond when needed. God even puts us in communities of people precisely because we need one another so much. We are mutually indispensable. Our responsibility is to help one another in times of need.

There is an irony here. God is able to heal by Himself. However, it is instructive that He often chooses to use other people and means in the healing process. There are many ways in which He heals, and most often, they involve people. He works His healing power through His people.

"You cannot read what God has to say about connecting with each other and be convinced that He wants us to face our pain with just Him and Him alone" (p. 30).

Exercise #5: Bible Study

Take your Bible and find the scriptures listed below. These verses make the strong point that God's preferred way for us to live is in community with one another, connected, and functioning as agents of healing and grace. After each reference, summarize in your own words what the verse says about being connected with one another.

1. Romans 12:5

_____

_____

2. Romans 12:15

_____

_____

_____

3. Romans 15:14

_____

_____

_____

4. 1 Corinthians 12:25

_____

_____

_____

5. 1 Thessalonians 5:11

_____

_____

_____

_____

6. Ephesians 4:2

_____

_____

_____

_____

7. Ephesians 5:21

_____

_____

_____

8. Hebrews 10:24

_____

_____

_____

9. 1 Peter 4:10

_____

_____

10. James 5:16

_____

_____

_____

_____

11. Galatians 6:2

_____

_____

_____

_____

HAMILTON'S EXAMPLE

Read again the story of Hamilton on pages 32–33. His is a great example of how isolation and secrecy work against our mental health. Hamilton's healing came when he stopped disconnecting and starting reinvesting with people.

> The reason that the choice to connect is the first choice is because God wants people in your life to bring about the benefits of the other choices. The other choices do no good for the hermit. You need others, and the alienation you experience in your pain blocks them off from you. So you must take a step away from your comfortable surroundings and allow others to minister to you and nurture you—no matter how difficult it is. (p. 33)

Like Hamilton and thousands of other people, independence seems to be the great goal of life. It's considered macho to say, "I don't need anyone else," "I am a self-made person," and "I will handle whatever comes my way." Some people might say, "All I need is just God and me," but what they really mean is, "I'll do fine by myself, and God can just watch over my shoulder."

Such cultural pride and arrogance doom us to relational failures, because we simply were not created to be that isolated. Besides, such an independent attitude is an illusion. It is not real.

Is There a Downside to Connectedness?

Just as the pride mentioned in the previous paragraphs sabotages our relationships with God and others, there are some risks in connecting to other people. People may be inexperienced in building relationships. Perhaps they have never had a close friend and don't know where to begin.

Your parents may not have known how to connect with others. Therefore, you are left without a model to follow. Or you might have made a meaningful connection with someone only to be betrayed or abandoned.

Perhaps you connected with someone who smothers you, stealing your autonomy and individuality. You may have befriended someone whose real goal is to dominate and control you.

There are risks involved in any relationship. Still, the value of being connected to others is positive and beneficial, justifying the risks.

Being connected in relationships is well worth the effort. We must not allow fear to keep us isolated and alone. God does not intend us to live that way.

Furthermore, as *Healing Is a Choice* makes clear, we often have to make connections with others despite our pain or disappointment.

We were created to live, grow, and prosper in interrelated, mutually dependent, godly communities.

JESUS SHOWED US HOW TO CONNECT

Jesus was one of the most connected people who ever lived. He developed His own support group, with whom He shared life for the better part of three years. Though crowds sometimes wore Him out, He still attended to the people—teaching, healing, even feeding them. He ignored societal boundaries that excluded women, children, lepers, and Gentiles. In fact, Jesus went out of His way to connect with such folks! He embraced everyone, even the most sanctimonious and legalistic in society. He saved the life of a woman caught in adultery. He restored the warped mind of a demoniac. He wept at the death of a loved one. He shared meals with tax collectors. He moved easily among His peers. Jesus connected without fear or reservation. He took the risks of reaching out and building relationships.

In the end, He was even betrayed by one with whom He had significantly connected. Still, it did not deter Him. He responded by dying for the entire human race, connecting us all by means of the cross.

If we ever needed an example of how to connect with others, it is Jesus. We may never replicate what He did, but we can try to be more like Him, especially in regard to connecting with people.

JOURNALING

Take a few minutes and think about chapter 1. Review it in your mind, or go back and skim the pages. Use the questions and spaces below to guide your journaling.

1. How do you connect with others?

_____

_____

_____

2. Have you been successful, or is it hard for you?

_____

_____

_____

3. Which parts of chapter 1 spoke most clearly to you?

_____

_____

_____

4. Did you see yourself in any of the examples mentioned in chapter 1?

_____

_____

_____

5. Did you have good role models to show you how to connect?

_____

_____

_____

6. Do you carry pain inside that you need to release? With whom might you do that?

_____

_____

_____

7. One of the best places to connect with others is a Christian church. Are you invested in a church? If not, how could you move toward connecting with a congregation?

_____

_____

_____

8. Have you experienced healing of any kind as a result of connecting with others? If so, how?

_____

_____

_____

9. Can you give up your pain and allow God's healing power to work in your life, regardless of how He may choose to express it?

_____

_____

_____

PRAYERFUL MEDITATION

Find a quiet, relaxing place where you are comfortable and un-interrupted. Take a few minutes and meditate on the information in chapter 1. Sit quietly and clear your mind of the day's events. Think about the goodness and greatness of God. Slow down your thoughts and focus on Christ. Ask the Holy Spirit to speak to your mind. Be patient. Listen quietly and wait for the Spirit to speak.

The Holy Spirit may want to encourage you to be bolder and more confident as you connect with others. He may want to challenge you to take the risk of being healed of past hurts. He may want you to roll your cares into His hands. Do you want to be healed? Jesus is able to do it.

PRAYER

Heavenly Father, thank You for the encouragement I received from this chapter. Help me to examine my heart and mind, and to identify the pain I may feel. From the power of Your Spirit, give me the courage to move toward connectedness with others and, ultimately, healing. Increase my confidence in You. Where I am weak and hesitant to act, give me strength. Increase my faith. Open my heart to others and give me a willingness to invest in Your people, the community of faith. I give You my life—mind, soul, and spirit. Through Jesus Christ, my Savior and friend. Amen.

2

THE SECOND CHOICE:
The Choice to Feel Your Life

THE SECOND BIG LIE:
"Real Christians should have a real peace in all circumstances."

THE LITTLE GIRL WHO COULDN'T FEEL

There are not many people who would see pain as a gift from God, but it is. In fact, it is at the point of pain that we often question God. There is a common belief that if He is real and if He loves us, He will keep pain from us. Most of us hate pain, and we do everything we can to avoid it, and rightfully so—by its very nature, pain hurts. If we are healthy and smart, we make the best decisions possible that will lead to the least amount of pain in our lives. Others do foolish things that cause great emotional pain and then rather than feel it, they deny it, drown it out with booze, calm it down with food, or whisk it away with a sexual encounter. They mask the pain and try to remove it rather than deal with its source. In the process, they question God's presence and power because of all the pain they have produced in their own lives. They will often view pain as a curse rather than as a gift.

Ashlyn Blocker's life is a fascinating study and dramatically demonstrates that pain is a special gift from God that protects us. Ashlyn cannot feel pain. Her parents knew there was something wrong when she placed her hand on a hot pressure washer and felt nothing. Ashlyn stood there, staring at her red and blistered hand, but she did not cry, and her mother knew they had a problem.

When her baby teeth came in, Ashlyn would wake up with swollen and bloody lips from chewing on them in her sleep. While eating, she unknowingly bites through her tongue. Her food has to be cooled because she cannot tell if it is too hot. They place ice cubes in hot soup to prevent the scalding of her mouth.

Ashlyn's mother said, "Some people would say that's a good thing. But no, it's not. Pain's there for a reason. It lets your body know something's wrong and it needs to be fixed. I'd give anything for her to feel pain."[1] What is true of physical pain and the body is true for emotional pain and the soul. Pain is a gift from God to let us know that something is not right, that something in our life needs attention and fixing.

When we feel our lives, we are tuned in to pain as it emerges and can resolve it before our lives begin to revolve around it. But if we are not allowed to or choose not to feel the pain, we will add hurt on top of injury and inflict further difficulty and conflict on our lives, just like the little girl who continued to injure herself. Pain is a gift. It is not one we actively seek, but when it appears in our lives, we need to react appropriately, rather than deny or neglect it.

LAURIE'S PAIN

Laurie was a member of a small, back-road church in east Texas, just outside of Tyler. The little building with its one-hundred-year-old steeple looked like something out of a painting of rural life in America. It looked as if it would be safe enough to attend church there, but for Laurie it was anything but safe. Laurie had attended the church since she was a little girl. She knew everyone and just about everything about everyone who attended there—everyone except her husband.

Although Laurie knew about the private lives of many of the members, she was unaware of the private life her husband had developed. Under her nose, in a small community, he had begun to see another woman. She may never have known if she had not found a receipt between the front seats of their minivan—a receipt from a nearby motel that she knew often rented rooms by the hour. There was no legitimate reason her husband would have been at that motel or paid for a room there.

Laurie had weathered many storms with her husband. She had stood by him as he lost job after job. Presently they were two months behind on their mortgage, and now she knew he was spending money on hourly motel rooms to have sex with someone else. The pain was almost more than she could bear. She felt too ashamed to tell any of her friends. She confronted him—motel receipt in hand—the minute he walked through the door. He immediately began to cry as she begged for an explanation. She screamed, "Why?" again and again as she beat on his chest and finally collapsed into a pool of her own tears. Her wretched cries of pain deepened his guilt and grief. It took nothing more than seeing his wife's broken heart to cause him to change.

He confessed it all to her. A coworker had come to him for comfort in the midst of her painful marriage, and he had foolishly become involved in their marital turmoil. He became the one she counted on for support and advice, and it had not taken long for them to jump into bed and consummate the affair. It had been going on for a relatively short time. He knew it was wrong from the beginning, but he had never felt anything so exciting, electrifying, and forbidden. He felt alive, desired, and sexual in her presence. He walked into her trap of seduction and lost his integrity for a few moments of feeling like a "real man." He was sincere and genuine when he told Laurie he would never see the woman again and would do whatever else Laurie wanted in order to show his remorse and recommitment.

He began to change. He stopped seeing the woman, and he began attending church as never before. He did what Laurie wanted and seemed to do it out of a sincere desire to become God's man and a man Laurie could be proud of. Everyone at church marveled at the radical change that came into his life. He was a living example of true transformation. He inspired others to take a second look at their own lives, and other men followed in his footsteps. Laurie seemed to have the husband of her dreams. People envied her to have a husband who had come around and was fully devoted to her.

But something else was brewing inside of Laurie, beneath the facade of love and acceptance. She was not a happy woman—she was angry. She was angry that her husband had broken their vows, deceived her as he did, and made her feel foolish if she started to wonder about where he had been. She resented the positive attention he was receiving. While she felt that he was a no-good, two-timing husband, everyone else seemed to admire him for his strong character. While she could hardly stand to be around him, other people wanted to stand with him in his remarkable recovery. She felt horrible about their marriage and felt horrible for feeling horrible. It was one huge dose of unfair life thrown right in her face.

The biggest problem for Laurie was that her husband received so much attention from just doing what he always should have been doing. He was applauded for being the man she had thought he was all along. Rather than anyone having sympathy for her, there was an expectation that she should be grateful. She could not handle that she had been the committed and dedicated wife, willing to stay with her husband after this radical betrayal, and no one seemed to care. No one gave her credit for doing the right thing every single day. Her anger and rage grew, and people in church began to see it. Comments started coming her way:

- "You should feel fortunate that he has made such a change."
- "Just trust God and let this be between him and God."
- "God works everything out to be good."
- "A Spirit-filled person would have a real peace about all of this."
- "Surely there were some deep problems in the marriage for him to have wandered as he did."
- "Surely after a couple of months you have worked through your disappointment."
- "Your anger is a sin you need to repent of."

All of these statements have an element of truth, but each one made the pain worse for Laurie. Each comment prevented her from doing what she really needed to do. Laurie needed to feel the full depths of her sorrow. She needed to feel the pain of betrayal and express that pain to a safe group of people, rather than skip over her emotions and declare "instant peace," as some in her church wanted her to do.

Holding in the pain and having no safe place to share caused Laurie to shut down. She stopped connecting with others, including her husband. She quit going to church and sank into a deep depression, and with the worsening of her depression came more ridicule and rejection from her church.

Laurie was not "allowed" to feel when she needed to feel the most. She needed to forgive her husband, but she did not need to do it instantly or superficially. She needed to find gratitude and peace, but that could not come immediately after learning of the betrayal. She needed to love her husband, but before she could act in a loving way, she needed to acknowledge all that she was feeling that was not loving, process it, and work through it so she could fill back up with love and acceptance.

WHAT WOULD JESUS FEEL?

The prophet Isaiah said that Jesus would be a man who experienced sorrow (Isaiah 53:3). We read of Jesus' experience in the Garden of Gethsemane, just before His crucifixion (Matthew 26). We hear Him ask His disciples to watch and wait with Him because He was so deeply troubled. He felt emotional pain to such a degree that He sweat drops of blood. Sweating blood only comes from feeling the deepest of pain, suffering, and sorrow. He was in the midst of great despair even in—and especially during—times of intense prayer with His Father. This was God as man, who today knows your emotional pain because He experienced it while on this earth. He did not minimize it or superficialize it. He felt it to the core of His soul.

I can't imagine a disciple present in the garden that evening saying any of the following to Jesus:

- "Jesus, stop feeling so bad. You should have a real peace about this."
- "Hey, Jesus, You are going to make us new Christians look bad if You act as if You are in pain when You are supposed to get over things quickly."
- "Jesus, how can You let something like this get to You? Be grateful for the fact that Your pain is going to save the world."

You see, Jesus knew the final outcome. He could see the marvelous result of His suffering. No one needed to tell Him that He would save souls by the millions. But He still had to work things out with His Father. He had to play out another scenario in which He did not have to go through the pain and agony. He had to reach a point of surrender, giving up His own comfort for the right to heal the rest of us from the eternal impact of sin. He was a Man of Sorrows, and it could be seen in vivid color that night.

FEEL—THEN HEAL

My point is that we must never shame a person who does not or cannot instantly feel the joy that awaits him or her on the other side of pain and agony. We must give them the kind of opportunity Jesus had to work through the pain and reality of suffering. If we do not, we push people into a place where they walk around with ungrieved losses and unresolved pain. This pain is never buried dead. It is buried alive and must be fed every day. It will drive a person to eat, drink, spend money, have sex, gamble, and do a thousand other things for relief. You must feel before you can heal, or you will stay wounded and in turn wound others who get too close.

We must never shame a person who does not or cannot instantly feel the joy that awaits him or her on the other side of pain and agony.

FINDING THE NEED BEHIND THE FEELING

Our emotions are gifts from God. They are indicators that something is wrong, not signs that we need to change instantly. Setting up a community where people feel the need to deny or hide their feelings does not allow those emotions to be used in the way God intended. Paul showed us that good can come from experiencing bad feelings. He wrote:

I am not sorry that I sent that letter to you, though I was sorry at first, for I know that it was painful to you for a little while. Now I am glad I sent it, not because it hurt you, but because the pain caused you to repent and change your ways. It was the kind of sorrow God wants his people to have, so you were not harmed by us in any way. For the kind of sorrow God wants us to experience leads

78

us away from sin and results in salvation. There's no regret for that kind of sorrow. But worldly sorrow, which lacks repentance, results in spiritual death.

Just see what this godly sorrow produced in you! Such earnestness, such concern to clear yourselves, such indignation, such alarm, such longing to see me, such zeal, and such a readiness to punish wrong. You showed that you have done everything necessary to make things right. (2 Corinthians 7:8–11 NLT)

Paul pointed out that sorrowful feelings led to making things right. Glossing over them or pushing them down or not expressing them would have eliminated a great opportunity for change and transformation. In Laurie's case, her feelings needed to be resolved, and they also pointed to some undone business. She was indignant about the notoriety of her husband's transformation, but she was left feeling incomplete. Why? Part of the problem was a lack of restitution on the part of her husband. Yes, he changed. Yes, he did all the right things, but he either forgot his wife's needs or overlooked them. Restitution was needed. He needed to show her in a profound way that he was willing to pay a price for what he had done. It is likely that Laurie would have been in a much better place sooner if he had developed a restitution plan.

If someone in the church had come alongside Laurie and gotten to the heart of her emotions, they would have discovered the lingering hurt and could have helped her resolve those feelings whether or not her husband did anything. They might have come up with a plan that would have made things right, if they had dug deeply enough into the situation.

What could Laurie's husband have done to make restitution? Here are some examples that might have helped with his wife's resentment and their disconnection. Not all of these would be healthy in every situation, but each could have been explored as an option to promote healing between Laurie and her husband:

- Her husband could have publicly honored her or openly confessed his devotion to her while admitting the severity of his sins.
- He could have volunteered to take care of the kids every Saturday for a year so she could have the day off to do what she wanted. Giving up golf, or whatever he did with his buddies, could have been his sacrifice for her.
- He could have saved money to send her on a trip with a girlfriend. He could have told her all the things he was willing to do without to pay for her time away for healing.
- He could have volunteered to keep the house clean for her. He could have served her in ways he had never served her before. His humble and contrite heart would have been a salve to her wounds.
- He could have sat down with her and asked her to consider anything he could do to make it up to her—and have given her time to thoroughly think it through.

I am sure there are many other things that could have been done to make things right. First, someone needed to come alongside Laurie to discover what was missing—other than needed time—in her healing journey. Even if her husband did nothing, she could have been helped through her despair rather than been shamed because of it.

RESOLVE OR REVOLVE

As I am writing this chapter, according to the video map on the screen in front of me, I am 35,651 feet in the air above Illinois, traveling into a headwind at 461 miles per hour, on a Frontier Airlines flight out of Philadelphia. I am returning from a five-day "Lose It for Life Institute" in Cape May, New Jersey. It was a life-changing experience for many of the 134 fellow strugglers who joined my staff and me. Their weights and sizes varied greatly, but most of them knew just about everything about weight loss, diet, and exercise. They were there to learn more than practical information on how they got to be the way they were and what they needed to do to change it. They were there to unlock some of the barriers and solve some of the mysteries that kept them heavy.

One of the most important parts of the whole experience was looking at, experiencing, and resolving feelings. They were hanging on to emotions they thought they had buried, because they had not fully felt the depths of their despair at some point in their lives. They had tried to bury their emotions because they were often told that to feel them would be wrong. They were probably instructed to develop a sense of peace or to get over it and move on, but they could not do any of that by just wanting to. They needed to feel the depths of their emotions in order to reach some state of resolution.

Many realized that if emotions are not resolved, their lives begin to revolve around those feelings, and they live in a constant state of pain, hurt, mistrust, anxiety, fear, and anger. Because these are not considered to be "Christian" emotions, they bury them. But they don't bury them dead; they bury them alive. Because they are not dead, the emotions demand to be fed, and feeding the feelings comes to dominate every area of life. Life revolves around their hurt, and they do everything in relation to their pain. They are controlled by their buried emotions, and when one or more of them surfaces, they redouble their efforts to stay in control.

They often had been told that food was their god, and many of them believed it. I challenged them on this thinking. I doubted that food was their god in the truest sense of what a god is. A god is anything that controls your life. It is the thing in your life that dominates it, controls it, and sucks the life out of it. Food does not do that, but unresolved feelings do. They came to accept that their feelings—their unresolved emotions—were so in control of their lives that they had become gods in the truest sense of the word.

I gave them a word picture involving the Thai restaurant across the street from my office. Just as you enter the restaurant, you can't help but notice that sitting on the floor is a statue of a fat Buddha. Almost every time I go there, just in front of the Buddha are some orange slices or some rice or some other type of food, laid out to feed the fat little god. I asked them to consider if that is what they were doing. The food is not the god. The feelings are the god. The food feeds the feelings and provides some comfort to the food eater.

The lightbulbs began to click on as I shared with them the need to feel and express emotions that have been pressed down, buried, and ignored; and until that was properly and thoroughly done, there was a good chance they would continue to feed those feelings with food. What would they be sacrificing to the feelings god? They would be sacrificing their bodies and the lives God intended for them.

They were paying a significant price and were willing to sacrifice their appearances and relationships because they refused to experience the full depths of the pain they were feeling. If food is used to feed unresolved emotions, it is in everyone's best interest that feelings be experienced and resolved so that a life is not wasted with a bodily sacrifice. Throughout those five days, I encouraged them to feel the depths of their emotions and to resolve their feelings so they no longer fed them and worshipped them.

If food is used to feed unresolved emotions, it is in everyone's best interest that feelings be experienced and resolved so that a life is not wasted with a bodily sacrifice.

Our feelings have a place, but they should not be the entire focus of our lives. That is really what those who suggest we do not need to feel are warning against. They are warning against a life in which everything is based on how we feel. By suggesting that people ignore their emotions, deny the depths of them, and attempt to move on, they create the very problem they are trying to prevent. So we must feel our lives and live them authentically, with nothing hidden and nothing buried. Living like that enables us to have feelings without being defined solely by them.

THE STATE OF NUMBNESS

Almost everyone has experienced a loss or a trauma so bad that they were numb and unfeeling rather than overwhelmed by the intense pain. The shock and numbness is a unique gift from God that allows us to survive the worst emotions. How else could a mother recover after delivering a stillborn baby she carried for nine months? How else could a father endure the news that a drunk driver has killed his young son? The severity of these emotions could cause a person to break with reality and totally break down. God gives us a natural response that—for a time—numbs us to the intensity and severity of the worst feelings. Gradually the emotions return, and we can slowly start to experience them, share them, express them, and then resolve them.

If we refuse to feel the emotions, we don't kill them—they are still there. We have them within us, and the pain lingers on. So we do for ourselves what God did in the beginning of the pain. We return to the state of numbness. We numb the emotions with food, drugs, alcohol, sex, gambling, stealing, or hundreds of other things we use as painkillers. When we refuse to resolve our emotions, we choose to carry them with us; each time they start to surface, we return to the numbing device of our choice.

We become hooked on the numbing device during the process of trying to return to the state of numbness. That dependency causes additional consequences and pain, and our lives spin helplessly out of control until we come to the conclusion that there is only one way out. We must finally feel the emotions we dreaded. We must reenter the pain, resolve it, and then move on with our lives, connected to others, feeling the reality of what we are experiencing right now, no matter how uncomfortable it is.

DYING TO SELF

We need to die to self, rather than trying to drown out our emotions or kill our feelings. Dying to self is an interesting concept. It is simple,

84

painful, and nonsensical to most of the world, but dying to self means we are willing to give up our entitlement to be comfortable. It means we are willing to be uncomfortable for the good of others and the purposes of God.

We are not healing our lives if we are protecting ourselves from feeling the emotions buried deep inside. We are infecting our lives rather than healing them if we avoid all contact and connection with others so that we don't develop additional painful feelings. We are infecting them with loneliness, isolation, and alienation. In order to heal, we must die to our most immediate desires and experience life as it is.

The choice to heal is the choice not to take a drink at the point of anger and rage. It is looking at the anger and rage as a sign that something is wrong and must be attended to. I live in the anger, experience it, explore it, and find out what is at the heart of it, until I finally resolve it in order to heal my life. The choice to heal means that rather than eating a carton of ice cream when I am anxious, I die to the urge to binge, feel the anxiety, live in it, discover its source, and then resolve it and experience a new level of healing. I experience the feelings, dying to my selfish urge to delay them, bury them, or smother them, and then I use them as a signal that I must do more work to clean out the emotional baggage from the darkest parts of my soul.

Misty and I are still laughing about her neglect of a warning sign in the midst of her busy life as an author and mother. I was driving her car to church one morning and noticed that on the dash was a light shining brightly under the words "Maintenance Required." I mentioned to her that it might be a really good idea to heed the warning of that light and take the car in and have the problem fixed. She believed there was something wrong with the indicator light and that it was the light that needed to be fixed. She totally denied that there might be something wrong with the motor that was causing the light to come on.

A few days later a loud clunk and some billowing smoke on the freeway ended her trip to work and the life of the engine. The intensity of the heat had cracked her engine because of the lack of oil. The oil drained away when a plug came undone under the car. The replacement engine cost twenty-five hundred dollars; the rental car to drive to and from work cost an additional four hundred dollars. This was money she did not have and time she could not afford to waste, but she paid the money and took the time to repair the car. None of it would have been necessary if she had merely heeded the warning light. All of us have done this in one form or another. I have been doing it many years of my life.

The painful emotions of anger, rage, guilt, shame, fear, anxiety, and grief are indicators that something down deep is wrong. They are God's built-in dash-light warning system, there to protect you from future destruction. Pay attention to them. Don't use excuses to hide them or bury them or numb them. Feel them. Learn to accept them as the price of being engaged in life and a natural result of living life to the fullest. They are a reality that all of us must face, because we will all experience loss, rejection, and hurt at some time or other. When we do, we must step into our emotions and feel them deeply so that we can let go of them and move on.

THE BIG LIE
"Real Christians should have a real peace in all circumstances."

Many are living the big lie that if we are real Christians, we should experience a real peace in all circumstances. The lie only serves to delay the pain that must be experienced as a gift from God. The gift of pain pierces through us, and we instantly know we have a problem to solve or a mystery to unravel. When someone we love dies, we have a problem to solve. We have to find a way to live without that person. We have to exist without his or her daily touch or frequent contact, encouragement, or nurturing. If we deny that pain, we don't solve the problem.

The claim of instant peace can lead us to constant and ongoing pain that will not die until we feel it, express it, understand it, and resolve it. The big lie prevents us from healing. It moves us into superficiality and fake connection. Feeling our lives and the pain in them allows us to connect in authentic and intimate ways.

I wanted to get away when the reality of my divorce hit. I chose Hawaii, and I am glad I did. There was a drive within me to experience Hawaii the way I wanted. It was a trip of defiance. I did not want to feel; I just wanted to go to act out my independence. If I was going to be left, then I was going to go and live the way I had always wanted to live for a couple of weeks in Hawaii.

I ate breakfast the way I wanted. I phoned my friends after a few days and told them I had three breakfasts in three days for less than three dollars that each took me three minutes to eat. I was free to eat as I wanted and was defiant in my freedom. Afterward I took my long board out onto the waves of Waikiki and, although I was a bit shaky, I surfed as long as I wanted and when I wanted. It was a dream trip during which I lived as I wanted to for the first time in more than twenty years.

The dream did not last long. Hawaii was full of memories; my wife and I had been there many times. She was all over it—we were all over it. There was not a place I could go without thinking of times we were there together and had an argument or were disconnected. The longer I stayed, the more the pain grew. I did not see it as a gift—it hurt.

The pain broke through the defiance of short breakfasts and long boards and laid me out flat on the bed of a dark hotel room. I felt sharp, searing pain from the bottom of my soul. I have never felt anything that bad and so incapacitating. There was no peace, because in my defiance I had landed myself in the heart of many memories that all seemed like a waste of time and effort. I felt the pain. I embraced it. I shared it with some friends. When I left, I was free from most of it. I was free because I had refused to fake peace when there was none.

You may be living some form of defiance. You may be showing the world that nothing gets to you. You may be avoiding pain while declaring you are at peace with God, yourself, and others. If that is the case, I invite you to feel your life and experience the worst aspect of pain in it so you can experience God in all of His glory. Pain leaves us empty so that we can fill up on God. If we don't allow that emptiness to lead us to God, it leads us somewhere else. We latch on to sick people rather than experience God's presence. We load up on sick people when we could have placed our burden in the hands of God.

We struggle and strive rather than allow God's power to energize us and do for us what we cannot do for ourselves. We seek forms of false intimacy with casual sex or romantic escapades rather than finding intimacy with God. We have affairs with the ungodly rather than connecting with God's healing community. We do all of this because we are defiantly declaring we are at peace when we are actually in tremendous pain and turmoil just below the surface.

INVITING QUIET

Today might be a good day to do a pain inventory and a feelings checkup. Perhaps you could find the time to get away, be still, and quiet your mind. If you do, ask yourself these questions:

- What am I afraid of?
- What is missing?
- Am I empty?
- What am I filling up on?
- Why am I refusing to feel?
- What feelings am I avoiding?

You may find that you can see a pattern of protection from the painful feelings you need to address when you take this kind of inventory. You may find yourself hiding from pain and hiding from others. You might see a tremendous amount of defensiveness on your part, and you might find yourself isolated and alone. If so, go further in your inventory and look at how fear plays into the style of living you have adopted. Discover what you are afraid of.

- Am I afraid of rejection?
- Am I afraid of being inadequate?
- Am I afraid someone might come to control me?
- Do I avoid doing things because I am afraid of failing?
- Am I afraid of doing nothing significant during my life?

When you have explored the fear, look at the anger:

- Do I hold a grudge?
- Am I angry because I feel controlled?
- Is my past in my present because of anger toward someone who hurt me?
- Am I seeking revenge in any form?
- Does my anger lead me to make negative statements about anyone?

Then in the quiet moments, take a look at the guilt and shame you bear:

- Am I feeling guilty about a current habit?
- Do I experience shame from something someone did to me?
- Am I knowingly involved in a sin?
- When I feel guilt, am I shutting it down with food or drink?
- Is there anything I could change to reduce the guilt?

In a quiet place, with a quiet mind, you may find the answers to questions you did not even know you were avoiding. You may find some areas that are sensitive and need resolution. You may discover that feeling your life is not something to avoid. You may find it quite bearable in the bad times and very enjoyable in the good.

THE RESURRECTION'S IMPACT ON FEELINGS

The foundation of the Christian faith is the belief that Jesus actually existed; lived here on earth to show us how to live; and then took upon Himself the penalty of our sins, died for them, was buried, and rose from the grave. A person who believes that and accepts Jesus is admitting that none of us have the ability within us to earn our way to heaven. We can never be good enough or accumulate enough to be with a holy God.

Jesus came so that we would no longer have to try to do what we cannot do. He paid the ultimate sacrifice with His life, and as a result we can have eternal life. Jesus said, "I am the way, the truth, and the life. No one comes to the Father except through Me" (John 14:6 NKJV). It could not be clearer that accepting Jesus as your Savior makes all the difference in the eternal world. But what about today and the way you feel?

The fact that Jesus died on the cross for you and rose from the grave has a lot to do with how you live today and how you feel. It was not just something that happened to affect your eternal soul. It is all about today. Today you do not need to continue in the guilt and shame that creeps up from your past, because Christ's death and resurrection have wiped the slate clean and have taken care of everything you have ever done that was wrong.

Today you do not have to be angry toward anyone. You can give them what God has given you through the death and resurrection of Jesus, and that is complete forgiveness. There is no need to be angry and live in bitterness when you can forgive, because Jesus forgave you. Today you do not have to fear the future. God has it all in His hands. Your eternity is secure, so your worst case is your best case. If you die, you will go and be with Jesus. You can be emotionally free in the present and find that living can be quite comfortable in spite of all the challenges to your own serenity.

When you put your trust in Jesus, your life becomes manageable, and your state of mind becomes enjoyable because your feelings are not raging out of control. You don't have to worry about anything when you trust God for everything (Matthew 6:25). There is no reason to be anxious about anything when you have placed your trust in God (Philippians 4:6). When you live this way, you are at peace with the world and yourself, and you are free to make the connections you need to make. You are free to feel the emptiness, the fear, and the anger because you know you will survive and that, in the end, all of these feelings will be resolved and in the hands of God. So every day you can turn over to Him a little bit more than the day before. You can feel your life, heal your life, and experience your life to the fullest.

Healing is a choice. It is a choice to feel your life.

CHAPTER 2 WORKBOOK QUESTIONS

THE SECOND CHOICE:
The Choice to Feel Your Life

THE SECOND BIG LIE:
"Real Christians should have a real peace in all circumstances."

IMAGINE WHAT MIGHT HAPPEN IF WE FELT NO PAIN. WE might say, "No pain? That would be great!" But the opposite is true. The absence of pain would create unimaginable problems. We might suffer serious physical illnesses and not be aware, because there would be no pain to warn us.

What could happen if there were no nerves in your feet, so that you could not feel anything as you walked about? Suppose you were running barefoot through the woods and stepped on several sharp pieces of a broken bottle. Your feet might suffer severe cuts with profuse bleeding. You might lapse into shock or even bleed to death, because there was no pain to warn you.

What if your appendix became infected, threatening to burst? Without pain to let you know something serious was happening, you might die from toxemia.

As we saw in chapter 2, Ashlyn Blocker is a small child who was born with an ailment that prevents her from feeling pain. As a result, she is often in danger of hurting herself. Her food must be cooled, and ice cubes are dropped into her soup so she won't burn herself. Her mother said, "I'd give anything for her to feel pain."

How ironic! Most of us hate pain. We view it as something to be avoided. It hurts. The bottom line is that we view pain as bad. Given the choice, human beings move as quickly as possible from pain to pleasure. Yet Ashlyn's mom desperately wishes her child could feel pain!

The truth is that pain can be very helpful. How often have you gone to your doctor or taken a sick child to the clinic, and the attending physician asks, "Where does it hurt?" Pain gives the doctor direction as she looks for the source of illness. Pain is not the enemy.

The Second Choice:
The Choice to Feel Your Life

Key Scripture: *Your promise revives me; it comforts me in all my troubles.*

—PSALM 119:50 NLT

The powerful truth is, "When we feel our lives, we are tuned in to pain as it emerges and can resolve it before our lives begin to revolve around it" (p. 72).

Pain can be all-consuming. It demands our total attention. It's hard to deny or push aside. Culturally, we seem dedicated to doing everything possible to eradicate pain. Billions of dollars are spent to prevent or alleviate it. The unwritten goal seems to be: do anything possible, at any cost, to avoid the feeling of pain.

However, whether we deny it or medicate it, there is no guarantee that our pain will go away. It is there for a purpose. Until we've acknowledged and addressed the cause of our pain, we will continue to suffer its misery.

The psalmist experienced considerable pain in his life. He learned an important principle that we all should affirm: we are comforted in our pain by the truth that God preserves our lives (Psalm 119:50).

AN IMPORTANT PRINCIPLE

Earlier we read, "What is true of physical pain and the body is true for emotional pain and the soul" (p. 72). Pain can be physical, but it can also be emotional, psychological, and spiritual. In fact, emotional pain is often much worse than its physical counterpart. It can take root in our psyches and embark on a deadly mission to wound our hearts.

Typically, medications and treatments heal physical pain, but the pain we bear in our hearts and minds does not respond well to organic medicines.

Chapter 2 describes the challenge of dealing with emotional pain, as illustrated in Laurie's story.

Exercise #1: Laurie's Story

Read Laurie's story again (pp. 73–76). If you are studying in a small group, ask a volunteer to read it aloud.

Respond to the following questions in the spaces provided. If you are studying in a small group, discuss your answers together.

1. What was the source of Laurie's pain?

_____

_____

2. Laurie's husband confessed his affair, repented, sought forgiveness, and recommitted to their marriage. However, as he improved, Laurie seemed to get worse. What happened to Laurie?

_____

_____

3. What caused Laurie's pain to intensify, even as her husband recovered and was restored?

_____

_____

4. What did Laurie desperately need to do?

_____

LAURIE'S STRUGGLE WITH HER PAIN

Laurie's story is filled with irony. At a time when she thought all was well with her life, her husband's life was a disaster. When Laurie discovered his affair and confronted him, he did all the right things. He confessed, repented, apologized, and changed. As a result he felt better, cleansed and restored. People were amazed as they noted the positive changes in his life. In a weird way, he became a local hero. Bad guy makes good! He was the center of attention. Everyone assumed that Laurie felt great too; but she didn't! On the contrary, the better her husband did, the worse she felt. Why?

Laurie never had an opportunity to acknowledge and deal with her personal pain.

She needed to grieve, to be angry, and to process through the painful emotions caused by her husband's infidelity.

People failed to acknowledge her personal pain. Strangely, they encouraged her to deny it. So Laurie languished. She had done nothing wrong. She hadn't engaged in an affair. She had been faithful and committed, yet she was the one racked by pain.

The one thing Laurie desperately needed was to acknowledge and feel the pain that lay suppressed inside her. It made her miserable! Holding her pain inside, she shut down emotionally, stopped connecting with others, and sank into depression.

CONNECTING AND FEELING

At this point, one of the great values of *Healing Is a Choice* emerges. Remember that chapter 1 encouraged readers to reach out and connect with others who could help them heal. This chapter encourages readers to feel their pain. Yet finding the courage and commitment to experience pain often depends on those with whom we have connected.

We need to experience our pain rather than deny it. But we also need a safe environment in which to do it. That "safe environment" is our circle of loving, caring friends. We need those who will encourage us to feel and stay near us while we do. We need friends who will not be afraid when our emotions are uncontrollable, and who will remain until they subside.

It is practically impossible to feel and express one's pain without the support of those who love you and can provide a safe environment for your feelings.

Laurie was missing one important connection that trapped her in unresolved pain. Her husband was a changed man, for the better. He received great applause and praise for his reformation. He had done everything right, except address his wife's pain. Laurie's missing connection was her husband! Laurie was left to languish in pain. Her husband needed to connect with her feelings, and to acknowledge his role in causing them. "He needed to show her in a profound way that he was willing to pay a price for what he had done" (p. 79). Such an act of connection might have dramatically sped up Laurie's recovery.

EMOTIONS AND FEELINGS

This chapter focuses on the importance of facing and experiencing our emotions.

The *American Heritage Dictionary* defines *emotion* as "a mental state that arises spontaneously rather than through conscious effort and is often accompanied by physiological changes; a feeling."[2] Emotions are instinctive, innate patterns of behaviors. They come with us at birth. Emotions are the part of the consciousness that involves feeling.

The word *emotion* comes from a Latin word meaning "to move." Perhaps that is why we often refer to our emotions as "moving us" to tears, joy, excitement, and so forth.

Emotions come in a wide variety. Some are sad. Some are joyous. Some are frightening. People are very comfortable with some of their emotions but can become quite upset by others. Let's do a personal appraisal of feelings.

Exercise #2: Feelings Appraisal

Read through the list of emotions below, one at a time. After each word, describe your reaction(s) to the feeling listed on the line provided.

Example: Hope—Makes me feel upbeat. Inspires optimism.

Emotions	Reactions
Anger	
Despair	
Fear	
Hate	
Hope	
Love	
Sadness	
Joy	
Grief	
Guilt	
Worry	

If you are studying in a small group, use the following questions for discussion.

1. Which emotions would you describe as negative?

_____

_____

_____

2. Which emotions would you describe as positive?

_____

_____

_____

3. Which emotions would you describe as most destructive?

_____

_____

_____

4. Which emotions would you describe as most constructive?

_____

_____

_____

Take some time to analyze your responses. If you journal, you might consider using these questions in that process.

1. Which emotions do you experience most often?

2. Are the emotions you feel most often positive or negative?

3. Do you find that some emotions seem to be constantly present in your life? For example, do you feel sad most of the time? Fearful? Angry? Hopeful?

THE DANGER OF DENIAL

Far too many people try to bury their emotions because they were often told that to feel them would be wrong. Can you remember a parent or relative saying, "Don't feel sad," "You shouldn't be so angry," or "You're just a worrywart"?

Though it might be unintentional, such language is an effort to deny your feelings. Most likely, your parents or friends were uncomfortable with those feelings or felt it was inappropriate to express them. How sad! When people are denied their feelings, they get stuck in them. They feel isolated, disconnected, and emotionally paralyzed.

There is no easy way through emotional and spiritual pain. It cannot be denied, buried, or ignored. We can't magically erase it as we do the writing on a chalkboard. If we don't look our pain in the eye, experience it and process it, it can "store up" in us, and we become consumed with the effort to find something to relieve our pain.

To make matters worse, many people suffering from intense emotional pain try to self-medicate using drugs, food, alcohol, money, sex, gambling, reckless risk taking, and more. Sadly, these things never work, and they always compound the problem. It's like trying to cure lung cancer with an aspirin. Thus, pain increases.

Denying our feelings is a debilitating effort. It's much better to experience the pain and learn how to express it appropriately.

Rather than suppress feelings, we need to pay careful attention to them, because they are barometers of our mental health.

What people need most is a genuine cure, the kind that only comes from God's Holy Spirit and the connection of loving, caring friends.

Exercise #3: What Would Jesus Feel?

Jesus experienced a wide range of feelings, from anger to weeping to joy. He did not deny His feelings but felt free to feel and express His emotions.

Jesus acknowledged His feelings. He

- wept (John 11:35);
- was compassionate (Mark 1:41);
- loved people, and had deep personal affection for friends (John 11:3);
- was tired and worn out (John 4:6);
- laughed and played with children (Mark 10:16);
- was so angry with corrupt temple officials that He over- turned their tables (Matthew 21:12).

Read the scriptures listed below. Each one describes something about the pain and sorrow Jesus experienced. After each Scripture reference, describe in your own words what the verse means, and how it describes Jesus' experience of physical and emotional pain.

1. Isaiah 53:3–9

_____

_____

_____

2. Matthew 26 (the entire chapter, but especially verses 38–40, 42)

---

3. Matthew 27:46

One thing we learn from these texts is that Jesus knows what pain is like, because He experienced it personally. He is acquainted with grief and sorrow. Therefore, He can empathize with us in times of suffering, and He knows the appropriate way to respond.

Remember how important it is to be connected to others during times of pain. Jesus is "a real friend [who] sticks closer than a brother" (Proverbs 18:24 NLT). He has promised to stay connected to us: "I will never fail you. I will never abandon you" (Hebrews 13:5 NLT). When we are connected to Him, He will be with us as we experience the deep pain in our lives.

THE VALUE OF PAIN

Pain, for all its hurts, can be a positive thing. We deny it at our own peril. The apostle Paul wrote,

We can rejoice, too, when we run into problems and trials, for we know that they help us develop endurance. And endurance develops strength of character, and character strengthens our confident hope of salvation. And this hope will not lead to disappointment. For we know how dearly God loves us, because he has given us the Holy Spirit to fill our hearts with his love. (Romans 5:3–5 NLT)

Consider the positive impact of pain. It gets our attention. Break a finger, stub a toe, suffer a migraine headache, or experience the rejection of a close friend, and you will pay attention!

Pain is a great motivator. When we experience it, we are moved to action. Our full attention will focus on getting medicine, reconciling a broken relationship, or doing whatever is necessary to get relief.

Pain gives us direction. If we are enduring a high fever, have lost a job, or have experienced a divorce, pain moves us toward healing, spurs us to find employment, and pushes us to make a fresh start.

Pain prompts us to connect with others. It is true that some folks, when enduring great pain, turn inward and isolate themselves. What they need most are good friends who can reach out to them. However, most people seek the support of others from whom they can draw strength as they walk through the valley of pain.

Whether it is a physician, a health practitioner, a counselor, or a trusted friend, the need to connect during the pain-to-healing process is profound. A physician has the expertise to diagnose and prescribe medicine. A counselor can help us examine the emotional pain we endure and guide us toward the means of dealing with it. A friend stands solidly with us in our pain—supporting, praying, helping, and caring.

Pain may not feel good, but it is not always our enemy. It has the power to spur us on to emotional and spiritual growth.

THE SECOND BIG LIE:
"Real Christians should have a real peace in all circumstances."

There are some religious groups who teach that "true" faith means we will never be ill, experience failure, have financial problems, suffer marital difficulties, or have to endure pain or suffering.

In order to prove themselves faithful and live up to such impossible expectations, they have to engage in denial. They often construct a worldview that allows them to endure all manner of problems, while they publicly "confess" just the opposite. They experience intense emotional pain, but confess that all is well.

The notion that real Christians can move through life with uninterrupted peace is psychological denial written as theology.

In the real world, all people are subject to the human condition. We all experience pain, illness, trouble, fatigue, grief, and anger, just as Jesus did. We experience the full range of human emotions, good and bad. It's important that we understand this, so we don't feel compelled to hide our pain behind a facade.

We should acknowledge the difference between objective peace and subjective peace. Objective peace occurs in a religious context. It is the peace that we have because Jesus Christ died for us, and as a result, there is no enmity between God and us. We have the peace of God that passes understanding. It is a spiritual fact, and does not waver, even though we may have all sorts of human experiences, good and bad (Philippians 4:7).

Subjective peace is what we have been discussing. It relies heavily on human emotions. We feel settled, happy, and peaceful. Life is relatively calm. Our worries are few, our bills are paid, our relationships are healthy, and life's existential pressures have diminished. It feels great, but we know that, in a moment's time, subjective peace could be shattered. A car accident, financial failure, trouble with a child, losing a job, or experiencing a heated argument with a spouse can all disturb one's peace, and for quite a while.

Real Christians can have objective peace with God at all times, but no human being will experience subjective peace all the time. As mentioned above, all people are subject to the human condition.

Here is a very important fact: the quality of our mental health may depend on recognizing the important distinction between objective and subjective peace.

Exercise #4: Bible Study

The Bible consistently makes the point that we experience both the joys and pains of life. No one is exempt.

By listing the statements in 2 Corinthians 4:7–10, 16, 17 (NLT) under "Bad News" and "Good News" categories, we get a vivid picture of the contrasting nature of real life. In this paradigm, we see that life is about limitations, pain, and fragileness.

"But this precious treasure—this light and power that now shine within us—is held in perishable containers, that is, in our weak bodies" (v. 7 NLT).

At the same time, it is about hope, recovery, and victory.

"We are not crushed and broken" (v. 8 NLT).

Read through the list and note that we experience not only normal human challenges (Bad News) but also the grace and care of God (Good News).

Bad News	Good News
2 Corinthians 4:7	
But this precious treasure—this light and power that now shine within us—is held in perishable containers, that is, our weak bodies [we are fragile creatures],	so everyone can see that our glorious power is from God and is not our own.
2 Corinthians 4:8	
We are pressed on every side by troubles [life is filled with pressure], We are perplexed,	but we are not crushed and broken. But we don't give up and quit.
2 Corinthians 4:9	
We are hunted down, We get knocked down,	but God never abandons us. but we get up again and keep going.
2 Corinthians 4:10	
Through suffering, these bodies of ours constantly share in the death of Jesus	so that the life of Jesus may also be seen in our bodies.
2 Corinthians 4:12	
So we live in the face of death,	but it has resulted in eternal life for you.
2 Corinthians 4:16	
Though our bodies are dying,	our spirits are being renewed every day. That is why we never give up.
2 Corinthians 4:17	
For our present troubles are quite small and won't last very long,	yet they produce for us an immeasurably great glory that will last forever!

This way of looking at 2 Corinthians 4 helps us understand that the normal Christian life is impacted by good and bad, highs and lows, victories and challenges. This is real life, and it is very important for us to experience—to feel—all of it. At times it may seem frightening. Life can be very tough. But regardless of the circumstances, God is faithful and His Holy Spirit is always close to us, ready to help in our time of need.

A Pain Inventory and Feelings Checkup

The book suggests taking a pain inventory and feelings checkup (pp. 89–90), so let's do that.

Instructions:

Select a quiet place away from noise, crowds, and busyness.

Be still and try to quiet your mind so that you can focus without interruption. In this exercise, you may find answers to questions you did not even know you were avoiding. You may find some areas that are sensitive and need resolution. Or you may discover that feeling your life is not something to avoid.

Ask yourself these questions:

1. What am I afraid of?

_____

_____

2. What is missing?

_____

_____

3. Am I empty?

_____

_____

4. What am I filling up on?

_____

_____

5. Why am I refusing to feel?

_____

_____

6. What feelings am I avoiding?

_____

_____

Look at your responses. Do you see a pattern? Do you seem to be hiding from your pain? Are you failing to connect with others? Continue by answering the next set of questions dealing with fear:

7. Am I afraid of rejection?

_____

_____

8. Am I afraid of being inadequate?

_____

_____

9. Am I afraid someone might come to control me?

_____

_____

10. Do I avoid doing things because I am afraid of failing?

_____

_____

11. Am I afraid of doing nothing significant during my life?

_____

_____

If you answered yes to any of these questions, take some time and consider why you are experiencing the pain of fear. Analyze the question(s) until you can answer no to the questions. Next, answer the five questions below that deal with anger:

12. Do I hold a grudge?

_____

_____

13. Am I angry because I feel controlled?

_____

_____

14. Is my past in my present because of anger toward someone who hurt me?

_____

_____

15. Am I seeking revenge in any form?

_____

_____

16. Does my anger lead me to make negative statements about anyone?

_____

_____

If you answered yes to any of these questions, take some time and consider why you are experiencing the pain of anger. Analyze the questions(s) until you can answer no to the questions. Finally, answer the five questions below that deal with guilt and shame:

17. Am I feeling guilty about a current habit?

_____

18. Do I experience shame from something someone did to me?

_____

19. Am I knowingly involved in a sin?

_____

20. When I feel guilty, am I shutting my guilt down with food or drink?

_____

21. Is there anything I could change to reduce the guilt?

_____

_____

If you answered yes to any of these questions, take some time and consider why you are feeling shame and guilt. Think about the question(s) until you can answer no to the questions.

THE PASSION OF CHRIST

In 2004, Mel Gibson created a stir throughout the world by releasing a movie titled *The Passion of the Christ*. In the most graphic portrayal of the death of Christ ever produced, the movie confronted viewers with the brutal reality of Jesus' physical abuse and ultimate death. The movie was very nearly too painful to watch.

What is clearly conveyed is that Jesus chose to "feel" His pain. He did not run away from it or deny it. He felt it all. And the most scandalous thing is that He experienced the pain for us. He created a means by which we can deal with our pain, be it spiritual, emotional, or physical.

Thanks to Jesus, we no longer have a need to deny or suppress our pain. We can feel it and overcome it, and roll it over onto Him, because He knows how it feels and never leaves or forsakes us (1 Peter 5:7).

JOURNALING

Take a few minutes and think about chapter 2. Review it in your mind, or go back and scan the pages. Use the questions and spaces below to guide your journaling.

1. Why do we fear pain?

2. Has pain ever had a positive impact on your life?

3. What parts of chapter 2 spoke most clearly to you?

4. Were you able to personally identify with aspects of chapter 2?

5. How have you handled pain in your life?

6. Do you acknowledge and feel your pain, or do you deny or suppress it?

7. Does God use pain to shape our character?

_____

_____

_____

8. Have you ever experienced the consequences of denied pain?

_____

_____

_____

9. What pain might you be holding on to at this time in your life?

_____

_____

_____

10. How can you let go of that pain?

_____

_____

_____

PRAYERFUL MEDITATION

Find a quiet, relaxing place where you are comfortable and un-interrupted. Take a few minutes and meditate on the information in chapter 2. Sit quietly for a few minutes. Listen to your heartbeat and appreciate that you are alive and can feel.

Clear your mind and focus on Jesus Christ. Quietly sing or hum a favorite hymn or praise song. Think about the goodness and great-ness of God. Ask the Holy Spirit to clear the clutter and busyness from your mind. Be patient. Listen quietly and wait for the Spirit to speak to your mind.

The Holy Spirit may want to encourage you to be braver when it comes to feeling your pain. He may want to challenge you to take the risk of acknowledging your pain.

Experience the presence of Christ, who will gladly take your pain and help you bear it.

PRAYER

Heavenly Father, hear my honest prayer and my sincere concerns. At times, I am overcome with pain. People I love are hurting and I don't know how to help. My health is failing and I can't stop it. The quality of my work is slipping and I am afraid I won't be able to keep up. I feel distant from You. Sometimes I think I have more pain than joy. I need help. I need Your help. Thank You for the challenge and encouragement I have received from this chapter. Help me to acknowledge my pain, feel it, and then, with Your help, move toward peace and calm. Help me to examine my heart and mind honestly, and to identify the pain I carry from day to day. I acknowledge that healing my pain is a choice. From the power of Your Spirit, give me the courage to choose healing. Increase my confidence in You. Where I am weak and hesitant to act, give me strength. Increase my faith. I give You my life—mind, soul, and spirit. Through Jesus Christ, my Savior and friend. Amen.

He will wipe every tear from their eyes, and there will be no more death or sorrow or crying or pain. For all these things are gone forever.

—Revelation 21:4 NLT

3

THE THIRD CHOICE:
The Choice to Investigate Your Life in Search of Truth

THE THIRD BIG LIE:
"It does no good to look back or look inside."

ARE THERE SOME THINGS YOU ARE DOING THAT ARE CAUS-
ing you to be separated from others and from the life you could be
enjoying? Are there areas of your life that are full of conflict and
struggle that you wish would just go away? Have you ever walked
away from a conversation or a fight wondering why you did what
you did or said what you said? Almost everyone has, but not everyone goes through the pain and struggle of getting to the "why"
behind the choices that are causing problems, conflict, and emotional turmoil. We heal our lives as we begin to search for truth
about why we do what we do and why we feel the way we feel.

When two very hurt and unaware people come together in marriage, the result is often a complete and total disaster. The outcome
is usually not good when neither person is willing to take a look
and discover the truth about him- or herself and the situation they
are stuck in. I came in contact with thousands of men in struggling
marriages when I wrote *Every Man's Battle* with Fred Stoeker.

There were all sorts of mind-boggling and amazing dilemmas. E-mails poured in about pastors who were cross-dressing at home and soccer moms who had left their families to ride cross-country with truckers they had met on the Internet. It was as if there was a dramatic movie in every e-mail. Some common patterns emerged in the midst of all the drama. The pain was common, and the structure of the relationships was common. One of the most prevalent was the overweight wife married to the sex-addicted husband.

She is overweight and out of control. In her anger, she eats with him in mind, punishing him with her growing girth, calming her anger at him like an alcoholic on a binge with a fifth of vodka. She is anxious and angry and very disappointed. Nothing in the dream she wanted showed up after the marriage vows; it is more like a nightmare. In her depression she eats, because she has nowhere else to turn. She resents her husband and compares his inner life full of flaws and failures with the outer lives of other men. He always comes up short in her superficial analysis. Nothing he does is good enough, and every now and then she lets him know it. She does not want him to touch her, and the eating helps to keep her out of his clutches. Until he is willing to change, she will continue to live out her life the best she can with her food as the only thing that comforts her as a woman.

He is into pornography and lust—perhaps it has escalated to sexual addiction. He uses his wife's weight as an excuse. In his mind, she has let herself go with no regard to how she looks to him or others. He feels entitled to look at other women and believes it is normal and natural for him to do so. Nothing he does changes the situation; she is beyond his influence, and he has no ability to reach her or control her. He is angry and blames her for the immoral mess in which he finds himself. He thinks if she would just get her fat act together, he would be able to have the kind of relationship with her he has always dreamed of. But until she is willing to change, he will just continue to live out his life the best he can with his pornography as the only thing that makes him feel like a man.

I have seen this over and over again: two people unwilling to look at themselves and how they came to this horrible place, quick to point a finger and quick to blame each other. They are in a quagmire of anger and resentment, and both have chosen coping behaviors that stand to make matters worse. But there is another way. There is a way out for both of these hurting strugglers, but the way is not easy. It requires taking an honest look inside, investigating the past to discover the truth about today.

Today's truth for a woman like this often begins with her father, who laid the foundation for her relationships with men. Most likely her father was not a man who provided for her or connected with her deepest needs. In the absence of what he could have given her, she has expected her husband to make up for it. She does not know that is what she has done, but it is. She resents the man in her life today because he is unable to fill the void left by her uncaring father.

There are some other cases that are just the opposite. The woman might not be miserable because her father was so bad, but because he was so good. If her father was an amazing man, she may have been looking for someone who could measure up to her ideal dad—and no man can. So either way, good dad or bad dad, she looks to her husband to fulfill her, and he is not enough. So she resents her husband and compares him to everyone else until she is finally convinced that he is a loser.

For the man's part, there is a good chance that the mother in his past is influencing his present. His mother may have been ideal; she may have met his every need, so he is angry because he is married to someone unwilling to do that. There is also a chance he had a domineering mother who tried to control everything he did and held on to him too long. In fact, she may never have let go. In the current relationship, he projects all of his anger toward his mother onto his wife, and she cannot be his lover as he fixates on her as a representation of his mother. So he turns to images rather than to his wife. The images can be manipulated and controlled, and he can have a sexual experience without being evaluated or judged. He is angry with his wife and compares her to the images he worships, and she always comes up short.

MYSTERIES OF THE MIND

All of us have mysteries inside of us that need to be solved. In the situations above, when the mysteries are solved, there is an opportunity for the relationship to be healed. Insight and awareness lead to informed choices that can heal, but if no one ever stops to consider the "why" behind the actions or the feelings that lead to the actions, there is little hope for change or healing. It would be helpful for all of us to stop and take a look at life in the past, where we are today, and where it is all leading to in the future. The Bible challenges us to take a look inside: "Let us examine our ways" (Lamentations 3:40 NIV). Our ways are our habits, conflicts, character defects, and the patterns in our relationships. When you are willing to take a look, you may discover some areas that need work and that, when worked on, lead to healing.

There is a mystery of the mind to solve when you come to the end of yourself and feel as if you cannot go on. You can give up, or you can hold on and allow yourself more time to solve the mystery that is leading to your sense of being overwhelmed, alone, and desperate.

There is a mystery to solve when you lose something you hoped to keep. You can just move on, or you can investigate why it meant so much to you and how you lost it. Solve that mystery, and you may find that you won't lose so much in the future.

There is a mystery to solve when there is a divorce or the breakup of an important relationship. In fact, in this case, there are usually many mysteries that need to be solved—that was the case for me. I had to discover how I ended up divorced after twenty-one years of a tough marriage.

FACING THE TOUGH TRUTH ABOUT ME

When the reality of my divorce began to sink in, it was not easy to face the tough task of looking at how I had added to the difficulty in our marriage or how my reactions to problems had made things worse. It was a tough task to take a look inside while trying to defend my integrity and all I had done to try to make the marriage work. I said things like, "Sure, I contributed to problems, but I did not contribute to the divorce or the events that led up to the divorce." My point was that all of us in every marriage do defective things, but they don't always lead to divorce. I knew there were worse husbands in solid marriages, so I was not going to take the rap for the divorce.

I remember long conversations about what I had done to preserve the marriage and heal it. I sought counseling for myself and was in counseling when everything blew up. I was in a men's support group and Bible study. I was making an effort to fix what needed fixing in the relationship. I was willing, and I wanted those who questioned me to know this was not the case of a man just blindly going through his marriage unaware of the problems. I was aware of them; I just did not have the answers.

Some light began to creep into my soul in the midst of my self-justification and defensiveness. I began to realize that if I totally and completely defended everything I did in the marriage, I had a good chance of getting involved in another one just like it. I let a little bit of light come in through my counseling, because making myself feel good about what I had done in the past was not going to forge a new and healthy future for me. I had heard great things about a male counselor named Milan, and I was optimistic about what we might accomplish together. In our first session, he gained my confidence and trust while instilling some optimism about the situation. He said to me, "I can help you get your life back."

Oh, what wonderful words those were to me! I had lost my life and had lived for years in what seemed like a dark dungeon of isolation. I wept at the thought of having a new and different life. When the tears ended, I was ready to begin to take a look inside. I am indebted to him for much of what I see today and how I relate to others differently.

My counselor and I explored my patterns of interacting with others. It became obvious that although I loved to communicate from a stage and behind a microphone, and loved to connect with people in those forums, I was in reality more of an avoidant personality. I did not connect quickly with people and was not open to intimate connection unless I felt it was very safe. I became aware of how my leadership positions kept me disconnected from others. I realized how my schedule and the rush and busyness of it all allowed me to run from person to person without truly connecting on a deep and intimate level.

I began to look at people's reactions to me after I speak. Sometimes a great experience with the material I present can be ruined by a personal experience face-to-face with me afterward. It had always been hard for me to go from connecting with three hundred people or three thousand people to talking in depth to just one person. While the adrenaline is still in my system, it is not easy for me to settle down and focus on the serious nature of one person's problem. I am often stuck with the dilemma of someone wanting my undivided attention and my feeling disconnected and avoidant, needing about thirty minutes to calm down before I can connect.

That pattern had fed into the problems in our marriage. I hated being criticized, and I hated coming home to an uncomfortable house full of conflict. I dodged and ducked just to keep the peace. I followed a counselor's directions that allowed me to become even more detached. He suggested that my wife should never hear anything negative from me. He said all of my interactions with her should be complimentary and positive. It was exactly what I wanted to hear—I no longer had to express difficult feelings. All I had to do was hold in my horrible feelings and eke out some superficial positive ones. It was a survival technique that kept me from going crazy, but it did little to help the marriage. In fact, it hurt the marriage badly.

I stopped being a complete person when I stopped trying to express my feelings unless they were positive. I was half a man, and I believe I lost my wife's respect when I stopped standing up for what was right in the relationship. I avoided the conflicts I hated, but I prevented her from seeing me as a real man with real needs and feelings. Sure, I was following the advice of a counselor, but it was the wrong advice, and eventually I knew it. I followed it because it fit into the style of relating I had developed. I needed to change that style if I was going to have a different kind of relationship in the future. Milan helped me see that and helped me make the needed changes, but they were not easy to make.

DIVORCE RECOVERY

Divorce recovery became a time of connection for me. I connected with whomever I could, in ways I never had before. One example of that was Doug Wilson. Doug is a consultant for some of the most successful and wealthiest people in the world. I had known him for twenty-five years, but we had never spent much time together. He and his wife, Karen, bought a house in Laguna Beach shortly before my divorce, and that allowed me to get to know him a little better.

He and his wife are great athletes, and they invited me on a bike ride. I did not have a road bike, so I bought one. I wanted to connect with them. I wanted to have friends at levels I had never had before, so the bike ride was a way to accomplish that. Well, at least I thought it was. I was enthusiastic but unskilled, and before the ride was over, I had run into a pole—lacerating my arm, and bruising my hip in such a way that it still hurts a year later. I also fell over on the bike at least five times, because I could not unlock my shoes from the posts on the bike. One fall was right in front of an older man who said he had done the same thing years earlier and had to have his hip replaced as a result. I lay there on the pavement, looking up at him in great pain, foreseeing major surgery, thinking, *Well, at least I am connecting at new levels with Doug.*

I did learn to connect at new levels with Doug. He helped me look at the mistakes I had made and the problems I was experiencing. My hips were sore from our times together, but he helped to heal my heart. I looked up to him and respected him enough to listen when he pointed out something inside of me that he felt needed changing. I am so grateful for my times with him and my times with Milan, but they would not have happened if I had not been willing to see the disconnection pattern in my life and wanted to fix it. If I had not accepted the avoidant parts of me, I could not have repaired them. If all I did was defend my life as a married man, I never would have been able to prepare for a new life and a new future. I would not have been willing to risk that in a new relationship things did not have to be the same as in the old one.

After six months of solitude and grief, I began dating in the midst of exploring my disconnecting patterns and developing new levels of connection. They were not all dates, but at least I began to spend time with some people of the opposite sex. It was a bit scary at first, but I tried to make sure our dates took place around other people as much as possible, just to be sure I was not getting myself into a situation that was beyond my ability to handle. Some believe in dating, and others do not, but for me it was a wonderful and valuable experience.

I went out with about twenty people, but the person who made the biggest difference in my life was Misty. She was full of life and a people person who connected with almost everyone she met. People loved Misty. Everyone in my family loved her too. Madeline immediately grew close to her and began to hint that this would be someone who would make a great wife for me. I asked her why, and she gave me three reasons:

1. She thought Misty would make a very cool stepmom.
2. She liked her two boys, James and Carter, ages five and seven.
3. She said we would finally be a real family.

I thought those were wonderful reasons.

Misty won Madeline's heart and the hearts of all those who met her. She also won mine, but it was a challenge for me. As I recovered from the divorce, I realized that the most significant contribution I had made to it was when I chose to marry Sandy in the first place. At that time, I picked someone who would allow me to remain avoidant and disconnected. There was something comfortable about the criticism I received. I was used to it, and it gave me an ongoing excuse to disconnect. But with Misty it was different—she wanted to know about my life. She wanted to know details, and she wanted to be connected to all of my life. She wanted to know me deeply, and she wanted me to know her. It was exactly the opposite kind of relationship I was used to.

If I had not done some work on myself and been searching for the truth about myself, I would have let Misty go. I would have enjoyed the fun we had, but I would have fled at the thought of connecting at a deeper level. The relationship would have been very temporary if I had not been seeing Milan and getting advice from Doug and just hanging out with my friend Dale. The healing choice I made to look inside allowed me to stay with Misty when connection became uncomfortable. The work I did inside allowed me to work through the temptation to run, and instead stay and connect and share life in a deeper, richer way. I am so glad I did.

One of the surprises was the first time we had a real conflict. Misty and her boys had joined Madeline, me, and the rest of the family in Montana for Christmas. It was a magical time that none of us will ever forget, but over dinner one night I made a comment about the boys. I was truly joking, but in the joke, I insinuated that they were a little out of control. It was a dumb thing to say, and I knew it even as the words were coming out of my mouth.

The one-hour ride back to the cabin was not a pleasant one. Misty was angry and hurt, and rightfully so. My immediate thought was that I would be paying for this blunder for quite some time. The next morning I did not know what to expect when I saw her. Wondering about her mood and wanting to tackle the problem early, I went to her room and knocked on her door. To my surprise she was smiling, and she walked right up and gave me a hug. The prior evening was over and done with; I would not be paying a price for it. She had worked through it and forgiven me. It was done, and I was amazed.

Now you might think that would not be a problem, but it actually was. In my marriage, I did dumb things all the time. I blew it, Sandy would get mad, and I felt as though she would stay angry for days or even weeks. I had the perfect excuse to stay disconnected when one of these incidents came up and I was in the doghouse. I did not have to endure the uncomfortable burden of intimacy, because we were separated over my mistake or insensitivity. That allowed me to live in my own world of isolation and alienation.

Now I was in a relationship where I was not banished from the kingdom for weeks or months. I was experiencing connection that even an argument could not undo. It was a new experience, one that I was uneasy with, but it was my first experience as an adult in developing an authentic relationship with a woman. I would never have been able to do that if I had not taken a look inside to discover the truth about myself.

MY OWN "WHY"

Part of the healing for me was discovering my own "why." I needed to look back at my history to discover why I had developed this pattern of avoidance and disconnection. I did not want to live that way, so I wanted to go back to the roots of it and see if I could unearth the source. If I could, perhaps I would be able to establish new levels of connection and intimacy. I wanted to, and I was willing to work for it. I may not have hit on all the reasons for my disconnection, but I believe I found some major influences.

The first came from my father's family. My grandfather was not exactly what you would call a touchy-feely person. Sure, he cried over soap operas, but I don't think he had much insight into what others were feeling, or that he cared. There was a lot of respect for him, but not a lot of connection with him. He raised my father, along with the rest of his boys, with boards, belts, and switches. It was all about correction, staying in line, and getting with the program. My father did the same thing with us, and he did it to an extent that I believe was abusive. He spanked us too hard and too late in life, and every whack of a board or belt pushed my brothers and me away from each other and away from him.

There were also disconnecting factors from my mother's side. Her father had committed suicide, and it was not something she was comfortable talking about. In fact, until I was in junior high school, I thought he had died of a heart attack. When I learned the truth, I felt like an outsider, and disconnected. Family secrets do that to people. The suicide had also created some problems with Mom's ability to connect. She was in survival mode, and it was not easy for her to connect deeply when she had a shameful secret about her father.

Mom and I were talking one day about how much more help parents have today than when she was parenting her three boys. She loves listening to Dr. Dobson and heard him explain that when a child talks about having a horrible day or feels as if all of life is horrible, just connect with him over it, tell him how sorry you are that he is having a rough time, and then move on. Mom reminded me that if any of us ever talked about life being less than great, she and Dad would try to talk us out of it or convince us we were ungrateful and needed to change the way we felt or the way we saw the whole world in general. We were essentially told that our feelings were wrong, instead of our parents respecting or acknowledging our feelings. The rejection of my feelings became another excuse for me to disconnect, rather than my feelings serving as a point of connection.

There was another reason for my disconnection that had nothing to do with my parents or my past. It had to do with the decisions I made and the mistakes I made, and I made a lot of mistakes. I chose to do the wrong thing over and over again. I had a secret life in high school, in college, and through my twenties. I did not share all of who I was; I hid most of myself. Rather than accept that I had a dark side, a promiscuous side, and a rebellious heart, I cut myself and others off from it. I was split rather than fully integrated into a healthy whole.

I separated out that part of me that I did not want to be known. I hid it, and in so doing I hid myself from the people closest to me. As a result of wanting to hide my sins and mistakes, I disconnected and began the avoidant lifestyle very early in life. I got by with it, but not knowing I was living that way hurt me. It was my work with Milan that began the process of changing. The discovery of the truth about myself led to healing that could not have come any other way.

YOUR TRUTH

More important than the truth about me is that you discover the truth about you. Perhaps that is why you started this book and are still reading. You really do want to learn and allow that insight to lead to healing. Maybe you have suffered a severe blow and are trying to recover from a divorce or a death or a loss of a job or something even more traumatic. Perhaps you are tired of not healing from some abuse in your past. Sexual, emotional, or physical abuse is still influencing too much of what you do, and you are ready for healing. If you are, you have to look within and discover some things about yourself that are not so pleasant. You have to solve the mystery of why some who have been abused move on, but you have become stuck. Are you willing to take a look inside? Don't you want to know what it is within you that is driving you, or driving you crazy? Wouldn't you like to see some of the destructive patterns you have developed and change them for good? If so, let's take a look.

Open Up Your Life

Every person has blind spots. Not foggy spots. Foggy spots are those spots we are not clear about. We know they are there, but we just can't quite grasp what they are all about or how to make them go away. Blind spots are different—blind spots are areas we do not see at all. We are not in denial over them, because we don't even know they are there.

You may think you are fully aware of all aspects of your being, but you are not. There are some areas that have mysteries to be solved that you cannot solve on your own, because you do not see the problem. You are completely blind to the reality of what is there, and the only way you will be able to "see" is with the help of others. They will help you uncover the truth that you would probably deal with if you just knew it was there. But first, before you ask for help with what you don't see, take a look at what you do see. Open yourself up with your own scalpel and take a look at what you can see.

Taking that look is called many things: "self-examination" by some, and "self-confrontation" by others. It is taking your life and holding it up to the light of truth and seeing what is there. Many twelve-step and recovery groups call it "taking a searching and fearless moral inventory." It is time spent looking at your faults and defects, writing them down, and seeing what they reveal about you. There are many ways you can do this, but I can simplify it for you. Following are twenty questions that will aid in taking inventory of your life:

1. Starting as early as you can remember, who were the people in your life who hurt you?
2. Was there anything you did to bring on that hurt, or were they solely responsible?
3. What was your reaction to that hurt? Did you forgive them, hold on to a grudge, or try to seek your own revenge?
4. Is there any way you could have altered your reaction to the hurt?
5. Starting as early as you can remember, who were the people in your life whom you hurt?
6. Did they do something first that hurt you, or were you acting without provocation?
7. Who have you hurt the worst? Arrange your list of those you hurt in the order of the most damage to the least.
8. What was your reaction when you first realized you had hurt each person?

9. What have you done to rectify the problem caused by your hurtful actions?

10. Is there anything you could do to make restitution?

11. Are you aware of your five greatest strengths? Write down what you think they are, and then ask five other people to tell you what they think they are.

12. Are you aware of your five greatest weaknesses? Write down what you think they are, and then ask five other people to tell you what they think they are.

13. What have you done to misuse your strengths? Have you been a good steward of them or have you wasted them?

14. What have you done to use your strengths well? Ask the same five people as in the previous questions where they have seen you use them well.

15. What have you done to correct or work on your weaknesses?

16. What could you do to work on them? Make a list.

17. What could you do to make restitution to those you have hurt?

18. Who could help you walk through a path of forgiveness toward those who have hurt you?

19. Write down a plan to contact those you have hurt, begin contacting them if it would not cause greater damage, and take notes on the things they tell you about yourself as you discuss the past.

20. Ask someone to be your partner in truth. Ask that person to help you discover the truth about yourself and motivate you to continue to work on the areas that need help.

If you take these twenty steps, monitoring how you feel along the way and journaling those feelings and other insights, I believe you will come to know yourself better. You will be taking what you know and using it to uncover what you do not know.

AT LEAST ONE OTHER PERSON

Once you have completed the twenty steps, you will have information about yourself that will be helpful to understand more about yourself and make it easier for someone else to understand you. Take that list and share it with another person who loves you, is wise, keeps confidences, and is committed to helping you become the best person you can be. Tell that person that you want honest feedback. Let him or her know that there are no points off for truth. You can handle the truth; invite that person to share it with you.

As you go through life, you want to be sure that there is at least one other person who has heard you confess your sins and shortcomings. You need to be sure that at least one other person has heard your full story—warts and all. You also need to be sure that there is at least one other person on this planet who is allowed to tell you the truth about yourself.

Tear down those protective walls so that at least one other person can tell you what you need to know about yourself.

Often the rich and famous become poor has-beens because they protected themselves from truth that might be uncomfortable. We all find ways to shield ourselves from painful realities. We create a world of people around us who do not dare tell us what we really need to know for fear that they might be banished from the kingdom. If you have done that, tear down those protective walls so that at least one other person can tell you what you need to know about yourself.

You also need to be sure that on this planet there is at least one other person who is praying for you. Satan is real, and there is supernatural warfare going on right now. Prayer is a supernatural means of fighting the enemy, who wants nothing less than the complete worst for you. Find a person, through your church or the Internet or friends, who has a strong prayer life, and ask that person to pray for you as you search for the truth about yourself. Make certain that you are also praying. Pray that God will reveal all things to you that you need to know to grow more like Him. Prayer is a supernatural tool to uncover the blind spots and begin to grow.

THE BIG LIE
"It does no good to look back or look inside."

The big lie that you might use or others might throw up to you is that it does no good to look back or look inside. My father was that way. He was very positive but had a very small life of introspection. To him, you just messed up and picked yourself up and never talked about it. You just moved on. We are to "press on" according to Scripture, and to look back is less than to press on (Philippians 3:12 NIV).

There is a verse in Hebrews that admonishes us to throw off any encumbrance that would weigh us down and prevent us from achieving what God has called us to do. Don't listen to the big lie. If you are riddled with guilt, shame, remorse, anger, rage, anxiety, or fear from your past, you need to do some work to solve the mystery of why these feelings exist.

These things are the encumbrance or the burden you need to throw off. Do it before it is too late. Do it before there are more broken hearts and broken relationships. Do it before you miss one more day of living as God would have you live. Do the work, and don't listen to anyone who would tell you it is destructive. Become the best student of yourself. Know yourself so that you can come to know all that God has planned for you, and you can live within that plan.

BREAKING THROUGH LIMITATIONS

Most of us want to believe we can break through our denial, shine a light on all of our blind spots, and develop new insights into ourselves without the messiness of working with someone else. The fact is that you have to have someone else help you. I have suggested that you get help from a trusted friend, but sometimes it requires more than a layperson's experience to help you see where you need to make changes. Sometimes you have to accept your limitations and reach beyond yourself and your friends and seek treatment from a professional.

Helping your life by getting treatment might be the most important step taken. We will explore that choice in another chapter, but before you go there, there may be some additional work in the area of feeling that could set you free to heal. As you have explored the truth about yourself, you may have uncovered some ungrieved losses. In the next chapter we will look at the importance of grief in the healing process.

Healing is a choice. It is God's choice, but there are choices we can make to ensure we experience the healing God has in store for us. Healing is a choice to discover the truth about yourself and solve the mysteries that lie within. Today is a great day to begin to heal or grow deeper in your healing by discovering new truth about yourself.

Healing is a choice. It is a choice to investigate your life in search of truth.

CHAPTER 3 WORKBOOK QUESTIONS

THE THIRD CHOICE:
The Choice to Investigate Your Life in Search of Truth

THE THIRD BIG LIE:
"It does no good to look back or look inside."

AUTHOR PETER GILLQUIST DESCRIBES A FOOTBALL GAME AS "20,000 people in the stadium who desperately need exercise, watching 22 people on the field who desperately need rest!" How true! Imagine you are attending a football game. Several times during an average game, the offensive team will run a play in which a fullback, probably weighing 220 pounds or more, will get the ball and begin charging downfield toward the goal line. It's a simple play, and all teams have it in their playbooks. From the moment the fullback gets the ball, the play is utterly simple. He runs with all his might toward the goal. His blockers get in front of him to clear the path. All eleven players on the opposing team move toward the fullback and do everything in their power to tackle him, preventing him from scoring. The opposing players are all impediments to the fullback, who is trying to score. Each impediment can potentially tackle him, but if the play unfolds as planned, the blockers will remove the impediments and the fullback will score. Statistically, the defensive team is more successful than the offensive one, so the runners are most often tackled and stopped. The impediments work!

Just as the fullback faces impediments on his journey to the goal, we all face impediments as we strive for a full, healthy, productive life. Conflict is an impediment, as is the tendency to disconnect from those who can help you.

If you haven't already noticed, the theme of connecting your life with others' is sewn into each chapter of this book. Being connected to others is an important means of finding the healing we need. Disconnecting and isolating ourselves is a strategy that dooms us to failure. Typically, when a person isolates himself, he becomes his own adviser, and that usually dooms him to receive faulty advice.

We need to be connected to trusted friends who will be honest and objective while loving and caring for us.

We move toward God because we know He loves and cares for us. We move toward family and friends, hoping for the support and love they provide. We move toward friends who care for and support us as we deal with painful issues.

People who understand the value of connectedness move as quickly as possible to a loving, supportive group who can help them deal with troubling issues.

It is not uncommon for some people to intentionally put impediments in the road to healing. Rather than make a choice to heal, they make a choice to hinder their healing. The impediments they place in their path keep them separated from others and diminish their spiritual and emotional health.

Why do we build impediments to healing? Why would we sabotage the very things that could most help us? Why are we sometimes our own worst enemies?

The answer lies in the fact that many people go marching through life without ever dealing with their tendency to create impediments. They repeat the same mistakes and build the same roadblocks over and over. Their behavior becomes instinctive, a habit that causes continual pain.

They ignore the one thing they most need to do, which is to examine why they keep making choices that result in pain and turmoil.

We heal our lives as we begin to search for truth about why we do what we do and why we feel the way we feel.

One of the reasons premarriage counseling is so important is that it requires a couple to examine their lives prior to marriage. They must deal with past relational hurt and be sure that it is healed. When two very hurt and unaware people come together in marriage, the result is often complete and total disaster, so each person must confront his or her hurts and work toward healing in anticipation of marriage.

Taking unresolved conflict, unaddressed emotional pain, and unresolved issues into marriage is to fill the road ahead with impediments.

Exercise #1: *Who Are Your Friends?*

How do you determine the people with whom you are connected? Take a few minutes and think about your closest, most trusted friends, those who could share your deepest concerns. List their names in the spaces provided. If you have only one friend, use one line. If you need more lines, draw them in. Beneath each friend's name, describe in a couple of sentences why this person is valuable to you, how you are connected, and how being connected to them makes you a better person.

1. Friend:

Why he or she is valuable to me:

2. Friend:

Why he or she is valuable to me:

3. Friend:

Why he or she is valuable to me:

4. Friend:

Why he or she is valuable to me:

If you did not list anyone, you might consider your need to cultivate new friends.

Read Proverbs 18:24 in several translations (New Living Translation, King James Version, and New International Version). Each version gives a slightly different perspective about friendship.

- The KJV encourages each of us to seek friends by reaching out and being friendly.
- The NIV encourages us to find a close friend who would be closer than a natural brother.
- The NLT says there are "friends" who destroy each other, but a real friend sticks closer than a brother.

The important point is to connect with others who will be true friends and provide support and care when needed.

THE THIRD CHOICE:
The Choice to Investigate Your Life in Search of Truth

Key Scripture: *Instead, let us test and examine*
our ways. Let us turn back to the LORD.

—LAMENTATIONS 3:40 NLT

THE UNEXAMINED LIFE IS A PROBLEM

Healing Is a Choice gives us ten important choices to make and ten lies to reject. The choice in chapter 3 is to investigate your life in search of truth.

Left to our own notions, we often lapse into self-centeredness and isolation. We often do hurtful things to ourselves and to others, then walk away shaking our heads, wondering why we do such things. We know hurtful, angry words damage our relationships, but we utter them just the same. We desperately need to figure out why we do the things we later regret.

Chapter 3 reminds us that we heal our lives as we begin to search for truth about why we do what we do and feel the way we feel. Without introspection, we keep repeating our mistakes and sabotaging our most important relationships.

Jeremiah was most likely the writer of Lamentations. The book begins with a summary of Jerusalem's sorrows and moves quickly to Judah's hope for God's mercy.

That pattern describes most of us. We experience failure, pain, and sorrow in life. It's tough. It often depresses us and impacts our behavior. We long for relief and desperately need to recover and do life a different way.

Like Jeremiah, we look with anticipation for mercy, grace, and healing. Like ancient Israel, we have choices to make. We can languish in our sorrow, or we can make a choice to heal.

If we make the choice to heal, then we need to examine our lives in order to know where to make corrections and improvements. It is a wholesome effort to stop and take a look at life in our past, present, and prospective future.

It is very interesting that both the Old and New Testaments address the idea of self-examination. Jeremiah encourages us, "Instead, let us test and examine our ways. Let us turn back to the LORD" (Lamentations 3:40 NLT).

In the New Testament, the apostle Paul challenged his readers to "examine yourselves to see if your faith is genuine. Test yourselves. Surely you know that Jesus Christ is among you; if not, you have failed the test of genuine faith" (2 Corinthians 13:5 NLT).

Self-examination is a theme in both Christian spirituality and philosophy. In 399 BC, Socrates uttered the most famous quote about self-examination. In a lecture to the people, he stated that based on his persistent questioning and study of the populace, he had determined that "the unexamined life is not worth living."

That statement has become a fundamental tenet of all philosophical quests. He further explained that the citizens of Greece spent their lives pursuing material things, without asking whether they were actually important. Socrates warned that if people failed to examine their motives and actions, they would never know if they were doing the right thing. His words sound like they were meant for us.

Ironically, the unexamined life may be our own. So many people arrive at adulthood without ever truly examining themselves. As a result, their lives are often a mess.

All of us have mysteries inside us. We don't understand why we do some things. We are shocked by the thoughts presenting our minds. We need help to understand why we do the things we do. Consider how easily we fall into negative relational patterns.

COMMON PATTERNS IN DYSFUNCTIONAL RELATIONSHIPS

There are common patterns in human relationships. They are common and identifiable. Read pages 118–20 again. The following common relational patterns are described:

1. An overweight wife is married to a sex-addicted husband.

2. A woman whose father did not provide for her or connect with her deepest needs expects her husband to make up for it.

3. A woman is miserable because her father was so good. She looks to her husband to fulfill her, but he is not enough, not as good as her father.

4. A husband whose mother met his every need is angry because his wife is unwilling to do that.

5. A husband whose mother was overbearing and domineering projects all his anger toward his wife.

6. A wife is sexually rejected by her husband, who sees her as domineering like his mother. Unable to feel sexual toward his wife, he turns to pornographic images that give him a sense of control.

7. A husband and wife grow increasingly apart. Anger has melted into indifference. The husband compares his wife to pornographic images on the computer, and in his comparison, she comes up short, rejected and alienated.

Notice that these patterns are all examples of disconnection. They drive people apart rather than connect them.

Exercise #2: What Are Your Thoughts?

Use the space provided to answer the questions. If you are studying in a small group, use the questions as a discussion guide.

1. How do relationships like those described above occur?

_____

_____

_____

2. How can marriages that begin with so much hope and optimism fall into such turmoil, conflict, and disappointment?

_____

_____

_____

3. Why is it so hard for people to become involved in the self-examination that might heal their lives?

_____

_____

_____

The answers to these questions reside in the minds and hearts of the two people involved. They brought themselves to the marriage, with all their "baggage" from the past.

We need to carefully consider the "why" behind our actions and feelings. Why do we do what we do? What is motivating us?

MYSTERIES OF THE MIND

Humans are complex, mysterious creatures. We can function in a relatively normal way. We can maintain relationships with a modicum of affection and commitment. We can tolerate huge amounts of relational pain.

On the other hand, we can make lifelong commitments to other people. We are capable of incredible acts of self-sacrifice and compassion.

Throw into that mix the fact we are capable of doing strange and unexpected things with no plausible explanation. The mysteries in our minds can damage the most important relationships we have.

But there is good news! Healing is a choice, and we are capable of making healing choices. Healing these mysteries requires us to look into our past and present and future and consider why we do what we do. We must identify the defective patterns in our relationships and correct them. Such work turns mysteries into knowledge and gives us hope.

THE THIRD BIG LIE:
"It does no good to look back or look inside."

As you begin to examine your life, there are plenty of people who will say, "Forget that! The past is behind us. You don't gain anything by looking back." It is possible for someone to be "stuck" in the past. Something so traumatic happened to a person in the past that he was left with unresolved issues. They are burdened by the residue of the past: guilt, shame, remorse, anger, anxiety, fear, mistrust, and more. Thus, they cannot move forward. These people dwell in the past. By definition, *dwell* means to "live" or "reside." Thus, they spend their entire lives dwelling in the past. However, there is a huge difference between introspection and living in the past. Introspection allows us to look at our past, learn from it, and then move into the future with new strength. The old cliché "We learn from our mistakes" works only if we pause to look back and examine them. It is a wholesome, productive effort from which most people benefit greatly.

Scripture encourages us to forget "the past and [look] forward to what lies ahead" (Philippians 3:13 NLT). The point is that we should have a future orientation.

The big lie suggests that there is nothing to be gained by looking back or looking inward. In fact, just the opposite is true. Our mistakes tell us where we don't want to go again. If we accept the big lie, we are forever doomed in our past.

ENCOUNTERING THE TRUTH ABOUT YOU

It is important that we discover the truth about ourselves. That might be one reason you are reading this book. You sense you are not whole. You wish you could change the destructive patterns of your life. Are you willing to examine yourself?

The truth is that you may need help. Most of us are reluctant to identify our own weaknesses and problems. We're not sure how to deal with them. We fear they may intensify if we expose them. We are afraid people will reject us if they find out what we're really like. However, as we mentioned earlier, "The unexamined life is not worth living." We will be healthier and better off if we do the hard work of examining ourselves and taking steps to change.

TAKING A SEARCHING AND
FEARLESS MORAL INVENTORY

There is a process by which we can take a careful self-examination. It requires "taking your life and holding it up to the light of truth and seeing what is there. . . . It is time spent looking at your faults and defects, writing them down, and seeing what they reveal about you" (p. 131).

Instructions:

There are twenty questions listed below. They will assist you as you conduct your inventory.

You do not have to share this with anyone (though it might be helpful to show a trusted, connected friend who can provide validation through a second opinion).

Offer complete answers with plenty of information. This is not a test!

You won't be graded. You do want as complete a picture as possible.

Take as long as you like. If this work seems exhaustive or is painful, just do a few questions at a sitting.

Again, you are in control of the process, but be very honest with your responses.

1. **Starting as early as you can remember, who were the people in your life who hurt you?**

_____

_____

_____

2. **Was there anything you did to bring on that hurt, or were they solely responsible?**

_____

_____

_____

_____

3. What was your reaction to that hurt? Did you forgive them, hold on to a grudge, or try to seek your own revenge?

_____

_____

_____

4. Is there any way you could have altered your reaction to the hurt?

_____

_____

_____

5. Starting as early as you can remember, who were the people in your life whom you hurt?

_____

_____

_____

6. Did they do something first that hurt you, or were you acting without provocation?

_____

_____

_____

7. Arrange your list of those you hurt in the order of the most damage to the least.

8. What was your reaction when you first realized you had hurt each person?

9. What have you done to rectify the problem caused by your hurtful actions?

10. Is there anything you could do to make restitution?

11. Are you aware of your five greatest strengths? Write down what you think they are, and then ask five other people to tell you what they think they are.

_____

_____

_____

_____

12. Are you aware of your five greatest weaknesses? Write down what you think they are, and then ask five other people to tell you what they think they are.

_____

_____

_____

_____

13. What have you done to misuse your strengths? Have you been a good steward or have you wasted them?

_____

_____

_____

_____

14. What have you done to use your strengths well? Ask the same five people as in the previous questions where they have seen you use your strengths well.

_____

_____

_____

15. What have you done to correct or work on your weaknesses?

_____

_____

_____

16. What could you do to work on them? Make a list.

_____

_____

_____

17. What could you do to make restitution to those you have hurt?

_____

_____

_____

18. Who could help you walk through a path of forgiveness toward those who have hurt you?

_____

_____

19. Write down a plan to contact those you have hurt, begin contacting them if it would not cause greater damage, and take notes on the things they tell you about yourself as you discuss the past.

_____

_____

_____

_____

20. **Ask someone to be your partner in truth. Ask that person to help**
    you discover the truth about yourself and motivate you to continue
    to work on the areas that need help.

_____

_____

_____

_____

AT LEAST ONE OTHER PERSON

On June 12, 1987, President Reagan made a speech that helped contribute to the downfall of the Soviet Union. He spoke directly to the Soviet premier and said, "Mr. Gorbachev, tear down this wall!"

That is what we need to be saying to one another. Let's tear down the walls that disconnect us from one another and have for so long confined us in our pride, shame, and anger. Walls often do more harm than good.

I am going to ask you to do something that takes great courage. Now that you've finished your twenty questions, select one person who loves you, will keep your confidence, and is committed to help you become the person God wants you to be. That person should be someone who cares for you, despite the way you sometimes are! Ask that person to give you honest feedback, and let them know you can handle the truth. Everyone needs one person in their life who will always love them and tell them the truth.

JOURNALING

Take a few minutes to think about chapter 3. This chapter is so personal in many ways, but the fact is that we have to be personal with one another if we ever want to be authentically connected. Take some time and write about your friends and the impact they have had on your life.

PRAYERFUL MEDITATION

Consider asking a friend with whom you are very connected to join you in prayer. Find a quiet, relaxing place where you are comfortable and uninterrupted. Take a few minutes and share your thoughts from chapter 3. Share the things that left a strong impression on you. Pause and thank God for the information you gained. Point out one or two things that you think might be a challenge. Ask the Holy Spirit to empower and enable you to apply those things in your life. Sit quietly for a few minutes and listen to the Holy Spirit. Feel your heartbeat and thank God for the life He has given you. Ask how you can commit your life in service to Jesus Christ.

Think about the love and faithfulness of God. Ask the Holy Spirit to speak to you about your life. Be patient. Listen quietly and wait for the Spirit to move. Ask the Spirit to help you evaluate your life to be sure you are walking in faith. Ask the Lord to provide you with good friends with whom you can grow spiritually. "Give all your worries and cares to God, for he cares about you" (1 Peter 5:7 NLT).

PRAYER

Heavenly Father, hear my honest prayer and my sincere concerns. At times I feel trapped by my past. I've had overwhelming pain, and even some guilt and shame. I don't always know how to interpret the events of my life, or reinterpret them. There are some things in my life I simply cannot change. Thank You for the challenge and encouragement I have received from this chapter. Help me to acknowledge my pain and then, with Your help, move toward peace and calm. Help me to examine my heart and mind honestly, and to identify the pain I carry from day to day. I acknowledge that healing my pain is a choice. From the power of Your Spirit, give me the courage to choose healing. Increase my confidence in You. Where I am weak and hesitant to act, give me strength. Increase my faith. I give You my life—mind, soul, and spirit. Through Jesus Christ, my Healer. Amen.

REJOICE AND SING!

If you know this chorus, sing it to conclude your devotion. If you don't know it, select a song or hymn of your choice.

THE STEADFAST LOVE OF THE LORD

The steadfast love of the Lord never ceases.
His mercies never come to an end.
They are new every morning, new every morning.
Great is Thy faithfulness, O Lord.
Great is Thy faithfulness.

4

THE FOURTH CHOICE:
The Choice to Heal Your Future

THE FOURTH BIG LIE:
"Time heals all wounds."

BIG DREAMS

Did you have great dreams for your life that have never come true? Did you believe that you would grow up, easily discover who God chose for you, marry that person, make a lot of money, have great kids who were never a problem, and then just continue to live happily ever after? Perhaps your dreams were even bigger and bolder than that. Was your dream to be a star of the stage or screen? Were you told you had great talent and you should go for it and make it to the top? Was your dream to live a peaceful life teaching at a university with the security of tenure, writing bestseller after bestseller? Did you have big dreams that never came true? I did. All the things I mentioned here are dreams of mine that never came true.

Most men have big dreams to conquer something or to achieve greatness. We do our best to rise above the circumstances of our births and childhoods, but we rarely do. We rarely outearn our parents or outachieve them. The fire of a parent who is great is often but a smoldering ash in the child expected to fill the shoes of a great leader or of a great minister. Most of us end up with mundane lives, just struggling to get by. We thought we would make a difference, but we fall short of our own expectations and often the expectations of others. Men become trapped in a sense of failure because the dream is not fulfilled, and the desire to make a difference dies.

Married women often end up in the same kind of trap. I think it is very common for women to believe that they will grow up and marry someone close to being a prince. They believe he will be handsome and always treat them with gentlemanly manners. They dream of long talks and intimate details of a day set apart. When that dream does not come true, they live a life filled with great disappointment. Every day becomes drudgery, living with a man so far beneath who and what they wanted and believed would be there for them. Each day becomes another day of hurt feelings and unmet expectations.

HURTS AND HOPELESSNESS

There are others who do not have dreams, because they have been hurt so badly they don't believe dreams come true—at least not for them. You might have been abused or neglected as a child, and it is still influencing who you are today. Someone might have been evil to you and taken advantage of you and then made you feel like an object, a piece of meat—anything but a whole person. You may have been hurt because someone close to you died. The anger from that loss may still be there.

You might be a person with a physical defect. You might have an illness or a handicap that you despise and wish would go away. In fact, you pray every day that it will go away, but it never does. You feel neglected by God, hurt and hopeless as you struggle through life.

I have talked to and worked with people who have lived for decades in the pain of shattered dreams and broken expectations. They are still suffering at fifty or sixty because of something that happened when they were a child or a teenager. Whatever it is, they have never gotten over it and moved beyond it. It is still working on them, eating at them, and robbing them of the life they could have.

The abuser who touched them physically continues to abuse them emotionally, because they have never moved beyond that hurt. They have chosen to allow the person who took away their innocence to take away their dreams and hopes. Oh, how I hurt for these people. If you are one of these, I long for you to do some very hard work and get beyond the struggle in which you are stuck. I don't want that person to hurt you one more day. I want you to experience healing that will totally free you from any influence the abuser could have on you. I am praying right now that this will be the choice that will set you free.

DRAGGING THE PAST INTO THE FUTURE

Anytime we drag our past into the future, we have some grieving to do. When we refuse to grieve, we hang on to the weight of life that slows us down and robs us from finding our lives. I discovered that a piece of my past was affecting all of my future. You may wonder how I could have made this mistake. There are times I wonder that myself, but let me tell you how my life in high school hurt me deeply for many following years.

I have written about this before, but I want to share it with you again. In high school, I had a girlfriend who was beyond belief.

She was tall and blonde and beautiful. Her laughter lit up my soul. I could not believe she loved me, but she did. We went to special places with her parents, and I experienced things that my parents never could have provided for me. We were a dream couple, and our picture ended up on the cover of the yearbook. We even had our own television show. I had fun with her and cared a great deal for her, but I cared for one other person a lot more—me.

I destroyed the relationship, and she broke up with me because of my selfish behavior and my obsession with myself. It was a loss such as many people experience after being married for years. It was a loss no one understood. They thought it was puppy love, but for me it was the love of a lifetime—at least it was at that time. So I suffered in silence, never admitting to anyone that I was devastated by the loss I had caused.

I became ill and anxious. I tried to control things, tried to get her back, but nothing worked. Later in college, for a brief time, we got back together, and I even botched that. I lost the person who meant so much to me and could not get her back. I often felt God had protected her from me. All of these emotions piled up on each other left me with an obsession and a pain that controlled what I did for years in the future.

She was a year younger than I. I attended Texas A&M so that I could stay in the same town with her. I couldn't attend the same school when she left for SMU, so I enrolled at Baylor, close to Dallas. I was so in love with her, and I could not let go. I dated her cousin just to be close to her. I could not let her go. At least I *would* not let her go. I found myself making decisions based on what she would think about me. Pain and loss were with me every day.

You would never have known it. I was always the life of the

party, but my pain was there. I refused to share my secret life of hurt and pain, so I isolated myself from others. No one was allowed in, and the wall I built grew thicker and thicker. All of that happened because of a high school love that I could not revive.

Years later, in a counseling session with a man I trusted, I finally opened up about my feelings concerning my high school love. I was embarrassed, but I knew I had to talk about it. He handled it as if it had happened yesterday and as if it were the worst kind of hurt he had ever dealt with. He invited me to do something that I am inviting you to do. He invited me to make the tough choice to grieve the loss and let go of it. He invited me to allow my life to go on without my lost love being part of my reality. He invited me to accept life as it was. He invited me to heal my future.

HEALING YOUR FUTURE

The Bible tells us not to worry about tomorrow, because tomorrow has enough trouble on its own. Once it arrives, tomorrow could be full of more trouble than today, so don't bring that trouble into your life ahead of time (Matthew 6:34). It is great and godly advice to not worry about your future, but it is also good advice to heal your future so that tomorrow will have as few problems as possible. Some people never stop to think about how they might heal or fix their future. There are some very practical ways to make your future the best possible. The Bible tells us to look at the ant for a lesson in healing our future:

Take a lesson from the ants, you lazybones. Learn from their ways and be wise! Even though they have no prince, governor, or ruler to make them work, they labor hard all summer, gathering food for the winter. (Proverbs 6:6–8 NLT)

Someone might read that and say that the ant was a bit worried about winter. Knowing the reality of something and preparing for it—doing the work—is not worry. A way for the ant to heal his future winter is through preparation and making provision. He can infect his future with laziness that will result in an empty stomach and death. It is during the harvest season that the ant chooses to take healing action that will heal the winter. Each of us can do the same thing.

We can make the coming years more secure by storing away some money. We can enrich our future years by building strong relationships that will last us a lifetime. We can grow a loving family who will take care of us in the final years of our lives. We can also plant some healing seeds that will produce a harvest of peace and serenity. Grieving heals our future. Doing the tough work of grieving plows the fields and softens the soil for a healthy harvest of connected relationships and for living a life with purpose and meaning. When we grieve, we come right alongside Jesus, follow His example, and do exactly what He did.

THE UNGRIEVED LOSS

When we resist grieving our losses, we drag our pain with us all through our lives. Karen is a stark example of what happens when we do this. She had an irresponsible father who was so self-obsessed that he never gave thought to the effect he was having on the lives of his children. He was disappointed when Karen came along—he had wanted a boy and was stuck with a girl. Most dads get over their loss of preference with the first glance at the baby—but not him.

When Karen was old enough to understand, her dad let her know that he had wanted a boy. He never acknowledged her in front of others as his daughter. He referred to her impersonally as "the girl who lives with us"—meaning his wife and him. As far as Karen can remember, he never shared any love with her. She felt dejected, like an outcast. Eventually her father left the family and started a second one with another wife.

Karen made her way through school as a loner. A kind college counselor reached out to her and helped her integrate into college life. She attended a workshop on forgiveness a few years after college graduation that helped her to forgive her father but did not help her to get fully beyond her desire for him to step up and be her dad. At one of our workshops, we had a question-and-answer session with our audience. Karen came to the microphone for help. As she stood before us, she wanted to know if she had done all she could do to win back her father.

Karen tearfully told us the sad tale of finally tracking him down in another town. She called, said she wanted to see him, and asked if he could drive over. He said no. Then she asked if he could meet her halfway. Sobbing, she told how her father said he did not have time to even meet her halfway, and how she got in her car and drove the full distance to see him. Karen phoned when she arrived, but her father said he did not have enough time to see her. She felt hurt, abandoned, and completely rejected.

We talked about her need for him to be her father. She said that everyone needs a dad; we told her, "Not that dad." She was still hanging on to the belief that he might come around, that he might change and become the father she had always wanted. We knew that she had never grieved the loss of her dad. Her tears showed how fresh the wound was; they showed that she had never healed her future. She needed to heal her future, because this man was still way too much in her present and in her future. Grieving would be the only way she could let go.

You might think it awfully hard to give up on a father. I can't think of too many things more difficult, but what were Karen's choices? She could accept reality, grieve the loss, and let go of the expectation; or she could spend her life feeling the pain as if it were yesterday. Grieving allows you to move on, free of the pain and agony. The deep tears turn to a sniffle, then to a lump in the throat, and then to a passing thought. Grieving takes the vulture who abused, abandoned, or neglected you and turns it into a gnat who can be easily batted away. The reality of it is always there, but it does not interfere with the way you live your life.

ACQUAINTED WITH GRIEF

Jesus was "a Man of sorrows and acquainted with grief" (Isaiah 53:3 NKJV). That presents the question, what would He be grieving over? Perhaps it was the loss of a perfect world. Perhaps He grieved the loss of the position He held and gave up to put on an earth suit, come down here and live as we live, and die for us. That was a pretty great loss—a throne in heaven.

Perhaps Jesus grieved the loss of all who did not believe in Him and chose their own way. Perhaps He even grieved about the mistakes I would make and longed for a closer relationship in which I would depend solely on Him and not on my own instincts and strengths. Perhaps He grieved the loss of your allegiance, or the future He had picked out for you that you turned down. I don't know what He grieved, but I know that He was full of grief and experienced the very thing many of us must walk through.

That Jesus walked where we need to walk gives me comfort and courage at the same time. I can share in His suffering, and I can bond with Him as I go through the grief process. I can be confident that He knows how to comfort me, because He has been there and experienced it all. I can also rest assured that it is the right thing to do. If we are called to be full of happy talk all the time and have a smile on our faces all the time, then I do not think Jesus would have been termed "a Man of sorrows and acquainted with grief."

UNGRIEVED LOSSES

Are you struggling with ungrieved losses? Are there things in your past that you continue to struggle with to this very day? If so, those losses can be grieved, and you can walk into a new future free of despair and suffering. First you have to do some exploration of what those ungrieved losses are. It was not difficult for Yvonne to figure out; she knew exactly what was troubling her. A friend of the family had molested her many years ago when she was a young child. Now at age fifty, she remained overweight and girlish in her style. *Homely* would be an accurate description. As Yvonne worked through the issues of her weight, she accepted the theory that she wanted a boundary to prevent her from ever being used again in a sexual way. What she established instead was a wall that was impenetrable by *anyone*. She let no one in, because no one was safe.

Every day Yvonne relived the pain of being ignored by her parents and then being noticed by a close friend of the family, who repeatedly used her. She hated the man and hated the thought of his touch. She thought about it every day. She would see a man who looked like her abuser and then obsess over him. Along the way something happened to her—she lost her tears. She could not cry, no matter how sad the event. It made her feel heartless and less than alive not to be moved by what moved others. She was a sweet woman. Yvonne's life had been spent taking very small baby steps in order to heal.

As she worked on her past, she went through the process of forgiving the man who had molested her. Yvonne pretended he was sitting in an empty chair in the middle of a room, and she told him what she had felt. She shared her hurt, and she demanded the chair to tell her why. She screamed for help for the first time. She felt and experienced it all over again, but she never cried.

The tears did not come until Yvonne moved into the area of grieving what she had lost. For years she thought she had lost her virginity. She had not, because she had been raped; she was not a willing partner. Technically she was still a virgin, and she came to realize that. There was still one thing she had never grieved—the loss of her innocence.

She remembered how naive she had been before the molestation, how her thoughts were sweet and good and positive. She reflected on happy days with friends that turned into sad days sitting alone in her shame. She began to see how her life had changed so dramatically and all that she had lost. Some things she would never remember, because she pulled out of life and developed a cocoon of protection. She lost the little girl she was, but she never grieved the loss. The damage done to her became the centerpiece of her life. She was defined by it and could not move beyond it until she forgave the man and grieved the life of safety and security she had never known. So Yvonne grieved.

Yvonne worked with her counselor, telling stories of what her life could have been like. She described dates with boys and summer afternoons spent comfortably by a swimming pool. She made up tales of romance she might have lived out. She described a failed fantasy that had been inside her mind for many years. And then she began to let go of it. She was willing to see beyond it. She was willing to admit that it was a heavy burden she had carried with her and dump that burden into a sea of the tears that began to flow again.

Yvonne exchanged her girlish smile and her inner rage for gut-wrenching sadness, sorrow, and grief over a lost life. It took days for her to feel the full depths of her grief, but each time she was with her counselor or writing in her journal, she walked deeply into it. She felt the pain and allowed herself to be comforted through it. She allowed her sister to hold her and rock her as she let the tears flow. Yvonne left every session feeling less and less of a burden to carry. Eventually her grief set her free.

TRADING YOUR EMOTIONS

"I tell you the truth, you will weep and mourn while the world rejoices. You will grieve, but your grief will turn to joy" (John 16:20 NIV). On the other side of grief there is joy. Inside of silent grief and unspoken pain, joy is robbed. Finally, grieving is a decision to heal your future and replace your pain with joy. You trade the nagging pain that does not go away for deep, sharp, grieving pain that dredges out the emotional waste of your life and leaves you free to find and experience joy. In grieving there is a cleansing through feeling what lies buried beneath, and there is a freeing from letting go of what has been a constant companion. The pain felt now removes the curse of pain in the future. It is resolved and no longer needs to be fed or minded or protected.

The losses and the feeling of living a life of "less than" are traded for the gains and the freedom that come from living through the reality of loss. The disconnected alienation is traded for a feeling of connection, belonging, and community. Dependency on your own resources and survival tactics are traded for a trust in God and a dependency on Him and His way. The feeling of naïveté is replaced and traded for wisdom and understanding. That insight is used to go beyond just connecting with others to reaching out and helping others. Grieving allows you to trade the emptiness of your protected world for the fullness of life with others. Old feelings and old ways are traded for a new life.

DEFENSES AND PRETENSES

So how will you know you are making progress? How will you know that you are truly working through the grief rather than just digging up old hurts and dwelling needlessly on the past? You will know because you are starting to give up on some of your defenses and defensiveness.

We protect ourselves from more pain when we have not fully experienced our grief. We arrange our lives so that we will not have to endure more than we can bear, so we defend our ground by not allowing others to speak truth into our lives. If they do, we push them out of our lives. With the losses grieved we are more willing to listen and hear the truth. We are no longer living on the "edge of overwhelmed," so we allow people to connect with us at deeper levels. We notice that we are able to live through the vulnerability of connection.

We also begin to notice that we have less and less need to present ourselves as something other than who we really are. We stop putting up walls of pretense. The little lies that deflect people from the real life we are living are no longer required. We notice when we are not totally truthful, and we do it less and less. We have no need to hide behind the old facades that protected us from hurt but prevented us from knowing the life God had for us.

THE BIG LIE
"Time heals all wounds."

The big lie is that time will heal your deep wounds. "Bide your time and one day you will awaken and feel better" is the false hope of this lie. I have not found it to be true in my own life or in the lives of others. In fact, it is just the opposite. Time seems to infect the wounds that are already there. The longer we live with them, the greater their damage, but we want to believe we just need time. What we need is time well spent resolving our pasts and healing our wounds.

How you mark your time can be the most powerful healing choice you can make. Will you spend your time alone and hurting on your own? If you do, there is not much chance that the wounded mind that got you there is going to help you out. That mind will just drive you further and further away from where you could be—from where God wants you to be. If you want time to be healing, you seek out the places where healing occurs and spend your time there doing the work required. Refuse to believe or live in the lie that time is going to heal you. Time will fade the pain and lighten your despair, but it will not heal. Move out of the time cure and move into a healing community where you can grieve your losses, let go of them and your expectations, and grab on to the life that is available.

CLEANSING POWER

The stripping away of who we want to be and who we pretend to be brings us to just who we are, and we discover that who we are is enough. We are created uniquely and wonderfully with all of what we need. We mess that up, and others attempt to mess it up for us, but grief is a cleansing power that takes care of the mess, no matter where it came from. The psalmist said, "My soul weeps because of grief" (Psalm 119:28 NASB). He was not just shedding tears; he was cleansing his life of the past. He was healing his future. He was letting go of what was and what might have been and reaching for what is and what is to be.

In this deep cleansing process, we reach a point where we realize that we are no longer holding on so tightly to the little world we have created. We realize that we are able to let go. We let go of the past, we let go of the unmet expectations, and we let go of a concept of God in which He is supposed to protect us from all hurts and pain. In the deepest forms of grieving, we let go and we find healing.

Do you need to let go? Do you need to fall back in the arms of God and allow Him to heal you? Do you need to express your feelings and protest to Him? Do you need to ask Him for power to let go? If you do, and if you persevere with Him, He will grant it because, according to His Word, it is what He desires for your heart.

Healing is a choice. It is God's choice, but we can make choices that allow the healing He has for us to be manifested in our lives. Healing is a choice to let go of our past hurts by grieving them, and grieving is a choice to heal the future.

CHAPTER 4 WORKBOOK QUESTIONS

THE FOURTH CHOICE:
The Choice to Heal Your Future

THE FOURTH BIG LIE:
"Time heals all wounds."

THE MAN OF LA MANCHA IS A MORALISTIC TALE ABOUT A fictional character, Don Quixote. The story is delightful and filled with Christian themes. In 1972, Joe Darion wrote a song, "The Impossible Dream," for a stage production of the story. Mitch Leigh wrote the music, and the song is now widely known and performed throughout the world. Read the words:

THE IMPOSSIBLE DREAM

To dream the impossible dream,
To fight the unbeatable foe
To bear with unbearable sorrow
To run where the brave dare not go
To right the unrightable wrong
To love pure and chaste from afar
To try when your arms are too weary

To reach the unreachable star
This is my quest
To follow that star
No matter how hopeless
No matter how far
To fight for the right
Without question or pause
To be willing to march into hell
For a heavenly cause
And I know if I'll only be true
To this glorious quest
That my heart will lie peaceful and calm
When I'm laid to my rest
And the world will be better for this
That one man, scorned and covered with scars
Still strove with his last ounce of courage
To reach the unreachable star

Darion's song has Quixote describing his dream to do something great with his life. Listen to some of his dreams: "fight the unbeatable foe," "right the unrightable wrong," "love pure and chaste," "fight for the right," "be willing to march into hell for a heavenly cause," and die in peace.

Quixote was a dreamer. His dreams were noble and righteous. They guided his life and inspired his quest.

What kind of dreams did you have early in life? You might have dreamed of being a great orator or a professional athlete. Perhaps you imagined being a talented musician, becoming a teacher, or having a happy family. Did you set your sights on becoming an entrepreneur, creating businesses of your own? Have you dreamed of doing something great for the people of the world by giving your life in service to the poor, sick, or imprisoned?

Sometimes other people have dreams for you. Your parents may have told you that you'd grow up someday to be a minister or a doctor. They might have told you that you could be anything you wanted to be, so go for it! For most people in this generation, the dream of our parents is that we will do better than they did. They have extraordinarily high expectations for us.

What kind of dreams do you have today? Maybe you've faced the fact that some of your early dreams will never become real. You've discovered that you can't throw a ninety-mile-an-hour fastball across the inside corner of the plate. You're not comfortable speaking in front of crowds. Academia is not where your interest lies. The nine-to-five business day is not your style.

There is nothing wrong with having great dreams, as long as we don't hold them too tightly. A dream is just that. It is an imagined future, not a reality. Many of our dreams never materialize. If we hold too tightly to them, we set ourselves up for hurt, disappointment, and failure. We may become despondent about our future, fearful that our lives will have no significance. Our dreams become losses.

Some people have their dreams stolen from them. They spend their entire lives grieving its loss. Still others grieve the loss of a childhood stolen from them by a molester, or a disease, or a disability. Life is filled with losses. Our challenge is to acknowledge our losses, grieve them, and then move on as best we can into the future.

THE FOURTH CHOICE:
The Choice to Heal Your Future

Key Scripture: *So don't worry about tomorrow, for tomorrow will bring its own worries. Today's trouble is enough for today.*

—MATTHEW 6:34 NLT

DRAGGING THE PAST INTO THE FUTURE

Some people are very different from those mentioned in the introduction. They never had an opportunity to create dreams. As children, they were demoralized and told, "You'll never amount to anything" and, "You're no good!" Their spirits were broken early in life, and they lost the capacity to have hope for the future. Their past is filled with emotional scars that are not yet healed.

Some people had dreams they let slip away.

1. **Read again the story on pages 159–61. To experience deep love and then lose it is an incredible loss. If we believe that the loss is a result of our own behavior, the pain we feel is compounded with guilt. Often it is simply too great to reveal, so we hold it inside, hidden from the world. We experience emotional pain that is just as intense as physical pain. We need to diagnose it, treat it, and let it heal, so that our future will be healthy.**

2. **Take a moment and answer this question: What are some of the deep losses you have experienced that continue to cause you emotional pain? If you are studying in a small group of connected friends, you**

might want to discuss this together. However, be sure everyone is comfortable with public discussion.

_____

_____

_____

_____

_____

_____

Here is an important truth. We each must make a healing choice to grieve our losses and let them go.

William Shakespeare wrote, "What is past is prologue."[1] By that he meant that it is possible for us to continually reintroduce our past into our future.

We cannot take past hurts and losses with us into the future without painful consequences. We have to accept life as it is. Doing that, we heal our future by removing from it the constant pain of our past. Thus, the future is less encumbered. We are free to look ahead without regret. We recover hope, because we make a choice to heal the pain of the past.

The events in our past are tied to memory, and we are born with good memories, so releasing past hurts can be a challenge. These are necessary losses. _Healing Is a Choice_ makes the point dramatically on page 162: "When we resist grieving our losses, we drag our pain with us all through our lives."

Exercise #1: *Thinking About Grieving*

Who thinks of grieving as a good thing? Normally, it's extraordinarily sad. However, appropriate grieving can be one of the most healing events in life.

Read Karen's story on pages 162–64 again. Answer and discuss the following questions. If you are studying in a small group, discuss your answers together.

1. Why did Karen's father reject her?

_____

_____

_____

_____

2. How often did Karen's father reject her?

_____

_____

_____

_____

3. Is it likely he did this more often than Karen's story recounts?

_____

_____

_____

_____

4. How must Karen have felt throughout life, having never received affection from her father?

5. How did you feel when the story noted that Karen's father never called her by name?

_____

_____

_____

6. How do you react to Karen's repeated attempts to get her father to acknowledge and meet with her?

_____

_____

_____

7. Karen never grieved the loss of her dad. As a result, she could not move toward the future without her dad casting a long shadow over it. She had to take him out of her future. How did she do that?

_____

_____

_____

Healing Is a Choice describes the important decision Karen made. "She could accept reality, grieve the loss, and let go of the expectation;

or she could spend her life feeling the pain as if it were yesterday. Grieving allows you to move on, free of the pain and agony."

She could not change or control her father. The awful reality of his rejection would always be there, but Karen's choice to heal ensured that it would not interfere with her life any longer. She chose to leave the past behind and move courageously into her future.

JESUS AND GRIEF

We should be very thankful that Jesus came to us in human form, so He could identify with us in every aspect of our lives. What would we do if Jesus could not identify with out grief? It's such a painful and debilitating emotion. How would we be able to bear it?

Not only did Jesus understand grief, but He was well acquainted with it. "He was despised and rejected—a man of sorrows, acquainted with deepest grief" (Isaiah 53:3 NLT).

It makes us wonder how much grief Jesus witnessed during His earthly ministry, and how much He attended to. It was, no doubt, more than we can imagine. Some of His responses to grief must surely be assumed in the passage that says, "Jesus also did many other things. If they were all written down, I suppose the whole world could not contain the books that would be written" (John 21:25 NLT).

We are comforted by the fact that Jesus understands our losses and our grief. He is familiar with the attending emotions and struggles. He is guiding us toward a better future. However, we must cooperate with Him and accept His help.

From a biblical perspective, God always has something to say about our lives and, specifically, our future. The words He spoke to Jeremiah have relevance for every believer: "'For I know the plans I have for you,' says the LORD. 'They are plans for good and not for disaster, to give you a future and a hope'" (Jeremiah 29:11 NLT).

Remember that God has plans and dreams for your future too. As a man of sorrows and grief, He identifies with our suffering. As a man of courage, He gives us strength to face our losses. Because He wept, we can freely express our emotions. Because He has experienced life as we have, we can call on Him for help. After all, He cares deeply for us. Because He lives, we can always face tomorrow!

DEALING WITH UNGRIEVED LOSSES

On pages 165–67, we read another story of how choices to heal impact our future. This is the story of Yvonne. Take time to read it again. Yvonne's process of grieving her losses and moving into the future gives us ten objective points to consider:

1. Explore your ungrieved losses. Try to be specific regarding the issue(s) troubling you. As a child, Yvonne was molested by someone close to her family.
2. How does the problem continue to impact your life? Yvonne realized that she remained overweight and homely at age fifty. She was not taking care of herself. She acknowledged that she used her weight as a boundary, protecting her from being used again sexually.
3. Is there collateral damage? The wall of protection Yvonne created became a barrier preventing anyone from getting too close to her. It helped her feel safe, but her isolation was part of the collateral damage inflicted on her by the molester.
4. Are you stuck in your memories? Yvonne suffered daily

memories of the molestation and her parents' failure to protect her. She ultimately became obsessed over them.

5. Are your emotions failing you? Gradually, Yvonne began to feel disconnected from her emotions. She stopped crying, even in appropriate settings where crying was expected and embraced.

6. How is your anger impacting you? Yvonne began to work on her past.

7. Have you taken the first steps toward forgiveness? Yvonne took the first steps in trying to forgive the molester. She began to envision him in an empty chair. She would tell him (the empty chair) how she felt, demanding that he (the empty chair) tell her why he had hurt her, and finally screaming for help. She felt deeply, but she still did not cry.

8. Have you reached the core issue? For Yvonne, it was the loss of her innocence. She remembered how sweet and happy and cheerful she'd been prior to the molestation. She began to feel her losses. She began to realize how much the molester had taken from her. He had stolen her childhood and almost four decades of her adult life. She realized that her entire life was being defined by one event.

9. Have you grieved? Finally, Yvonne faced the weight of pain she had borne for years. She felt emotional pain at its deepest levels: grief, sadness, and sorrow. She was able to cry again. She grieved the loss of those years. Yvonne worked hard with her counselor. She wrote and wrote in her journal. She made progress.

10. Do you sense that you are recovering? Eventually, Yvonne's grief set her free, so that she could move confidently into

the future. She made one of life's greatest exchanges. She traded her grief for joy!

Perhaps you have gone through an experience similar to Yvonne's. How are you doing? Look back at the ten stages in Yvonne's journey and ask yourself, "Where am I in those stages?"

If you are struggling with letting go of grief, remember that God is on your side, loving you and assisting as you make choices to heal. He sends the Holy Spirit to minister to you in your time of trouble and pain. Consider the comfort He offers from His Word: "The LORD is good. When trouble comes, he is a strong refuge. And he knows everyone who trusts in him" (Nahum 1:7 NLT). "Give all your worries and cares to God, for he cares about what happens to you" (1 Peter 5:7 NLT).

A DIVINE EXCHANGE

Listen to these words: "I tell you the truth, you will weep and mourn while the world rejoices. You will grieve, but your grief will turn to joy" (John 16:20 NIV). Let those words resonate in your mind. Let them take root. Take a few minutes and memorize them. "Your grief will turn to joy!" "Your grief will turn to joy!" Can it be? Really? The answer comes from the heart of God. He says, "Yes!"

When you make a healing choice to grieve, you open the door to a brighter, hopeful future. You trade pain for joy. You leave isolation and disconnection with people behind and exchange it for the joy of friendship and connectedness. You give up a way of life that doesn't work very well for a way of life that is productive. You trade an old way of living for a new way.

DEFENSES AND PRETENSES

All this sounds great, and it is! However, for people who've suffered great pain most of their lives, it is important to know when they are truly working through the grief and moving ahead, rather than just digging up old hurts.

You will know you are healing as you give up *defenses* and *pretenses.*

We need defenses to protect ourselves from more pain when we have not fully experienced grief. Sometimes this is referred to as "being defensive" or using a "defense mechanism." It's really about protecting ourselves from additional pain.

A practical example might sound like this: A dear friend notes that you seem depressed and are not physically taking care of yourself. You might respond by saying, "I feel great and there's nothing wrong with the way I look!" Instead of being open to the friend's honest observation, you shut the other person down with an emphatic denial. Case closed! No discussion!

Defensiveness is a barrier that prevents us from being honest. It is a means of not allowing another person to speak truth into our lives. It often pushes those who love us most out of our lives. They may become reluctant to tell us the truth about ourselves in the future, so we become more disconnected from one another.

Defensiveness is a common problem in human relations and always impacts them negatively. However, defensiveness is even more destructive when a person suffers from unresolved pain and grief.

Pretense comes from the same root word as *pretend.* A pretense is a false appearance or action intended to deceive. It is presenting ourselves as something other than what we are. A good friend might say, "You seem sad today." A pretentious response would be to put on a big smile and say, "I can't believe you'd say that! I've never felt better in my whole life."

We could create another example from Yvonne's life. A friend might say to Yvonne, "You must be very angry toward the person who molested you." If Yvonne wanted to be pretentious, she might respond, "Oh, it's really no big deal. I'm over it now and I'm doing fine!"

People use defenses and pretenses to protect themselves from having to face the truth.

Defenses and pretenses block those who care about them from helping. The consequences are dangerous, because people are driven away, causing the hurting person to be further disconnected from friends and loved ones. Increased disconnection leads to further isolation and more pain. And the cycle repeats.

A sure sign that people have engaged the grief process and are healing is that they feel less need to be defensive or pretentious. The defensive lies and denials are no longer needed. The truth becomes less frightening. We are not afraid that the truth will cause people to reject us.

Exercise #2: Thinking About Defenses and Pretenses

If you are studying alone, use the spaces below. If you are studying in a small group, use the questions below for discussion.

1. Can you recall a time when you have been defensive? Describe.

_____

_____

_____

2. Think about your feelings during the event described above. What caused you to act defensively?

_____

_____

_____

3. Can you recall a time when you acted pretentiously?

_____

_____

_____

4. Think about your feelings during the event described above. What caused you to act pretentiously?

_____

_____

_____

THE FOURTH BIG LIE:
"Time heals all wounds."

This is one of the great lies among human beings. A more accurate statement would be, "Time changes all wounds." A man had surgery on his knee to repair cartilage tears. In time, the wound from the surgery healed, but the damage in his knee increased. He developed acute arthritis and severe pain. Ultimately, he required knee replacement surgery. In his case, time did not heal the knee.

In chapter 2, we learned an important principle: "What is true of physical pain and the body is true for emotional pain and the soul" (p. 72). If time does not heal all physical pain, it's not likely to heal emotional pain.

Time changes wounds, but the changed wounds are usually bitterness, hatred, denial, rejection, and a cold absence of emotions.

What is accurate is that time heals all wounds that are treated appropriately. We need to spend time working on our past wounds. Both Karen and Yvonne were finally able to deal with their pain when they sought help from people trained to assist them.

This book is about healing choices. The most important choice is the powerful decision to act. Make a decision to stop being alone and suffering in silence. As long as you isolate yourself, there is not much chance for healing and growth. After all, you're stuck in the same place, with the same thoughts and the same patterns and the same behaviors. You're isolated! You simply cannot do the same things over and over and expect different results. The pattern must be interrupted. Make a decision to find the places where healing occurs. Make an appointment. Keep it. Do the work required. Being proactive leads to healing!

Your only other option is to remain in the same place and hope that time will cure you. Take it from thousands of people. Time will not heal you. Time will only make your pain last longer. Grieving your past and letting it go will heal you. Then, you can face the future with confidence.

We should be very thankful that we live in a time when Christian counseling is a viable option for so many people. Christian counseling is a discipline taught on scores of campuses. Christian psychiatrists, psychologists, and counselors are present in most localities across America, and more are being trained now. They are there to help you.

WHO ARE YOU?

At the beginning of this chapter, we read about Don Quixote, who wanted to "fight the unbeatable foe," "right the unrightable wrong," "love pure and chaste," "fight for the right," "be willing to march into hell for a heavenly cause," and die in peace.

Quixote was a dreamer. His dreams were noble and righteous. They guided his life and inspired his quest.

Most of us have dreams and goals we establish early and try to fulfill. However, many of us get derailed along life's path. People hurt or abuse us. They take our dreams away from us. We suffer failures and losses. Some are so severely damaged that they get stuck in their pain for years, even decades. Sometimes we inflict pain, suffering, and defeat on ourselves as a result of bad choices.

It's important that we don't live with our losses and failures. We must remember that the One who loves us most has sent us a powerful message in His words to us: "Now glory to God, who is able, through his mighty power at work within us, to accomplish infinitely more than we might ask or think" (Ephesians 3:20 NLT).

JOURNALING

Take a few minutes and review chapter 4. It is an important chapter with information to help hurting people and to help you minister to others. Have you experienced significant pain in your past? Did someone you loved cause it? Did the events leave you scarred? Have you repeatedly attempted to figure out a way to deal with it? At what point will you leave it behind and move on? Take time and write about your painful experiences and the impact they have had on your life.

PRAYERFUL MEDITATION

Find a quiet, relaxing place where you are comfortable and uninterrupted. Ask the Holy Spirit to reveal pain you may still be experiencing from events in your past. Be patient and wait on the Spirit to speak to your mind. God wants you to acknowledge your pain, grieve over it, and have the courage to move boldly into your future. Remember that He has promised never to leave you or forsake you. Remember that He was despised and rejected, acquainted with grief. He knows how you feel. He knows the memories that continually torment you. He knows how you sometimes are triggered by events to remember past hurts. He has compassion on you and wants you to experience healing.

Are you willing? Will you face your pain, grieve, and walk into the light of a new life?

Ask the Holy Spirit to help you grieve. Let Him speak to your heart and mind. Then ask Him to give you courage to change. Sit quietly for a few minutes and listen to the Holy Spirit. Thank God for the life He has given you. Thank Him because He is able to redeem the past.

Think about God's love and faithfulness. Imagine yourself being happy, unburdened, and filled with joy. That is how God wants you to be. "Give all your worries and cares to God, for he cares about you" (1 Peter 5:7 NLT).

Prayer

Heavenly Father, hear my prayer. I have endured so much pain for so long. I am worn out and want to move on with my life. Please help me. Send Your Holy Spirit to give me strength to deal with the wounds from my past. Help me to grieve instead of pushing things down deeper into my mind. Give me release from the emotional bondage I feel so often. Give me courage to allow others to help me. Lead me toward people who will accept and connect with me. Thank You for the challenge I have received from this chapter. I choose to take healing steps today. Please stay close to me as I take these steps. I truly want to be healed. You are the Great Physician. Do Your cleansing, redeeming, restorative work in me. Increase my confidence in You. Increase my faith. I give You my life—mind, soul, and spirit. Through Jesus Christ, my Healer. Amen.

REJOICE AND SING!

If you know this chorus, sing it to conclude your devotion. Its words of healing can strengthen your heart. If you don't know it, select a song or a hymn of your choice. Use it to worship God for a few minutes.

SAY THE NAME (OF JESUS)

Say the name of Jesus. Say the name of Jesus
Say the name so precious, No other name I know
That can calm your fears and dry your tears
And wipe away your pain.
When you don't know what else to pray
When you can't find the words to say . . . say the name
Jesus, Jesus, Jesus, Jesus, He's gonna make a way.

5

THE FIFTH CHOICE:
The Choice to Help Your Life

THE FIFTH BIG LIE:
"I can figure this out by myself."

ONCE YOU HAVE INVESTIGATED YOUR LIFE, SEARCHED FOR the truth in your life, and grieved the losses, you are ready for the choice to reach outside of yourself and help your life. When the truth leads to the reality that help is needed, choosing to get help is the next right thing to do. It takes courage to seek out, obtain, and utilize whatever resources you need to treat the untreated areas of your life. But not everyone has the courage. Not everyone is willing.

Just the other day, I spoke with a very bright thirty-five-year-old man. Well, I said he was bright—by bright, I mean brain capacity—but in a sense he has proved he is not very bright at all. This man has a very high IQ and is a microbiologist and nuclear physicist—or at least he has the degree and the experience to be one. He is, however, a postal worker who drives his route alone in a truck, comes home to an empty house without even a pet, watches television, goes to bed, and starts the whole process all over again the next day.

He suffers from social anxiety. People drive him away or up the wall. He is uncomfortable every moment he is around others. This discomfort often leads to inappropriate interactions, which have caused him to lose job after job. Following his last job fiasco, he saw a newspaper ad about joining the postal workforce and has been able to hold down a job as a traveling postal worker for a few years. He has been able to earn a consistent paycheck, but he is miserable.

It is difficult to show up day after day and do a good job as a postal worker if you are called to be a microbiologist. Many of our listeners are postal workers who tune in every day as they deliver the mail, and they love their jobs. Some love being outdoors, and others feel a sense of connection to the people they deliver mail to; they are energized by the job. It would be a very difficult job, however, if you believe that everything in you was designed for microbiology. Postal delivery would be a very tough job if you have memories of wanting to know details about how things work and spent hours as a boy looking at leaves and seawater and anything else you could fit under your microscope.

I asked this man with an IQ far beyond mine, who has the ability to study and focus far beyond my ability, "What have you done to help yourself feel more comfortable around other people?" He had done nothing. He had never sought any help for himself. He had never Googled "anxiety" or searched the yellow pages to find a counselor. He listened to *New Life Live,* but he had never called 1-800-New-Life to explore the possibility of getting a counselor. Throughout his struggle and pain, he held on to the notion that he would one day figure out the answer and help himself live the life he wanted. At his age, however, the rut he was living in was growing deeper and deeper. Perhaps talking to me was his first step toward helping his life.

COUNTING ON THE SICK MIND

I am all for us feeling good about ourselves and being grateful for the gifts God has given us. I am amazed at the wonders of His creation that we call man and woman. Our brains alone are beyond my ability to comprehend. The more I learn about computers, the more amazed I am at the one living just above my brow. I am all for building ourselves up with positive self-talk about how great a creation we are and how marvelously talented we are. Those are really nice things for us to do, but in the midst of our happy talk, we need to accept the glaring reality that we each, to some degree or another, have a sick mind. Its wiring and chemistry might be functioning perfectly, but it is functioning in the human state of perpetual sickness that takes us down paths we do not want or need to travel.

In the midst of our happy talk, we need to accept the glaring reality that we each, to some degree or another, have a sick mind.

"Right in front of every person is a path that is very wide and easy to follow" (Proverbs 14:12; author's paraphrase). As far down that path as you can see, it seems to be a very pleasant and pleasurable way to go. You end up in the midst of death and destruction, however, when you take that path to where you want to go. That path is not the path of truth, it is not the path of wisdom, and it is not the path of God. It is the path of the sick mind.

The mind we use to do so much is a defective organ. It is so sick that microbiologists end up delivering mail. Pastors end up selling stocks and bonds. Married men end up in relationships with prostitutes. Women end up living like doormats. Geniuses end up behind bars. Wealthy people shoplift. Healthy people gain 180 pounds. Mothers hit the children they love. Fathers molest the children they always dreamed of treating better than they were treated. Teachers end up selling insurance. Counselors end up in inappropriate relationships with those they wanted to help. Fun and exciting people end up bolted to the security of their own homes, unable to walk out the front door. The sick mind does all this and more.

People can watch their lives fall into complete disarray and confusion. They can experience confusion and hopelessness for years and yet still believe that they must and will find a way to help themselves. Perhaps they have heard the term *self-help* and, without exploring what that really means, think that there are a lot of people succeeding because they have figured out how to help themselves. Nothing could be further from the truth.

Self-help is not really *self*-help at all. Self-help that really helps is God help; it is group help; it is expert help. It is anything but a person's sick mind finally finding the path to a great and wonderful life. The sick mind that leads us down the wrong path is not going to somehow find the right path one day. In order to find that path, we must seek help beyond ourselves. We must reach out and find the treatment we need.

THE SOONER THE BETTER

If your sick mind is causing you distress, the sooner you get help for it, the better. In the meantime, your body is harming itself, including harming your mind. In *Newsweek*, September 27, 2004, there was an excellent sidebar on page 46, by Josh Ulick. He explained in the sidebar how the body can harm itself if we do not relieve the problems of our past and our conflicts. The problem comes from our ability to spring into action when there is great danger. A chemical reaction occurred that set the body into action when a caveman saw a threat to his family or himself. That was good for his family and him, but it is not so good for us if we do not see the problem and respond to it properly.

Today, rather than having supernatural strength "to kill the rhino," we sit and stew in our own juices, because for us there is no rhino. When the body senses a threat, it gets ready for action. First, the hypothalmus gland secretes a substance called CRH that stimulates the pituitary gland. The pituitary secretes the ACTH molecule, which travels to the adrenal gland. The adrenal gland releases cortisol, a hormone that helps keep blood sugar up and give the body extra energy to act. If you were a cave dweller, with rhinos all around, you would be thankful for the boost. If you are an accountant, however, you might become restless and not know how to respond to the chemistry set exploding inside your head.

Additionally, there are other responses that kick into gear. The adrenal glands produce epinephrine, which increases heart and breathing rates for better fighting and defending. Blood pressure rises as well, as the legs and arms receive extra blood for more energy. All of this dissipates as the threat is killed or runs away into the bushes.

Today most of us don't face rhinos. Some of us might have bosses that wear on us and never give us a break. If we do, the lingering effects of the stress hormones can be quite damaging. Our memories become impaired. The immune system is weakened. High blood pressure and stomach ulcers are common. Skin problems and digestive difficulties also follow. It is in our best interest to deal with the problem as soon as possible, so the adverse side effects have as little opportunity as possible to damage us.

SICK STRAY DOG

Would you do more for a sick stray dog than you would do for yourself? Most people would help a stray dog that was in trouble. If you saw a dog on the side of the road that had been run over or was wounded or sick, you would probably help that dog. If you are like most people, a helpless, whimpering puppy would be hard for you to leave dying and bleeding in the street. Most people would determine the appropriate available treatment, and a trip to a local veterinarian would not be too much trouble. If you would do that for a stray animal, why wouldn't you do it for yourself? There are many reasons.

You might be embarrassed to seek help; it would be a sign of weakness for you to walk into a counselor's office or attend a Celebrate Recovery group. You would be "found out," and the last thing you want is for someone to know you have a problem. So you protect your problem and your image, but you ruin your life in the process. At least you prevent your real life from beginning. Rather than admit a limitation or allow anyone to know that there is a broken part of you, you continue the masquerade and avoid any place where people go to get help. You may view the decision not to get help as rational, but it is part of the denial that a sick mind uses to remain unhealthy.

If the stray dog on the side of the road was a person, you would not put much stock in that person's assessment of his own injury or his direction for treatment. If a person's leg has been torn off by a hit-and-run driver and you see it across the road, you don't listen to the person tell you he will be all right; he will just walk home; he just needs a minute to get himself together. You know the severity of the injury. You can see the evidence, and it does not look good. The hurt person is in denial or shock or something other than a state of reality that would lead him to get the help he needs. It is no different for the person limping past the counselor's office or the pastor's suite or the recovery group while saying to him- or herself, "I am going to be just fine, one day, eventually, sooner or later, down the road, not too far away." If that is you, you need to pull over, reach out, and get the help you need.

This condition of self-deception is addressed quite plainly in Proverbs 3:5–7. The passage directs you not to lean on your own understanding. Do not trust yourself. Do not be wise in your own eyes. Do not fool yourself into thinking you have the answers and will figure it out. It is an admonition to move out of your own understanding and seek help and insight from someone else who may be able to help you with the deep wounds that must be treated, and the sooner the better.

WOUNDS

We all have wounds of one sort or another, and the sooner we get help for them, the better. Right now I am guilty of not doing the very thing I am suggesting you need to do. The computer I am typing on is sitting on my left leg, which was badly hurt about two weeks ago while riding bikes with my daughter. I crashed into a lady coming up behind me because her bike was so expensive that it didn't make noises like ours did. I had no idea anyone was riding along behind us, because I heard nothing. I pulled to the right—right into her path. As I realized the situation, I yanked back left, falling over the top of my bike while the brake handle plunged into my left thigh.

I can still feel the torn muscle that probably needs to be sewn back in place. I did not have time to take care of it when it happened; I thought it was going to heal, but it still hurts. Now I will have to visit the doctor's office, and they probably will have to rip up some places that healed improperly that could have easily been sewn up if I had come in the day of the accident. As a procrastinator, I thought it was something that would get better with time. It did not, and you won't either.

We need to treat the wounds sooner rather than later. When we don't treat the wound, the wound infects other parts of us and spreads out into other relationships. The abused may become an abuser if the abuse is not treated and resolved. The abused may experience the abuse over and over again until that wound is properly treated. Lives can be wasted because something that hurt at age sixteen is still not resolved at twenty-six or forty-six. At some point, a person starting to experience pain in the soul, the way I experience pain in my leg right now, must decide that it is no longer acceptable to allow the problem to go untreated. Outside help is required if hope is to replace the gaping wound.

WISE COUNSEL

Reaching out to get the help you need does not come only in the form of a recovery group or a counselor's office. Many times the help you need can be found at the local church. But for it to be effective, you need to be part of that church and involved in it. If you have gone to work on your connections and have become part of

dealing with might seem like a huge vulture hovering over your head or perched on your shoulder. You cannot do anything without being aware of that huge presence dominating your thoughts and treatment. The goal of treatment would be to shrink that vulture into the size of a gnat. You would know it was still there, but it would not be in control. It would not be the dominating force in your life.

One of my biggest problems resulting from a huge struggle with attention deficit disorder is following directions, or at least trying to follow them. I can get lost going to places I have been many times before; I am hopeless. A friend of mine was riding with me one day and saw the turmoil I was going through and knew my desire for vultures to become gnats. My good friend said, "Steve, make it a gnat, make it a gnat." That was a good reminder.

I was allowing the struggle to take hold of me and was participating in vulture-controlled living. I needed to regain my focus and shrink the vulture of misdirection down to the manageable size of a gnat. Although it is easy to do that while driving around, it is much more difficult to do that with problems you have had for years. Treatment will help you RISE above the vultures in your life and learn to turn them into gnats.

RISE is an acronym I use to summarize the benefits of treatment and give some direction in what to do while you are in treatment:

R Reduce the stress in your life by learning some new
   management skills.
   Reduce conflicts that cause inner turmoil and difficulties
   in your relationships.
   Reduce the negative patterns that have set in over your
   lifetime.

Reduce the substances you use to help cope with the pain in your life.

I Increase your self-awareness and how you affect people who interact with you.

Increase your awareness of your feelings.

Increase your understanding of yourself and why you do the things you do.

Increase your connection with others.

Increase your assertiveness in a way that draws people to you rather than repels them.

Increase the healthy influences in your life.

Increase your time alone with God in the Bible and in prayer.

S Substitute positive emotions for negative ones.

Substitute the willingness to risk for fear.

Substitute humility for arrogance.

Substitute acceptance for anger.

Substitute peace for anxiety.

Substitute surrender for control.

E Eliminate addictive behaviors.

Eliminate a critical and judgmental spirit.

Eliminate certain repetitive sins in your life.

These are just some of the areas you can work on in treatment and some of the outcomes you can expect. If you look at the list of outcomes above, you can see that it would be a pleasant way to live.

You have to ask yourself what is standing in your way of getting the help you need. Do you really want to be healed, or have you grown too accustomed to the brokenness? Are you dependent on living in bondage, or are you ready to live in freedom? When you reach a point of no longer justifying the sickness in your soul, you are ready to seek the help that can heal it.

TREATMENT OPTIONS

You might think of psychological or psychiatric help as the only way a person with some emotional problems can get help. You may have seen a movie or two that depicted a sick institution full of psychotic people, compared yourself to them, and decided that you would never be in bad enough shape to go that route. An institution is far from being the only option for help. It is something that very few people ever need and is not something to be afraid of.

When I first began graduate work in counseling, I sought a place where I could work with severely pathological patients—a place people were not coming to get help with a marital problem or something similar, but a place where people had reached the end of their own inner resources and needed someone to take care of them. I found that place at Fort Worth Neuropsychiatric Institute in 1977 and was hired by Dorothy Grasty, the director of nurses. I began as a psychiatric aide, cleaning toilets and doing whatever else was needed. It was a great experience that affected everything I have done since that time.

The institute was a safe place for healing. People there cared deeply about the patients, and the patients got better. It was not like anything depicted in movies out of Hollywood. I worked with thirty other institutions across America. I saw what went on in these facilities, and it was good treatment. If you ever are faced with having to be admitted to a facility to protect yourself or others, you do not need to be afraid. These places are truly places of healing. Like any institution, there are some that are not so great and a few that might just be in it for the money, although there is very little money in it these days. For the most part, however, you can trust that there is a helpful place waiting for you if you need the most extreme form of treatment from an institution or inpatient facility.

If you ever are faced with having to be admitted to a facility to protect yourself or others, you do not need to be afraid. These places are truly places of healing.

There are many other forms of help and treatment that are much less extreme. You may need medication to help you think clearly or feel appropriately, and a psychiatrist can help you with that. A psychologist or a licensed marriage and family therapist can provide counseling or therapy. As mentioned earlier, a pastor who is trained in counseling may be the perfect resource for one-to-one therapy. Group therapy involving others with similar problems, conducted by a licensed therapist, may help you relate to others and uncover areas within yourself that need work. All of these are more formal types of treatment.

Some of the most helpful treatment does not come from a trained professional. There are many options outside of a professional's office that don't cost anything and have been used by thousands for transformation and healing. Self-help groups such as Alcoholics

Anonymous or Alanon meet all across this country and around the world. Celebrate Recovery is a growing Christian recovery resource that can be found in about three thousand churches. Anyone who struggles in some area should locate a group specific to his or her struggle and at least give it a try.

There are other options. Retreats and workshops can help a person get on the right path to healing. At New Life we conduct intensive retreats for women whose husbands have been involved in sexual sin. We call them "Every Heart Restored." We offer "Every Man's Battle" for the men who have struggled with lust and sexual sin. For people struggling with weight, we offer "Lose It for Life." For those who have been abused or been abusive, "Healing Is a Choice" is the workshop that came out of this book. All of these are great treatment options that can help transform your life.

"They offer superficial treatments for my people's mortal wound" (Jeremiah 6:14 NLT). Take this scripture as an admonition not to do this to yourself. Treat your wounds appropriately rather than superficially. Get the help that you need before the wound further infects you or those around you. Treat deeply what needs treating rather than just giving it the minimal amount of attention needed—hoping it will eventually go away. You are worth the effort, and God will honor your efforts to get the help you need to heal what is broken in your soul.

THE BIG LIE
"I can figure this out by myself."

The big lie that you may have been telling yourself is that you can figure this out on your own. I don't think so. I think if you could, you would have done so by now. With all the pain and struggle you have endured, I believe you would have figured it out and put the fix in place. You have not because you cannot. Although you might see that as a weakness, the greatest act of strength you can exhibit is to admit you don't have the answer within you and to turn to someone who does.

In a Gatorade commercial, athletes drink the orange or green variety, work up a huge sweat, and orange or green sweat beads pop out everywhere. Then comes the question, "Is it in you?" When it comes to the answers to fixing your life, the answer is, no, you do not have it in you. The answers to your problems are not there. The sick mind that led you down the path of sickness will not lead you to a place of health and wholeness. You are not going to figure this out. Not even reading this book is going to be enough. You will have to reach beyond what is in your head and reach out for the help you need—it is not in you.

There are some really good things that are in you. There must be some desire to live a better life, as evidenced by picking up this book. You must not love the rut you have dug for yourself. You want out, and that is good. You have sought and are acquiring new information. But my fear is that you are hoping that you will finally become smart enough to figure it all out on your own, by yourself. If that is the motive for reading this book, it could backfire on you.

If this book lifts you out of your desperation enough so that rather than shutting down or wanting to jump off, you continue down the wrong path, then you are ill served by this book. If you walk down that wrong road with new information, you are still living with the false belief that one day you will figure it all out on your own. For you, this book becomes a tool to keep you isolated and lonely in your broken state.

If this book motivates you to reach beyond yourself to get help from someone who can see a perspective that is different from a sick mind, then you will have begun the journey toward healing. You don't have it in you, but someone else does. Reach out and get the help you need. Help your life, and your life will never be the same. If you don't know where to turn or who to call, call us at 1-800-New-Life.

Millions of people choose to stay in the despair and anguish that have become their constant daily companions. You don't have to be like them because healing is a choice. It is a choice to find the treatment you need and help your life.

CHAPTER 5 WORKBOOK QUESTIONS

THE FIFTH CHOICE:
The Choice to Help Your Life

THE FIFTH BIG LIE:
"I can figure this out by myself."

AT THIS POINT IN OUR JOURNEY THROUGH *HEALING IS A Choice*, you may have noticed a progression of healing steps, as follows:

- Chapter 1 established the importance of being connected to others.
- Chapter 2 explained the importance of feeling your life, especially your pain.
- Chapter 3 taught you to investigate your life and search for truth in your life.
- Chapter 4 emphasized the importance of grieving your losses.
- Chapter 5 emphasized the very important decision to reach outside yourself and help your life. You need help to heal. You need a healing team that includes yourself, appropriate friends and family, professional caregivers, someone from your faith community, and, most important,

God. The truth you must face is that you are not going to heal yourself.

Writing in 1624, the pastor-poet John Donne penned these words: "No man is an island, entire of itself; every man is a piece of the continent, a part of the main."[1]

Donne's point is that no one can exist on his or her own, cut off from the rest of society. To use Donne's illustration, there are no human islands!

When Donne preached and wrote, most of Europe was moving toward isolationism. Nations were not seeking to be interconnected with one another. They were worn out from fighting and wanted to be left alone to form little island-nations all over Europe.

About that same time, Sir Thomas More wrote *Utopia*, which described an island-nation that prospered in its isolation. The irony of More's book was that the citizens of Utopia did not prosper because of being isolated. Rather, they prospered because they relied on one another. They were interconnected.

What is the purpose of this brief history lesson? I mention it because there is a strong comparison between John Donne's point and the theme of chapter 5.

You are not an island! You may have constructed a protective barrier around your life to protect yourself from future pain, but it is not helping you. You were not created to be alone, and you need to be connected to others in order to be healthy.

There is, however, one thing you can do to be healed. You must make the healing choice to reject isolationism and to engage those who can help you.

One of the most important lessons to be learned in *Healing Is a*

Choice is that we need to be connected with others. None of us do very well with life alone. If we are dealing with serious emotional, spiritual, or psychological issues, withdrawing into isolation usually exacerbates the problems. Think back on the stories we've read. Rachael's condition improved as she began to connect with friends and, ultimately, good counselors. Laurie suffered because her husband failed to connect with her in the most vulnerable and painful time of her life. Karen withdrew into isolation due to lifelong rejection from her father. Yvonne spent more than forty years disconnected from her feelings and other people due to childhood abuse.

The truth is both simple and profound. We are not created to live isolated and alone. We are not meant to live without companionship. We are meant to live connected to family, friends, and others in an interdependent community.

If we withdraw and isolate ourselves, we suffer the consequences. When the investigation of our lives reveals that we need the help of others, then making a healing choice to reach outside and help our lives is the very best choice we can make. It takes courage to make that choice and commitment to see it through to its conclusion. Making such choices is a powerful way to help our lives.

THE FIFTH CHOICE:
The Choice to Help Your Life

A SICK MIND?

We live in a culture filled with people who desperately want to believe that, "I'm okay" and "You're okay!" Television hosts and celebrities tell us that all we need to live happy lives is to reach deep inside and draw out the emotional power. They tell us that "all the answers to your problems are inside you." Such cultural jargon usually does more harm than good. It's spoken out of context, misrepresented, and misapplied, and it often leads to compounded failure in people's lives.

Thus, *Healing Is a Choice* makes a very blunt statement on page 193. It reads, "In the midst of our happy talk, we need to accept the glaring reality that we each, to some degree or another, have a sick mind."

We rarely know how to solve our problems. None of us are perfect. We are all somewhat damaged. From a theological point of view, our damage results from the fall. As a result we have a sinful nature that needs healing. Jesus Christ, the Great Physician, heals our nature. From a sociological point of view, we are also somewhat damaged. No one had perfect parents or perfect adults around all the time. Consequently, we are somewhat damaged by those who raised us and those who interacted with our lives. Circumstances may have damaged us, as in the example of a child who becomes ill and must be bedridden for long periods of time, or a young person who is abused and must deal with the consequent pain for long years.

To some degree, our minds are sick and need healing.

THE ESSENTIAL CHOICE

We now reach a critical point in the book. We read that "right in front of every person is a path that is very wide and easy to follow" (Proverbs 14:12; paraphrase). The New Living Translation is even more emphatic: "There is a path before each person that seems right, but it ends in death." What's the point?

As we arrive at the decision to help our lives, we have a healing choice to make. We can take the wide, easy path. After all, it looks inviting and easy to manage. There don't seem to be any impediments in the way. We think, *This will be a breeze!*

But wait! People have taken that path before and gotten into deep trouble. That wide path is deceptive and filled with danger. We are warned not to take that path. But we think, *It's wide and easy. Why would we even consider another way?*

Jesus answered that question in Matthew 7: "You can enter God's Kingdom only through the narrow gate. The highway to [destruction] is broad, and its gate is wide for the many who choose that way. But the gateway to life is very narrow, and the road is difficult, and only a few ever find it" (vv. 13–14 NLT).

So, the choice is clearly stated. If we take the wide, easy path, we are headed for trouble. It is not the path of truth or wisdom. It does not lead us to God or the healing we need. It will not solve the problem of our sick minds. Consider some of the consequences listed in the book for those who take the wide, easy path:

- Microbiologists end up delivering mail (pp. 191–92).
- Pastors end up selling stocks and bonds.
- Married men end up having affairs.
- Women end up living like doormats.
- Geniuses end up behind bars.
- Wealthy people shoplift.
- Healthy people gain 180 pounds.
- Mothers hit the children they love.

The book offers more examples of people's lives falling apart as they head down the wide, easy path that Jesus called "the road to destruction." This is where our sick minds lead us.

How Do You Make Choices?

People make choices every day. Sometimes they are insignificant (*What kind of toothpaste will I use?*); at other times they are critical (*Will I contact a Christian counselor to help me with my growing depression?*). Each of us makes hundreds of decisions daily. How do you approach the decision-making process? Is it instinctive, deliberate, or both?

Exercise #1: Making Choices

Answer the questions below. If you are studying in a small group, discuss them together.

1. How do you determine the value of your choices? What makes some choices more important than others?

_____

_____

_____

_____

2. How many choices do you make in an average day that positively impact the quality of your life?

_____

_____

_____

3. Do you have a process or strategy you use when making choices? Describe it.

4. List a few of the most important choices you've made in life. After each one, describe whether the choice was a good one or turned out to be a mistake.

(a) _____

_____

(b) _____

_____

(c) _____

_____

(d) _____

_____

5. Think of past choices. Perhaps you chose not to attend the state university in order to enroll at a Christian college. Perhaps you chose to give a year of your life to Christian service rather than accept a wonderful job offer you received. Maybe you chose to marry a

dedicated Christian man rather than the nonbelieving man who swept you off your feet. Can you recall decisions you made that involved declining a great choice in order to make a choice in favor of something better?

_____

_____

_____

_____

If we reject the choice of the wide and easy path, then what road should we take?

Clearly, the right option is what Jesus called the "narrow gate" (Matthew 7:13). The outcome of following Jesus' path leads to healing, health, a meaningful life, and joy. It's the road that ends in a good, productive life.

The discussion about choices of paths is addressed beautifully in a poem titled "The Road Not Taken," written by Robert Frost, one of America's greatest and most prolific poets. Read the poem carefully, perhaps more than once.

THE ROAD NOT TAKEN

Two roads diverged in a yellow wood,
And sorry I could not travel both
And be one traveler, long I stood
And looked down one as far as I could
To where it bent in the undergrowth;
Then took the other, as just as fair,
And having perhaps the better claim,

Because it was grassy and wanted wear;
Though as for that the passing there
Had worn them really about the same,
And both that morning equally lay
In leaves no step had trodden black.
Oh, I kept the first for another day!
Yet knowing how way leads on to way,
I doubted if I should ever come back.
I shall be telling this with a sigh
Somewhere ages and ages hence:
Two roads diverged in a wood, and I—
I took the one less traveled by,
And that has made all the difference.

6. What is the message Frost is trying to convey in this poem?

_____

_____

_____

7. Are Jesus and Robert Frost saying the same thing about the paths
they recommend? Explain.

_____

_____

_____

IS SELF-HELP AN OPTION?

Choosing the right path to follow is an important choice, one that will either hurt our lives or heal them. Following the wide, easy path is a road to pain, not healing. People's lives fall apart on that road. They stumble into confusion and hopelessness.

Yet thousands of people continue choosing the wide, easy path. Somehow, erroneously, they think that path will lead to health, or that they will magically find some sort of "self-help" solution to finally heal them. After all, isn't self-help a major industry in the United States? Yes, it is a big business generating huge amounts of money while healing a precious few people, if that! Just buy three books (you might not actually read them) and twelve tapes, and attend four seminars. Then, hopefully, you will be healed instantly. That may be an oversimplification. However, a significant number of Americans think that self-help will cure all their ills. Actually, it creates more problems, because all people have really done is stay on that wide, easy path. They are still rejecting the hard, healing path.

Our sick minds that lead us down wrong paths are not going to somehow find the right path one day.

As we are reminded, "Self-help is not really *self*-help at all. Self-help that really helps is God help; it is group help; it is expert help" (p. 194).

WARNING! NO HELP LEADS TO POOR HEALTH, OR WORSE

Here is a very important truth: we need help to get on the right path, because we are not capable of doing it alone. We must seek help beyond ourselves and find the treatment we need. Otherwise, we could get sicker and increasingly harm our minds and bodies. The consequences are devastating.

Our bodies are not designed to tolerate the debilitating impact of unresolved conflicts and painful issues from our past. We sit in our chairs stewing over problems.

We can't seem to find solutions that work. We're frustrated, because we want to do something to solve our problems. Our bodies tense up, wanting to spring into action, but we sit immobilized. With no physical outlet, our bodies take a terrible hit, like a "chemistry set exploding inside your head" (p. 195).

NOTE: For more details regarding the physical damage stress can produce, read pages 194–96 again. You may also want to check the library or Internet for headings such as these:

"How Does Stress Affect the Body?"
"Stress and Your Health"
"The Effects of Chronic Stress on the Body"

There are common reasons why people do not seek the help they need, including:

1. They might feel embarrassed to seek help.
2. It would be viewed as a sign of weakness.
3. They would be "found out" (that they have a problem).
4. They've lost hope that anyone or anything can help.

There is no good reason to deny the help that is needed. In fact, we would actually call these excuses "denial." It never leads to healing. It always causes illness.

The word picture painted in the book is a sad reminder of how ill people become when they are in denial. The description is: "the person limping past the counselor's office or the pastor's suite or the recovery group while saying to him- or herself, 'I am going to be just fine, one day, eventually, sooner or later, down the road, not too far away'" (p. 197).

The truth is that we all have wounds, problems, and scars of one kind or another. So, the sooner we get help, the quicker we will be healthy and whole.

"Denial" is just another term for self-deception. Denial says, "You're the only one in the world who feels this way or has this problem, and you shouldn't let anyone else know about it!"

Scripture has a response to denial. It says, "Trust in the LORD with all your heart; do not depend on your own understanding. Seek his will in all you do, and he will show you which path to take. Don't be impressed with your own wisdom. Instead, fear the LORD and turn away from evil" (Proverbs 3:5–7 NLT).

These verses tell us to move away from our own understanding. In its place, we should seek the help of competent, trained professionals, while also seeking the connectedness of good friends.

If you tore your knee cartilage, you'd see an orthopedic doctor as soon as possible. You'd have to in order to walk properly. If you had appendicitis, you'd see an internist or a surgeon who could remove it before it poisoned your body and threatened your life.

If you are dealing with emotional, spiritual, or psychological pain, you should follow the same strategy. As quickly as possible, seek professionals who can best help you.

CREATE A RESOURCE DIRECTORY: AN IMPORTANT WAY TO HELP

Here is an exercise that will be helpful for you individually, and perhaps for your church. Every church should maintain an up-to-date referral list of professionals who are trusted and can be recommended as needed. Churches are often viewed as sources of information for people needing help. Churches are also primary centers of pastoral care. Even if you are receiving professional help, your church should be part of the healing team. You need a pastor who can offer solid biblical counsel and who can listen and pray with you. Churches and pastors are primary resources.

A directory makes referring easy. You will need to do some research, using a telephone book, medical directories, word-of-mouth recommendations, and firsthand information. Create as many categories as you need.

To begin building your directory, fill in the information below. Keep a personal copy and offer copies to your church and friends.

Psychologists and Professional Counselors

1. Name: _____ Phone 1: _____

   Address: _____ Phone 2: _____

   City: _____ State: _____

   Other Important Information: _____

2. Name: _____ Phone 1: _____

   Address: _____ Phone 2: _____

   City: _____ State: _____

   Other Important Information: _____

3. Name: _____ Phone 1: _____

   Address: _____ Phone 2: _____

   City: _____ State: _____

   Other Important Information: _____

Christian Counselor

1. Name: _____ Phone 1: _____

   Address: _____ Phone 2: _____

   City: _____ State: _____

   Other Important Information: _____

Psychiatrist

1. Name: _____ Phone 1: _____

   Address: _____ Phone 2: _____

   City: _____ State: _____

   Other Important Information: _____

Grief Support

1. Name: _____ Phone 1: _____

   Address: _____ Phone 2: _____

   City: _____ State: _____

   Other Important Information: _____

General Support Groups
(Cancer, Diabetes, Heart, Alzheimer's, etc.)

1. Name: _____ Phone 1: _____

   Address: _____ Phone 2: _____

   City: _____ State: _____

   Other Important Information: _____

2. Name: _____ Phone 1: _____

   Address: _____ Phone 2: _____

   City: _____ State: _____

   Other Important Information: _____

Hospice

1. Name: _____ Phone 1: _____

   Address: _____ Phone 2: _____

   City: _____ State: _____

   Other Important Information: _____

Crisis Pregnancy

1. Name: _____ Phone 1: _____

   Address: _____ Phone 2: _____

   City: _____ State: _____

   Other Important Information: _____

Financial Assistance and Counseling

1. Name: _____ Phone 1: _____

   Address: _____ Phone 2: _____

   City: _____ State: _____

   Other Important Information: _____

Substance Abuse Agencies and Groups

1. Name: _____ Phone 1: _____

   Address: _____ Phone 2: _____

   City: _____ State: _____

   Other Important Information: _____

TREATMENT

Acknowledging the genuine need for help in your life motivates you to put away the false hope of self-help and consider seeing a professional who can guide and assist you in the healing process. The decision to seek help is an important healing choice. When you get to this point, treatment becomes a viable option.

The specific goal in treatment is to grow in character and to become closer to Christlike living. However, there are other areas in which treatment would be beneficial. It could help resolve inward conflicts between Christlike character and contrary behaviors. It could also help you move toward consistency, doing the things you should do and rejecting the things you should not do. Consistency helps you live in conformity to your values and to be the same person in private that you are in public.

What are some treatment options that can be pursued? They run from extreme to mild, depending on the need. In the extreme, psychiatric or psychological help might be valuable. Occasionally, but not often, hospitalization might be necessary. The more common treatments include medication to help you think clearly. One of the chief duties of psychiatrists is to prescribe and manage medication.

A marriage and family therapist can provide much-needed treatment for broken relationships. A pastor trained in counseling might be very helpful in one-to-one treatment. The pastor can also combine good counsel with the wisdom of Scripture and personal prayer.

Group therapy is usually a productive option, because it affords group members the advantage of discussing similar problems. Many churches also have various kinds of support groups available to the general public.

There are effective treatment options that cost little or nothing and have proven records of success. These include Alcoholics Anonymous, Alanon, Celebrate Recovery, Divorce Recovery, and more. Helping your church develop a directory of resources like we described above will facilitate treatment and help.

A great advantage of participating in a support group is that you benefit from a structured treatment program while simultaneously enjoying more connectedness, which, as we have learned, is one of the more important aspects of our healing.

THE FIFTH BIG LIE:
"I can figure this out by myself."

Bluntly, the answer to this lie is, "No, you can't!" If you could figure it out, you would have by now. If you could heal yourself, you would already have done so. If you could make the pain go away, you would have done that long ago. You need help in the healing process. However, the one thing you can do is start the process, that is, make the healing choice to help your life.

The constant lie you will hear in your head is, *I can do this myself. I can do this myself.* You must tell yourself the truth. You can't. What you can do is run to those people and places that can help you heal.

Remember the last three lines in Frost's poem? They are:

> *Two roads diverged in a wood, and I—*
> *I took the one less traveled by,*
> *And that has made all the difference.*

The choice to help your life is the harder path, but it's the healing path.

JOURNALING

Take a few minutes and review chapter 5. It is a challenging chapter encouraging you to do the hard work of moving toward healing. Making such choices heals your life and changes your future. The good news is that Jesus is with you in the process. He understands our weaknesses and our reluctance to do what is best. Because He understands, He can truly help us. In your journal, explore the barriers we employ that keep us from being healed.

Prayerful Meditation

As before, find a quiet, relaxing place where you are comfortable and uninterrupted. Get a cup of coffee, some tea, or hot chocolate. Ask the Holy Spirit to reveal places in your life where you may be reluctant to seek help. If you are stubbornly resisting what you know in your heart you should do, then repent and resolve to change.

If you need to pursue treatment for any reason, pray about the options you have.

Be patient and wait on the Spirit to speak to your mind. God wants to guide you in this process rather than have you marching out on your own. Remember, always, His promise never to leave you or forsake you. He loves you and cares about everything that occurs in your life. He is compassionate and full of grace and mercy.

Are you willing to help your life? Will you face your pain and walk into the light of a new life?

Ask the Holy Spirit to help you make this courageous choice. Let Him speak to your heart and mind. Sit quietly for a few minutes and listen to the Holy Spirit. Thank God for the gift of life He has given you.

PRAYER

Heavenly Father, hear my sincere prayer. I worry that I won't ever be well. I often feel as if I take one step forward and two steps back. I'm up one day and down the next. I've forgotten what consistency means.

Please help me get some balance and truth back into my life. Please give me hope that life will be better . . . soon. Please send Your Holy Spirit to do a deep, inner work in my soul. I want to laugh and feel lighthearted again. Please give me courage to seek the treatment I need. Give me more friends. I'm tired of being alone. Thank You for the challenge in this chapter. I hear it and will do my best to respond positively. Please stay close to me as I take more healing steps.

Increase my confidence in You. Increase my faith. I give You my life; mind, soul, and spirit. Through Jesus Christ, my Healer. Amen.

REJOICE AND SING!

If you know this hymn, sing it to conclude your devotion. The words can strengthen your heart. If you don't know it, select a song of your choice.

'TIS SO SWEET TO TRUST IN JESUS

'Tis so sweet to trust in Jesus,
Just to take Him at His word;
Just to rest upon His promise,
Just to know, Thus saith the Lord.

Chorus:
Jesus, Jesus, how I trust Him!
How I've proved Him o'er and o'er!
Jesus, Jesus, precious Jesus!
O for grace to trust Him more!

O how sweet to trust in Jesus,
Just to trust His cleansing blood:
Just in simple faith to plunge me
'Neath the healing, cleansing flood!

Yes 'tis sweet to trust in Jesus,
Just from sin and self to cease;
Just from Jesus simply taking
Life and rest, and joy and peace.

Chorus:
I'm so glad I learned to trust Him,
Precious Jesus, Savior, Friend;
And I know that He is with me,
Will be with me to the end.

6

THE SIXTH CHOICE:
The Choice to Embrace Your Life

THE SIXTH BIG LIE:
"If I just act as if there is no problem, it will finally go away."

WHEN SANDY PHONED TO TELL ME I WAS ABOUT TO BE served divorce papers, I was filled with anger. I had hoped something could be worked out. For me, her filing was what the actual finalization of the divorce is for others. There was no turning back. She had no desire for reconciliation. There was just hurt and anger and an "every man for himself" mentality that set the divorce process into motion.

It was a mess, and it looked as though it would take every cent I had to get through it. I felt sorry for myself, but I felt worse for Madeline. My wonderful daughter deserved better than running back and forth from house to house; she deserved a home. I knew the statistics on kids of divorce, and I was very worried for her. I was determined to make decisions that would be the best for her in the worst of circumstances.

I wasn't just worried about Madeline; I was worried about me.

For days and days I fought off the reality of what this might do to me and to my calling as a minister, a Christian author, a speaker, and a radio talk show host. The last thing I wanted to be was a recently divorced one of any of those. I thought that perhaps if I did not say anything, it would just pass by, but I knew that would not work—especially since I had established myself as someone who was open and honest about his problems. I could not hide the horrible reality that I was going to be divorced.

I struggled with what to tell and how to tell it. The marriage had ended; the divorce was finalized, and I had not wanted to tell people about the divorce until it was done. I did not want a lot of people suggesting that we had not done enough to reconcile. Throughout that year, I told people that I was going through one of the most difficult times of my life. I asked them to pray for me, and many did.

Some figured out what was going on, and when they wrote and asked about it, I told them what had happened. Then I finally went on the air and shared that I was divorced. I let people know that it was not a result of my own moral failure. If they wrote or e-mailed, I told them the details of what I had been through. The board and my radio cohosts drafted and signed a letter that assured everyone that I had worked hard to save my marriage, and that they were sticking by me because there was no scandal, just a sad tragedy.

The letters and e-mails started pouring in. Everyone, with one exception, who was associated with New Life had very supportive things to say. Many were shocked, but there was so much encouragement. I was told that I would be used by God in a greater way than ever before. The cards and letters were extraordinary examples of God's grace coming through true believers. It was as if we had taught our listeners about the realities of life and taught them how to respond in the face of tragedy. They responded with such love and compassion that I was overwhelmed with gratitude. When I needed their support the most, they gave it willingly, and I went through a great year of healing and restoration. Some of the most healing forces came from Christian leaders whom I had respected for years.

SHOOTING THE WOUNDED

When I made calls to some ministry leaders, I did not know what to expect. Ed Atsinger, the head of Salem Broadcasting that owned many of the stations we were on, had just removed a major ministry from his network because of integrity issues. I sat down with him and shared what had happened. He sent an assistant out to make sure what I had said happened really did. I was not insulted that he had to check things out. He has a huge responsibility to keep people on the air who are "walking the talk." After he conducted his investigation, he told me I did not have a problem and that he would support me however he could. If it had gone differently, it could have been the end of my career on national radio, or at least the end of my time on some very powerful stations.

One of the most moving phone calls for me was with Dr. James Dobson. How do you tell the most pro-family, most anti-divorce person that your marriage is over? It was not easy. I respected him so much and always considered it a great gift to have had books published by Focus on the Family. Dr. Dobson talked to me as if I were his son—at least I felt his fatherly guidance on how to get on with my life. He told me that the Christian community is known to shoot their wounded but that I would not find that to be the case. He thought I would feel very supported and loved; his words were prophetic. The day Rick Warren, author of *The Purpose Driven Life*, appeared on the cover of a national magazine, Rick called me to check on me and encourage me.

Shortly after my conversation with him, a pro-life, pro-marriage group asked me to come and help them raise money through my speaking, and I told them of the divorce. They said they would check with their board to see if a pro-family and pro-marriage group could have a divorced person speak. The board met and then called to tell me to come. We raised more money for that organization that night than they ever had before.

When Jim Burns's HomeWord ministry had its first fund-raiser, I was slated to be the MC and help them raise money. I told Jim I would not be offended if a pro-marriage group did not want a divorced man as the MC. Jim said he would not think of changing me out. He knew I was the most pro-marriage person in the room after seeing what happens when you don't stay married.

We raised more than $500,000 at the fund-raiser, and I was blessed to have been part of it. I felt it was another example of God using me in spite of my circumstances and myself. But not every instance was as pleasant as these. There were those in the Christian community who seemed to think that getting a divorce, even if it was not your choice, was the unpardonable sin for a Christian leader or minister.

LEAVE NO MAN BEHIND

Early in the year I was asked to speak in Winnipeg, Manitoba, in Canada, for Promise Keepers. It was an honor to speak and to be given the responsibility for giving the altar call at the end of Friday evening. I wondered if I would do what I heard Billy Graham do and tell everyone that the buses would wait; but I did not do that. I spoke on the divided heart and how we have parts of us that get split off from the rest and that God wants us and calls us to have an undivided heart.

Toward the end, I suggested that many men there had never surrendered anything in their lives to God, and they needed to. To others, I suggested they had surrendered some things, but not all, and some of the unsurrendered things were destroying their lives. When I asked them to come forward and either surrender all of their lives or part of their lives, they came in droves. The men came in tears, bowed to their knees, and offered up to God the unsurrendered areas of their lives. It was an amazing evening.

Promise Keepers asked me to come back later in 2004 to another city. I was so moved by my experience in Winnipeg that I made sure I could speak again. But about a month before I was to speak, I got a phone call from Kirk Giles, the head of Promise Keepers Canada. He asked about my divorce and told me that a minister where I was speaking was raising a question about it. I told Kirk what had happened and that I did not need to come and speak. I offered to cancel so that he could have a great event without my divorce as a sideshow. He said he still wanted me to come, but he needed to verify the facts surrounding the divorce.

He looked into the divorce, calling my board members and others, and the end result was that they would stick by me. They were going to have me speak because they felt it was the right thing to do, no matter what the reaction of a local church. I will never forget those brave Promise Keepers standing behind me because they felt it was the right thing to do.

There were two things that astounded me about this Promise Keepers incident. First of all, the minister who had the problem with me never called or e-mailed me to ask about the details surrounding my divorce. He never called to say something like, "I love you as a man, a Christian, a brother in Christ, but I have some very strong feelings about divorce." I would have understood that, but obviously to this "concerned" person I was no longer a person; I was just a label or an issue. My e-mail address is in all of my books as well as the 1-800-New-Life number, where I can be reached by phone. It is just not that difficult to reach me if you want to talk to me. He never made an attempt.

The bookstore owner he approached made an attempt to contact me and succeeded. He e-mailed me and told me a local pastor did not think he should carry my books since I was divorced. I reassured him that I had done all I knew to do to save the marriage, and it was not a result of moral failure on my part. He was very understanding and told me he would stand behind me in every way and that my books would stay on the shelves.

The most astounding thing in all of this was the response of Promise Keepers. I told them I did not need to come. I told them I would be happy to bow out because their mission is greater than some divorced guy's struggle, but they did not uninvite me. After looking into my situation, they felt it right to continue to have me speak; I was so grateful. At the end of the night, the men walked the aisles in great numbers as I asked them to come down to the altar. There were so many people coming down in that packed place that we had to ask for pastors to come and help us. It was an amazing evening for all of us. The Holy Spirit was at work, and my presence or the lack of my presence had nothing to do with it.

Kirk Giles was the first speaker of the evening, and he played a clip from a movie about the Afghanistan war. A man had been shot down and the platoon went back into the town because they were trained to leave no man behind. It was a very moving story. Kirk followed up the clip with a talk on how men need to stick up for each other, fight for each other, and not leave each other behind. When I returned home, I wrote to Kirk and told him he practiced what he preached. I thanked him for not leaving this man behind; I was very grateful.

FACE, THEN EMBRACE

I hated being the source of a controversy like that. I hated that my divorce became an issue. Even though it is one of the few times I have known it to be an issue, it was hard to face. I wanted to stop speaking and just crawl back in a hole again. I had to face that; I had to face the fact that people would talk about it and reach their own conclusions, and I would never have a chance to let them know my perspective. I hated this part of my life; I just wanted it to go away. But I had to face it. If I was going to heal, I had to face it, accept it, and embrace it.

The "face it" part was difficult enough, but the "embrace it" part was something else entirely. I did not want to embrace it—that would mean making it part of me. It would mean accepting that my identity would always be connected to the word *divorce*. And in embracing that I would move into it rather than away from it and use the experience to help others rather than try to hide it to help myself. I did not want that level of acceptance of the thing I had tried to avoid for so long, but slowly I began to feel differently.

Some things happened that allowed me to pick up my life as it was and begin to embrace it and all the tough realities that went with it.

When I was in Indianapolis over the Christmas holidays last year, I attended Central Christian Church, pastored by Richard Clark. He gave a very interesting sermon about the need for Christ to become a part of you the way a cow does once you eat it. In a very humorous way, he told the congregation that since he had had a piece of steak, it had become part of him, that he was now part cow. He wanted Jesus to be integrated into our lives like that. He is very engaging, so I met him afterward. He told me he had just quoted Henry Cloud in a talk he had given. Henry is the wisest psychologist I know, so I was expecting something profound. He quoted Henry as saying, "We are all just so screwed up." I hope that does not offend you, but it is packed with truth. Richard and I laughed a little and nodded in agreement.

I began to think about that in a different way than I had before. We are all messed up, and I had been speaking about it and writing about it for some time. But now I had a chance to live it. All of my past struggles were just that—in the past. This was happening now, and I had an opportunity to walk through it with others who were struggling with divorce or with some other trauma. Previously, it was all about my college days, my promiscuity, or paying for an abortion, but now it was going to be about now.

I could do this because we really are all messed up, and this was just evidence of what I had been talking about. I had told people for years I was a fellow struggler, but I always left the impression that I had conquered all my struggles and now was living at a level above and beyond the rest. Embracing the divorce and walking right into it meant that I was truly stepping off any kind of pedestal I had crafted for myself and was going to connect with people in a more authentic and personal way.

I began to believe I could face this and embrace it. I could do this as a divorced man, a broken leader of a ministry, a single father, and a person who has always wanted to communicate truth in a realistic way. I started to tell myself that I could do this and started to believe it. I started to feel that God would be with me and there would be good times ahead.

So I embraced my new identity as a divorced person and began to connect with others in the same situation. I embraced the circumstances of being a single father and all that goes with that. I embraced the challenge of looking people in the eye and knowing they had questions and doubts. With the help of God, I could show them by my actions and my decisions about my future that I was worthy of their trust. This was not the end of life as I knew it as much as it was the beginning of life as I had never known it.

As If It Were Meant To Be

Insight and understanding do not come easily for someone like me. There are times when I have studied something for days, and then a new angle on truth will emerge, but sometimes it hits me at the oddest of times from out of nowhere. I was speaking to a group on the day Martha Stewart went to jail. I mentioned that we should pray for her as she entered her new "gated community." The joke got a good laugh, but then I began to talk about the gift of jail. I said we should pray, because really good things happen when people go to jail, and I prayed that for her.

Then, off the top of my head, I started talking about some examples of what happens when people go to prison. In the Old Testament, Joseph was in prison more than thirteen years. That was a huge chunk of his life, but it must have been the chunk that prepared him to be in charge of an entire nation. When you look back on the story, it seems as if God meant for him to be in prison all along. I don't think God wanted a man jailed for doing the right thing and not sleeping with the queen, but once he was, God went to work, and now it almost seems that was the plan from the beginning.

The apostle Paul wanted to win the world over to the Christian faith. Instead of being free to preach wherever he wanted, he found himself jailed. I don't think God intended for an evil government to jail the number one proponent of the faith, but if you look back at the story, it seems that is what God meant to happen. Paul, sitting there doing jail time, had nothing better to do than write letters. What might have seemed like a waste of time then, now seems like part of a well-thought-out plan. If you look at how influential Paul is in the church today and how much of the New Testament was written by him, it feels as though God meant for Paul to be in jail all along.

A more modern example is Chuck Colson. Colson went to prison for crimes committed during the Watergate scandal of the Richard Nixon era. I don't think God ever intended for Chuck Colson's life to spin down a path of crime and prison. When it did, however, God came along and made it look as if that had always been the plan. Chuck became a Christian and turned his miserable situation in prison into a ministry to others who found themselves stuck there. Prison Fellowship has now ministered to millions of prisoners and won millions to Christ as a result of the path Chuck Colson took. If you look back on it, it seems like God planned it that way from the start.

Whatever comes along, our mistakes or the mistakes of others, it seems God is there saying, *I can work with that if you will embrace it and allow me to handle it.* Joni Earickson Tada is another example of a prisoner. She became imprisoned by a wheelchair after diving into a shallow pond and breaking her neck. She is a quadriplegic as a result of one small judgment error. I don't think God ever intended that Joni break her neck. But once she did, He knew He could work with it, and He has in a glorious way. Because of Joni's courage in the face of no miraculous healing, many others with illnesses and handicaps have found the courage to continue on. They have not given up, because they have seen Joni writing, painting, speaking, singing, and living an amazing life. When you look back on it, you think it was meant to be that way from the beginning.

That was the substance of the talk I was giving; it was not intended to be, but it was. While still speaking, I had the idea that it was the insight I needed for my own life. If I embraced my life rather than try to segment it and split off the divorced part from the rest of it, I would one day look back at it and it would look as though God intended for the divorce to happen, even though it is the last thing He wanted. That is what brought me hope. It is a concept that can bring hope to anyone in the worst of circumstances. Embrace them, as horrible as they are, and one day you will look back and it will appear it was part of the plan, because God can work with anything, and He does.

I don't know what reality you are facing. I don't know what horrible thing you wish you could just make go away, but I am encouraging you to allow God to work with it. Don't deny it or try to cover it up. Embrace it, and embrace all of your life. He can use you greatly, and He can use your situation. Embrace it, and allow God to work with it while God is working on you. Your situation might be just as humiliating as Martha Stewart going to jail or as a Christian radio talk show host getting a divorce, but He will use it. He will make the best come of the worst if you will trust in Him to do so.

Your situation might be just as humiliating as Martha Stewart going to jail or as a Christian radio talk show host getting a divorce, but God will use it. He will make the best come of the worst if you will trust in Him to do so.

RADICAL ADJUSTMENT OF EXPECTATIONS

For most people, embracing one's own life comes down to making a radical adjustment of expectations. If you do not do that, you will always be hanging on to the life you thought you deserved or wanted. If you adjust your expectations, you can embrace life as it is and live life to the fullest, and you will discover that the life you have is more meaningful than the life you thought you deserved or wanted. You have to allow God to work with your mistakes and His desires for you. When you do and you embrace the different way of living, it becomes the best way of living.

This past weekend I went to see the opera *Tourandot*. I had studied opera as a music major at Baylor University. I wanted to be able to sing the deep arias of a bass baritone and did learn a few. For all of us in music school, the opera was the ultimate accomplishment. A great story line, combined with the music of a genius and the spectacular sets, could not be matched in any other art form. For me it was a goal worth striving for and if not that, then music comedy on

Broadway. That was the way I wanted my life to go. As I sat there listening to some of the most spectacular music I have ever heard, it occurred to me that opera could have been my life. But it could never have been as fulfilling as the life I have.

I am not walking around regretting not being a classical singer, even though it would be a lot easier to be a divorced classical singer than a divorced Christian talk show host. I am not still living in the days of pain when I realized my life would not be full of music and the stage. I am thrilled that this is the course it has taken, even in the face of a difficult divorce. I am trusting God to use even that, and I am embracing it. I am encouraging you to do the same.

Make a radical adjustment of your expectations. You expected to stay in control of your life and perhaps the lives of your children, but you were never in control. It was an illusion. You did what you could to maintain a feeling of control, but you did not have it. So you can adjust your expectations and relax a bit. Perhaps you have been shaking a fist at God because He has not delivered to you the life you wanted. You can adjust your expectations and embrace the life He has given you. You might have expected something close to perfect out of yourself. You could not deliver on that, so adjust your expectations. Accept your own humanity and limitations and allow God to work with you in spite of them.

EMBRACING THE ABRASIVE

Embracing your life means embracing all of it, including the people who make it difficult. I call these people "grace growers" or "character builders." They are used to help mold us into what God wants us to be. We hate the fact that they are even in our lives, but without them we would never come close to what God wants for us. These people who are so tough are actually a gift from God. Like me, you can probably look at the character you have developed and see that it did not get there from people being nice to you. It is there because of some very tough treatment by people who did not have your best interest in mind.

God allows these struggles, and in permitting them He uses them to advance His purposes and His kingdom. David, a man after God's own heart, would have never been the man he was if he had not been the victim of Saul's jealousy. It is the difficult things and the difficult people that make up the stories of our lives in a way that can honor God.

Remember the story of David and the giant? If David had taken on a third-grader, I don't think we would have heard much about it. The bigger the challenge, the more God can do with it, even when the worst outcome occurs. Alter your expectations and embrace the life you have, and you will live far beyond the expectations you had before. It just won't be in the form you originally wanted.

Eventually you become grateful that your life turned out the way it did. The tragedy might be the thing you needed to start to live life as God wanted. "Be anxious for nothing, but in everything by prayer and supplication, with thanksgiving, let your requests be made known to God; and the peace of God, which surpasses all understanding, will guard your hearts and minds through Christ Jesus" (Philippians 4:6–7 NKJV). If you want that peace, embrace your life. Drop your anger and bitterness over the way life is, and embrace it. Don't deny the reality of your life or attempt to rationalize it away. Embrace it and take up your life as it is. Give up the old life you thought you had or needed or deserved, and embrace what is before you.

Luke 9:23–25 tells us to give up what we thought we needed and discover what God has for us: "If anyone would come after me, he must deny himself and take up his cross daily and follow me. For whoever wants to save his life will lose it, but whoever loses his life for me will save it. What good is it for a man to gain the whole world, and yet lose or forfeit his very self?" (NIV). You may be holding on to something you were never meant to have, or holding on to a life you were never meant to live. Adjust your expectations, embrace the life you have, and discover what God can make of it—mistakes and all.

THE BIG LIE
"If I just act as if there is no problem, it will finally go away."

The big lie is that if you just act as if the hard realities are not there, they will eventually go away. This lie is not something you keep up in your head or down in your heart. This lie becomes a way of life. You live it every day, and it keeps you from a life that is full of meaning, purpose, and connection. You live in denial of who you are, and one day you find that you are living, or attempting to live, someone else's life. Rather than face each day as it is, you are trapped in living each day as you wish it was. In doing that you miss so much of what your life could be.

I could have swept my divorce under the rug and moved ahead, not talked about it, and hoped the problem would go away, but I would have lost so much of who I was called to be. I would have missed the chance to connect with single parents and those struggling just to find a decent date for some dinner conversation. I would have missed out on the opportunity to show others that my life is no different from theirs. I cannot predict the behavior or control the behavior of another. I can only do my best to handle what comes my way.

Shortly after my divorce, I went to a divorce care group and became part of the healing community. The second night I was there, a man came up to me and said he listened to *New Life Live*, and it had meant a lot to him. He said he almost had not come back the week before, but that seeing me there gave him the motivation to return. He said he was glad to see that we lived the lives we preached on the radio and did the very things we told others to do. He was just one person, but it was a great example of how embracing my real life, rather than trying to deny the tough reality of it, brought someone else closer to the real life he was meant to live.

I believe you will find the same to be true. I want to challenge you not to bide your time and simply hope that whatever you are dealing with will just go away one day. I challenge you to make it the centerpiece of your life. Chuck Colson could have ducked for cover and hoped that people would quickly forget he was ever in prison. Instead, he made it the focal point of his life, and the results for the kingdom of God are staggering. Perhaps there is an opportunity like that in your life, and to begin to live it, all you have to do is embrace your life and live it to the fullest, trusting God to bring the best out of the worst of circumstances.

Healing is a choice. It is God's choice, but we can stand in the way of the healing that God has for us unless we embrace our lives and the tough realities that we find within them.

Chapter 6 Workbook Questions

The Sixth Choice:
The Choice to Embrace Your Life

The Sixth Big Lie:
"If I just act as if there is no problem, it will finally go away."

Review

We have learned some very important truths about healing in the first five chapters. It is important to reinforce what you've learned, so you can apply it to life. Before we move to chapter 6, let's do a review exercise. Read each statement below and fill in the blank:

1. One of the most important relational needs in the healing process is to be _____ with others.
2. We cannot heal if we are in denial. We must acknowledge the importance of feeling our lives, especially our _____.
3. It is necessary for us to investigate our lives and _____ for truth in them.
4. In order to move successfully into the future, we must do the important work of _____ our losses.

5. There comes a time in the healing process when we must reach outside ourselves and _____ our life.

The answers are found on page 264. Check your responses to ensure that you have learned these important healing principles.

REDEMPTION

Redemption is a wonderful word, one of the best in the English language. Even better, it is one of the greatest realities in life. God loves to redeem. It's one of His best things to do!

Scripture is filled with examples of redemption. Consider the story of Joseph in the Old Testament.

After their father's death and burial, Joseph and his brothers returned to Egypt. The brothers were afraid Joseph would punish them for the way they mistreated him as a young boy. They had been very jealous of Joseph. Back in Egypt, they told Joseph that their father had left a message asking Joseph not to harm them. Then, they begged Joseph for forgiveness for what they had done long ago. Finally, the brothers went to Joseph, bowed low in submission, and volunteered to be his slaves.

Joseph was overcome with emotion and wept. He told them not to be afraid, because he would not harm them. He said, "'Am I God, that I can punish you? You intended to harm me, but God intended it all for good. He brought me to this position so I could save the lives of many people. No, don't be afraid. I will continue to take care of you and your children.' And he reassured them by speaking kindly to them" (Genesis 50:19–21 NLT).

That story is a perfect description of redemption. What Joseph's brothers meant for evil God turned to good! He redeemed Joseph's situation.

Joseph's brothers deserved to be punished for what they did. They had hoped Joseph would be killed. As it was, he suffered much as a result of their treachery. The brothers should have been severely punished. However, Joseph forgave them. Instead of punishment, he welcomed them back into the family. He redeemed their situation by paying the price of forgiveness, so that their relationship could be restored.

The theme of the greatest story ever told is redemption. It is the story of Jesus Christ, who willingly gave His life to redeem us, so we could become the sons and daughters of God.

Life is filled with stories of redemption. A father gives his life to save a drowning child. A mother works long hours in a tough job for many years, so her handicapped daughter can attend a special school and learn to live a normal life.

Culture is filled with examples of redemption. We find them in literature, music, media, and daily life. Scores of movies have redemptive themes, including: *It's a Wonderful Life*, *A Christmas Carol*, *The Shawshank Redemption*, *Dead Man Walking*, *Groundhog Day*, *A River Runs Through It*, *The Passion of the Christ*, and many more.

Literature provides its share of redemption stories as well. Think of Victor Hugo's *Les Miserables*, and C. S. Lewis's *The Chronicles of Narnia*. More books have been written with redemptive themes than we can possibly mention.

WHY WE NEED REDEMPTION

There is a kind of redemption that is objective and connected theologically to salvation. It has to do with an event, the redemptive work of Christ on the cross. Every person needs to experience that redemption. It saves us and incorporates us into the family of God.

However, there is another aspect of redemption that speaks to all of life. It is a reflection of what Christ did on the cross. It works in and through us, so that we have the power to be redemptive toward people and situations. It is a process more than an event.

Every person needs to experience that kind of redemption too. We need it because we are prone to fail. We make mistakes, suffer unintended failures, and sometimes deliberately hurt others. To be blunt, we tell lies, and we are not always honest in our relationships. We need some means to deal with all these failures. Redemption gives us that and helps to heal the deep pains of life.

We need it because we can become the victim of other people's choices, and that hurts deeply. This aspect of redemption provides the strength and ability we need to forgive one another.

Redemption is an important way of establishing a relationship with God and with others. Thus it is a vital part of the healing process. To accept redemption is a powerful healing choice. To be redemptive is a powerful healing act.

The most important healing decision we can make is to accept the redemption that God offers us through Jesus Christ. The moment we make that decision, we move onto the road of recovery and healing. Healing may be a long way ahead, but we've finally arrived on the right road!

Redemption is God's way of turning into good what was meant for evil (Exodus 50:19–21).

Redemption needs a reason. It is a response to something bad that has happened; sin, defeat, failure, betrayal, molestation, broken relationships, and rejection from loved ones. It allows us to forgive, restore, and have hope. It calls out to us to do the right thing.

We can be sure that when redemption is at work in our lives, things are moving in a healing direction.

A Tough Journey, a Healing Arrival

This chapter offers us a very personal and poignant story of how powerful redemption can be. Read pages 229–37 again.

This story of divorce, grief, and recovery asks an important question: "Does God use tragedy?" The answer is, "Absolutely!" How does He use it? He redeems it!

We are all broken in some way. We all experience failures of various kinds. After a great tragedy, redemption is our best hope at becoming useful again. It means that God can still use us in spite of our history or circumstances. Why? Because He redeems both! Remember: "God turns into good what is meant for evil" (Genesis 50:19–21 NLT; paraphrase).

The story in chapter 6 begins when divorce papers were served. It felt terrible for everyone involved. It had the potential to be controversial, and to a few people, it was. It took a while to fully accept the awful truth. I was a divorced minister. I hated it, but I had to face it. I knew people would be talking about it without any input from me to help them understand.

The lessons I learned through this process were truths that can help anyone going through a crisis, suffering a tragedy, or enduring failure. Ultimately, these lessons helped me arrive at a good place.

LESSON ONE: "FACE, THEN EMBRACE"

If we are going to heal, we must make the choice to face the truth of what is happening to us, accept it, and embrace it.

1. Can you remember a time in your life when you were forced to face a situation that seemed overwhelming and out of control? Describe how you felt in the space provided.

_____

_____

_____

2. How did you "face it"?

_____

_____

_____

3. How did you recover?

_____

_____

_____

When it comes to facing and embracing our problems, we really have no choice. The problems exist in reality, which we cannot change. Embracing them means we are accepting reality as it is. We may not like it or want it, but anything other than acceptance is denial. We have learned in *Healing Is a Choice* that denial is a destructive barrier to healing. Tolerating it is a willful choice against healing!

Having accepted a reality we cannot change, it is important to embrace it. Why would we want to embrace something that is painful? On the surface, that seems like a poor choice.

Why would anyone want to "embrace" divorce? Being divorced means that one's identity is forever changed. It's not unlike a person who loses a leg in an automobile accident. No one desires that, but it happens, and once it does, it cannot be denied or rejected without psychological consequences. The healing choice is to embrace the reality before us and accept that we are forever changed.

Embracing reality means we move into the experience rather than hide from it. It also means we accept the fact that our identity has changed in some significant way. That may be an undesired reality. You didn't want it, but it's there!

Think of some undesired reality you have faced. Answering the following four questions will help you examine your feelings and thoughts as you reflect on it. It is important to self-examine, so that you don't get stuck in negative emotions.

1. **Recall a time in your life when an undesired reality was thrust upon you. Perhaps it was a sudden, severe illness in your family, or even a death. Maybe it was the loss of a job, a divorce, or financial failure. How did you feel?**

_____

_____

_____

2. How did you respond to the event? Did you reject it at first or try to deny it was happening to you?

_____

_____

_____

3. Have you been able to embrace it? If so, how long did it take? Or, are you still in the process of accepting and embracing it?

_____

_____

_____

4. Since you embraced the new reality in your life, how have you felt?

_____

_____

_____

LESSON TWO: "WE'RE ALL JUST SO SCREWED UP!"

Are you offended by the term "screwed up"? Some of you may be. However, you might be surprised to learn that the phrase is listed in the *Oxford Dictionary*. It means "bungle" or "mess." Those two words have a number of meanings, including: trouble, mismanagement, work clumsily, state of confusion, and embarrassment. Put all those words together and you get "screwed up"!

It would be an error to say that we all have our act together. Most of the time, the exact opposite is true. Very few of us have our act together. Add to that the fact that human beings are an unpredictable lot. We do some unexpected and weird things without warning.

Our lives are not always as organized and well-managed as we'd prefer. Often, old wounds and emotional scars keep us "screwed up" and disoriented.

We suffer that condition due to sudden, violent, even evil acts perpetrated on us by people whose agenda was to harm. It wasn't so much what we did, as what people did to us. It's not surprising that some of us would be "screwed up." What is surprising is that some of us can cope at all. Sadly, many people can't.

We marry individuals we intuitively know are not compatible. We damage significant relationships, thus isolating ourselves. We make choices that result in long-term negative consequences. We're often "screwed up" from pretending that everything in our life is perfect when, clearly, it is not. We cover our pain with facades.

By definition, a *facade* is a deceptive outward appearance. In ancient Greek theaters, the masks worn by actors were facades. If they wanted to convey happiness, they wore a smiling facade. If they wanted to convey sadness, they wore a frowning one.

People still wear facades every day, often to mask what is really true inside them. They are covering up, hiding their real selves. Such masquerading is another way of being "screwed up" and pretending to be something other than what we really are.

Chapter 5 taught us that defenses and pretenses are debilitating obstacles to healing. They keep us in bondage. In contrast, Scripture teaches that "the truth will set you free" (John 8:32 NLT). Facades and lies imprison us in jails of our own design.

The good news of the gospel is that redemption is available. No one has to stay in the condition in which they find themselves.

Everyone has free choices to make each day that either heal us or hurt us.

Regarding divorce, facing and embracing it means that we refuse to live in denial. We remove the facades and defense mechanisms, and accept reality. With no facades to wear, we can connect with people as we truly are, in an authentic and personal way. We can accept the tag of "divorce," being a single parent, and the stigma people sometimes attach to us.

LESSON THREE: "AS IF IT WERE MEANT TO BE"

God specializes in paradoxes (opposites that nevertheless are true). An example is: "Whoever wants to be a leader among you must be your servant, and whoever wants to be first must become your slave. For even the Son of Man came not to be served but to serve others and to give his life as a ransom for many" (Matthew 20:26–28 NLT).

It is paradoxical how often God's people end up in jail. Good people don't belong in jail. Jail is for the "bad guys," not God's elect. Yet it happens, repeatedly. Consider a few of God's "jailbirds."

Joseph spent thirteen years in prison, a significant portion of his life. How could that possibly have been a good thing? Most of us would rail against such injustice. We'd demand a new trial. We'd hire expensive lawyers and protest. There would be a letter-writing campaign, and we'd inundate the legislature with mail. But Joseph accepted it and embraced it. He actually turned it into a positive experience in the long run, thus redeeming his situation.

In retrospect, we realize that God was in it. Surely God did not condone the injustice of it all, but once it happened, He was there unfolding His will as if it were meant to be.

Paul was familiar with jails. His heart's desire was to preach the gospel throughout the entire world. Instead, he spent an undue amount of time behind bars. Certainly, God's will for Paul was for him to teach, preach, and evangelize in as many places as possible. Prison kept interfering. However, once Paul was in prison, God was always there, unfolding His will as if it were meant to be!

Paul used his prison time to do a very simple thing, writing letters. Remarkably, those letters from jail became the backbone of the New Testament. We still read them today! In retrospect, it seems as if it was meant to be.

Chuck Colson is a contemporary example. He was sent to prison for committing crimes related to the Watergate scandal during Richard Nixon's presidency. Colson fell from a high position of power to a dismal prison cell. While there, he gave his life to Christ and created one of the greatest prison ministries in the world. God's desire was not that Colson would be disgraced and imprisoned, but once it happened, God began unfolding the events of his life as if it were meant to be.

Joni Eareckson Tada is another example. Her story involves a prison of a different kind. It has no bars. It is the prison of her disability. Joni broke her neck in a diving accident and became a quadriplegic as a result of one error in judgment. God did not intend for her to be imprisoned in a wheelchair, but once it happened, He turned it into something good, as if it was meant to be.

God wants to teach us that He can work with our failures, liabilities, and limitations, if we will embrace them and let Him lead.

Joseph could have spent thirteen years being bitter and angry. Paul could have become frustrated to the point of depression. Colson could have become hardhearted and vindictive. Joni might have given up hope and languished flat on her back. However, God had plans for them, as if it were meant to be all along.

Even in divorce, God is at work, changing circumstances, guiding, and empowering us. Most of all, He is redeeming, turning bad to good.

These examples give us hope that God can and will redeem the failures, mistakes, omissions, difficulties, health issues, and liabilities of our lives.

1. **Think of a time in your life when something happened that felt awful. It may have felt unfair. You didn't deserve it, but it happened, and you had to deal with it. Describe the event and the feeling you experienced.**

_____

_____

_____

2. **Describe something good that resulted from the events described in #1.**

_____

_____

_____

No matter how terrible your circumstances are, God is with you. You may have been abused as a child, betrayed by a spouse, molested by a relative, rejected by a father, or locked in an emotional prison filled with pain. The good news is that God never left or forsook you. He loves you, and He is working to turn all those trials and hurts into something good, as if they were meant to be from the beginning. Whatever horrible thing is threatening your life, allow God to work with it. He is the God of redemption. It is one of His best things to do!

LESSON FOUR:
"RADICAL ADJUSTMENT OF EXPECTATIONS"

At some point in our lives, most of us will need to radically adjust our expectations. We will experience obstacles, limitations, and circumstances that demand it. Things we once did without a second thought will no longer be options for us. If we don't make adjustments, we will be continually frustrated and angry.

We will reach an age where we can't run a marathon. We won't be able to eat the way we did when we were twenty-six. We will require more sleep. Our energy levels will decrease, if they haven't already! At work, we will be surpassed by younger coworkers.

If we don't make adjustments in our expectations, we will live with constant frustration. We will become emotionally and psychologically unhealthy.

However, we have a better option. We can make a healing choice to embrace life as it is. We can make needed adjustments, so we can live life to its fullest. We will do life in new ways, but it will be life, and it can be good!

Our fear is that any change or adjustment in expectations will diminish us. We view this kind of change as diminishment. We see it as failure and loss. However, there is overwhelming evidence that changes in life patterns are not the same as diminishment. As we get older, changes are important if we want to live successfully.

We must embrace the life God gives us at whatever stage we are in. The adjustments we make are necessary losses.

We must accept our own humanity, with its limitations, and allow God to work with us in whatever circumstances we find ourselves.

LESSON FIVE: "EMBRACING THE ABRASIVE"

Embracing and accepting life includes dealing with people who make life difficult. That's not great news, but it is a fact of life. *Healing Is a Choice* names these people. They are called "grace growers" and "character builders" for obvious reasons.

When we see these folks coming, we want to run for the hills. They drain us of energy and cry on our shoulders. Their problems are never resolved, and they bounce from one caregiver to another, wearing people out.

What are we to do with these people? Why are they in our lives?

In another example of divine paradoxes, God brings these people into our lives to shape our character. Abrasive people may offend us, but they also make us better people.

God allows such encounters to advance His purposes in us. "Grace growers" build strength in us we might otherwise never experience. "Character builders" toughen us, so we can endure the challenges of life as God uses us. David would not have become the man he was, except for his struggles with Saul.

Remember that Jesus said, "If any of you wants to be my follower, you must turn from your selfish ways, take up your cross daily, and follow me. If you try to hang on to your life, you will lose it. But if you give up your life for my sake, you will save it. And what do you benefit if you gain the whole world but are yourself lost or destroyed?" (Luke 9:23–25 NLT).

Healing Is a Choice offers this paragraph: "Remember the story of David and the giant? If David had taken on a third-grader, I don't think we would have heard much about it. The bigger the challenge, the more God can do with it, even when the worst outcome occurs. Alter your expectations and embrace the life you have, and you will live far beyond the expectations you had before. It just won't be in the form you originally wanted" (p. 242).

Think about the previous paragraph for a few minutes. Let it roll around in your mind. Consider each sentence. Then, respond to the paragraph by expressing your thoughts below:

THE SIXTH BIG LIE:
"If I just act as if there is no problem, it will finally go away."

The sixth big lie reminds us of pretenses. It encourages us to pretend that we have no problems, when in fact we are struggling mightily with them. This lie promises that by pretending, we can make our problems go away. That's not just a lie; it's a whopper of a lie!

If we pretend we have no problems, the ones we have and are ignoring will increase. The result will be more misery.

This lie is also an unhealthy crutch. You grow to depend on it. You wake each morning hoping this is the day it will come true. The lie becomes your constant companion. It keeps making grandiose promises to you each day, only to disappoint and frustrate in the end.

Problems rarely go away by themselves. No amount of pretending can hide the fact that this lie disappoints you day after day after day.

The answer is to overwhelm the lie with the truth. Face your problems. Don't try to cover them up or deny them. Call them what they are. Shine the light on them. Ask God to help you overcome them.

Remember that healing is a choice. It is God's choice, but we have a part to play.

We can stand in the way of healing by continuing to believe the big lie. However, there is a better option. We can embrace the life we have, with all its difficulties and challenges, and remember that God is redeeming us and our circumstances. God loves to redeem. Its one of His best things to do!

JOURNALING

Take a few minutes and review chapter 6. Note the strong emphasis on redemption. Take some time as you journal and record your thoughts about what redemption means to you. Consider the love of God that created redemption and offers it to us.

Review the big lie and think about how it tries to diminish the power of redemption.

Remember that healing is a choice, and redemption is one type of healing. How can you appropriate God's redemptive work into your life?

PRAYERFUL MEDITATION

As before, find a quiet, relaxing place where you are relaxed and uninterrupted. Maybe you have selected a favorite place by this time. Sit in a comfortable chair. Take a few minutes and think about the blessings of God. Ask the Holy Spirit to give you a genuine understanding of redemption. Think about how redemption changes your life and gives you hope. Remember that redeeming is God's best thing to do. He wants you to experience it at its deepest levels. Remember, also, that God redeems lives and circumstances.

Think about the sixth big lie. Have you ever believed it? If you believe this lie, you will be engaging in magical thinking, not spiritual truth.

Your quality of life depends on trusting God, not hoping your problems will just go away. God's Holy Spirit will direct you into all truth. Listen to Him. Inculcate His truth into your mind and heart.

God is always working in your life. As you look back, even being mindful of your struggles, you will see that your life is just as it was meant to be!

Be patient and wait on the Spirit to speak to your mind. Remember, always, His promise never to leave you or forsake you. He loves you and cares about everything that occurs in your life. He is compassionate and full of grace and mercy.

Are you willing to embrace your life? Will you accept it and use it for God's glory? It doesn't matter that you are scarred and wounded. He can still use you. Thank God for the gift of life He has given you.

PRAYER

Heavenly Father, hear my earnest prayer. I want to experience redemption at its deepest level. I worry that I may take it for granted and not appreciate the sacrifice that appropriates my redemption. Help me to realize that the life You have given me is good. Help me to remember that, regardless of what has happened to me in the past, You can always redeem it and make my life pleasing to You. I sometimes struggle with believing that You have totally forgiven me. I need help with that. I also have trouble believing that You still love me, considering some of the things I've done. I am not worthy of Your redemption, but I desperately need and desire it. Help me to believe and trust in the fact that You are working in my life every day, shaping it into Your plan. Help me not to resist that. Please send Your Holy Spirit to do a deep, inner work in my soul. I want to be genuinely filled with Your Spirit. Thank You for the challenge in this chapter. I hear it and will do my best to respond positively. Please stay close to me as I take more healing steps. Make me bolder and more attentive to Your will. I give You my life—mind, soul, and spirit. Through Jesus Christ, my Friend. Amen.

Rejoice and Sing!

If you know this hymn, sing it to conclude your devotion. If you don't know it, read the words and meditate on them.

I Surrender All

All to Jesus, I surrender;
All to Him I freely give;
I will ever love and trust Him,
In His presence daily live.

Refrain:

I surrender all, I surrender all,
All to Thee, my blessed Savior,
I surrender all.

All to Jesus I surrender;
Humbly at His feet I bow,
Worldly pleasures all forsaken;
Take me, Jesus, take me now.

Refrain

All to Jesus, I surrender;
Make me, Savior, wholly Thine;
Let me feel the Holy Spirit,
Truly know that Thou art mine.

Refrain

All to Jesus, I surrender;
Lord, I give myself to Thee;
Fill me with Thy love and power;
Let Thy blessing fall on me.

Refrain

All to Jesus I surrender;
Now I feel the sacred flame.
O the joy of full salvation!
Glory, glory, to His Name!

Refrain

ANSWERS TO REVIEW ON PAGE 245:

1. connected
2. pain
3. search
4. grieving
5. help

7

THE SEVENTH CHOICE:
The Choice to Forgive

THE SEVENTH BIG LIE:
"Forgiveness is only for those who deserve it or earn it."

I AM AWARE THAT YOU MIGHT BE ONE OF THE PEOPLE WHO picked up this book and started to read it in spite of the fact that you saw in the table of contents that one of the choices to heal is to forgive. That you are even reading these words is a miracle, because you have read a lot of stuff on forgiveness and understand everyone's angle on it, and none of it does one bit of good for you and your situation. You have been abused, mistreated, or neglected in such a severe way that you believe that forgiveness of that person or persons is impossible for you to experience. You are a good and kind and loving person, but there is one person you harbor a grudge against, and you plan on keeping it. The person does not deserve to be forgiven by you or by God. Anyone looking at what happened would say that you are totally entitled to your feelings.

If what I have described above is the way you feel, or you feel that way to a lesser degree, I am hoping and praying right now as I write this that this could be the time when everything changes for you. I am praying that as you read on I can help you walk through some steps and help you make some choices that lead you to the choice to forgive the unforgivable. And if you are someone who has not been hurt deeply, I pray that you will use these words to minister to someone else who is struggling because he or she is unable or unwilling to forgive. I pray that in the future if you are ever hurt deeply, you might come back to this chapter and use it to walk out of the anger, bitterness, and resentment.

THE MOST DANGEROUS THING ON EARTH

We live in a world where danger and terror are all around us. We live with uncertainty each new day because we never know what might befall us. Since 9/11 most of us have a little more fear that terror in the world might one day intersect with our personal world. There is something much more dangerous than a terrorist somewhere out there in the world who may or may not harm us one day. There is something worse, much worse than that. It is worse because it can exist within us and affect everything we do and the very person we become. That internal terrorist is called a "justifiable resentment."

A lot of people have resentments. Some just seem to have a bad attitude about life, and they lean toward resenting everything. They resent paying taxes, paying more than a dollar for a gallon of gas, or being asked by their church to give money to support the new building campaign. They resent the person they are living with. That person is not bad, but the "resenter" collects little things done over time and walks around with a huge collection of things to hold against the person. It makes him feel a bit superior, so he hangs on to everything he can find. Resenters go through life feeling negative about anything and everything. They have a problem, but it is nothing like what I am going to describe. These petty resentments are real resentments, but they are not the type that will kill you.

A *justifiable* resentment is the type of resentment that will kill you. It is not about anything petty. It is about real and horrible abuse or mistreatment. It is about a real-life event that anyone would say was terribly wrong, and most anyone would tell you that you are totally justified in feeling the way you do. Tenderhearted people will cry with you over it, and many probably have. All the evidence supports your feelings of anger, resentment, bitterness, and unwillingness to forgive. The other person does not deserve forgiveness, and no one wants him or her to have it. That is what I call a justifiable resentment.

Real resentment over real damage by a real person produces a justifiable resentment, and it becomes such a huge part of your life that it feels like a vulture sitting on top of you—a dark and dangerous presence that affects everything you do.

If the resentment was not justifiable, someone could just talk you out of it. A friend could tell you things he or she has told others who had a bad attitude:

- "Stop being so negative."
- "Look at the bright side of things."
- "Stop seeing the glass as half empty."
- "Start thinking more positively."
- "Look for the good in people."
- "Try accepting people for who they are."

These are the things people say to someone who just needs to make a few changes to make herself more comfortable and enjoy life more.

But none of those things apply to you, because you have something to hang on to. There is a date and a person and a trauma that really happened. It is your Auschwitz, and those who know of your terrible ordeal support your feelings. That is the problem—no one questions your feelings. Everyone feels horrible for you, so it is easy for you to hang on to the resentment. Anyone would, but you can't. You can't, because it is eating you alive. It is your own internal terrorist that is destroying your life, keeping you from living the best life possible. It is hurting your relationship with God and with others. You will be firmly rooted to your past and to your abuse as long as the justifiable resentment grows within you. Everything you do in life will lean up against your grudge. It will come to define who you are and limit what you can become.

Although it might be very difficult to imagine, you really can be free from that justifiable resentment. You can let it go and experience the healing power of forgiveness. You can choose to heal a very troubled area of your soul by choosing to walk through a path of forgiveness. And if you take this path, something very amazing is going to happen to you one day.

One day you are going to awaken and realize that everything in your life has changed. You will sense that you are no longer rooted in your past. You will realize that what once defined your life and your inner thoughts is no longer relevant to how you live your life. You won't forget what happened, but you will be aware of something with the magnitude of a gnat you just swoosh away. That little gnat is nothing compared to the vulture that now sits atop your head, talons deeply implanted in your heart. One day you will awaken and that vulture will no longer be there, and you will be free.

THE PHYSIOLOGY OF FORGIVENESS

The psalmist wisely stated that in the guilt of his sin and in the silence and covering it up, his "bones wasted away" (Psalm 32:3 NIV). He knew then what science is just now coming to accept. Guilt, resentment, sin, and silence have a physiological impact on a person. They all combine to create an emotionally and physically sick person, who misses the best of life because he or she is stuck in the past that cannot be changed.

Nothing will ever be enough to make up for what happened. Nothing will take the place of the years or decades that were eaten away because there was a wrong done. Whether it was done by you or to you, if you have held on to the guilt and refused to allow forgiveness to work its supernatural healing effect, your body has felt the effects of a lack of forgiveness right along with your mind.

In a recent article in *Newsweek*, the authors began by making a statement of truth that the psalmist knew long ago: "Persistent unforgiveness is part of human nature, but it appears to work to the detriment not just of our spiritual well-being but our physical health as well."[1] There was a time when the medical profession would have steered clear of a study about forgiveness. Forgiveness was a topic to be handled by the religious community. Even the field of psychiatry was uncomfortable with looking too closely at forgiveness because it was such an issue of faith, but today it is a widely studied topic in the clinical field. In 1997, there were only fifty-eight published studies on forgiveness. Today there are more than twelve hundred published studies. That is a huge leap for the subject of forgiveness. There is even a foundation called the Campaign for Forgiveness Research.

One of the things you will see from all of these studies is that the Bible teaches truth about forgiveness. Scripture documents the devastation from sin and the ongoing destruction when sin is not forgiven. Jesus died for our forgiveness. A price had to be paid; a sacrifice made for us to be forgiven. The same applies when we forgive. We have to sacrifice our right to resent or hold a grudge. We have to die to ourselves to ensure that we can live in peace within ourselves and with others. Sometimes it is the hardest thing imaginable to do, but in truth it is not. Living with the ill effects of unforgiveness is much worse.

Dr. Dean Ornish has helped many people adjust their lifestyles by eating differently. He has helped people lower their cholesterol and their weight by eating better and living better. He does not just stop with what a person puts in his mouth. He also wants to help with what resides inside his heart and soul. The man who has helped people stop eating so much red meat regards anger and vengeance as red meat consumed by the soul, and forgiveness as the healthful tofu of living.

Dr. Ornish said, "In a way, the most selfish thing you can do for yourself is to forgive other people." In other words, there is not a long list of things you can do that are better for you than to forgive, but it is a choice that you need to make every day.

The physiology of forgiveness works for you to stop the "wasting away" that the psalmist mentioned. When you open up about your own sin and accept God's forgiveness for it, you begin to change your physiology. When you forgive someone else for something he or she did to you, the change is in your "heart," as in your soul— but it is also in your *heart*, as in the big red muscle pumping inside your chest.

The studies show that there are at least a couple of ways that forgiveness produces an instant result for you. Instantly, you reduce the stress in your life. It is not easy maintaining bitterness, hostility, hatred, fear of being hurt, and anger all in the same body while trying to present yourself on the outside as a normal and healthy human being. These emotional states come with increased blood pressure, hormonal changes that lead to cardiac disease, and impaired immune function. There is evidence that neurological function and impaired memory may also result. The lack of forgiveness is a potent internal cocktail that you administer to yourself to your own detriment every day.

The lack of forgiveness is a potent internal cocktail that you administer to yourself to your own detriment every day.

One study took twenty couples that were in trouble in their relationships and compared them with twenty other couples that had healthy and happy relationships. The study included blood work to help determine the physiology of the two groups. As would be expected, the healthy and happy couples' health was reflected in a healthier chemistry in their blood. The couples that were angry and resentful showed higher levels of cortisol, a hormone that gives us great strength and power under stress but destroys us when it lingers in our systems long past a crisis. When the unhappy couples were asked about their relationships, this destructive chemical shot up. As a result, the couples living with ongoing resentment and bitterness will have more health problems than those in the healthy and nurturing relationships.

"It happens down the line, but every time you feel unforgiveness, you are more likely to develop a health problem," said Everett Wortington, executive director of Campaign for Forgiveness Research. That is a bold statement about a direct link from our unforgiveness today to creating health consequences in the future. Forgiveness is a part of healing our future as well as helping us live a great life today.

Resentment and bitterness cut us off from others and make us suspicious and fearful of relationships. Resentment isolates us and creates a loner mentality. It becomes the ultimate wall between a healthy social network of family, friends, neighbors, and community, and us. You shed people when you refuse to forgive. You need to develop a new way of thinking and relating rather than live a life where you feel entitled to hang on to grudges.

You can choose to live as a forgiver. You can choose to make your whole life work better for you by incorporating the repeated act of forgiveness into the person you are. Charlotte van Oyen Wityliet, a researcher at Hope College in Holland, Michigan, said, "Forgiveness should be incorporated into one's personality, a way of life, not merely a response to the specific insults."[2] If you have created a life where the grudge is common and resentment lingers in many of your associations with others, the choice to forgive is the choice to heal your future and to heal who you are right now.

As I have stated before, I know you feel justified in whatever it is you feel anger, bitterness, and resentment toward. There is no justification you can make, however, that will ever make it right to live without finding a way to forgive every person who has or will hurt you, including yourself. The benefits of forgiveness are too great to live without.

HAVING TO PRACTICE WHAT I PREACH

Earlier I wrote about how I had miraculously been able to experience forgiveness through my divorce. I can tell you that any remnants of the hurt and pain is much like a gnat, and I really can just swoosh it away. The vulture shrank fairly quickly, and I am grateful for that. That experience was very much unlike another experience I had where I developed a pure and genuine justifiable resentment. And there was no miraculous healing relief in any form. I brought it home with me, and we lived together for quite a while. It was very difficult to give up.

What happened to me was something I would never have imagined possible in my earlier years—being cheated out of a large sum of money. I felt betrayed, abandoned, and the fool. I did not handle the loss well. It was something that left me with a justifiable resentment that I needed to get rid of. In order to do that, I followed a path that I hope will help you.

First, I had to accept the cold, hard reality that my "you can't do this to me" stance did not do me any good or move me along in the healing process. I had to accept that I was not in total control of my life and to humble myself to the reality that I was not all-powerful.

Second, I had to face the reality that I had no power to prevent what happened. I had to accept my powerlessness. It was hard. I thought I was invincible, unstoppable, and somehow beyond this kind of treatment. I had to trade my false belief that "it could never happen to me" for the painful reality that I was weak and vulnerable and without power.

The next area of grief work I had to experience was in relation to God. I had to accept and grieve the fact that God chose to allow it to happen. God could have stepped in. Others have been part of miracles, and I could have been part of one. God could have intervened. I had to realize that I was not immune or protected from everything in this world. God loved me, but He was not going to step in every time I got in a tough spot. That is always one of the hardest parts of getting beyond the hurt, pain, and resentment. We all at some point must come to accept that God did not jump in and act on our behalf.

Next, I addressed the fact that I will never be the same. In many ways this event will impact me forever. It was not easy to accept that nothing I could do would undo the damage or bring back what I had lost.

Finally, I had to determine that, no matter what, I had to pick up my life and move beyond this. Otherwise it would be the focus of my life, and it could even control my life so much that it would become a false god in my life.

I discovered that I could actually forgive, that I could free myself by turning the outcome over to God, who owns the cattle on a thousand hills. In other words, I can trust that no matter what, I will be okay. It was a positive decision for my life to let it go and move on.

I did not move on immediately. For a while I felt anger, rage, disappointment, regret, and envy. I allowed myself to feel those feelings; I took time to share them with others. As I shared them, their power began to disseminate. Their ugliness was starting to be replaced with peace and calm and an acceptance of the reality. I was able to lay down all of those "shoulds."

What I have described is a process, not an event. Someone could have told me to forgive and move on, and I might have tried to do it, but it would not have been complete. I needed all the steps to reach a point where I could forgive and feel no ill will in my heart. That has happened, but there was one final act of forgiveness I had to take care of before the process was to be completed.

THE PERSON HARDEST TO FORGIVE

The last step in completely getting over this loss and living in forgiveness was to forgive myself. The ordeal was not entirely my fault, but I still needed to forgive myself. I needed to forgive myself for not seeing it coming. I needed to forgive myself for not handling the situation perfectly. I needed to forgive myself for being a normal human being who could get involved in something and not come out smelling like a rose.

Perhaps a better way of stating it would be that I had to accept myself with all my flaws. That acceptance was the end result of the forgiveness process. When the acceptance was there, the forgiveness was in place, and I could finally move on. I could move back to a closer relationship with God and experience His love. "His compassions fail not. They are new every morning" (Lamentations 3:22–23 NKJV). His compassion understood my plight and pain, and His love was there for me with each new day.

YOUR LOSS VERSUS MINE

I know my story is probably nothing compared to what you have been through. Your story might be about memories that you wish you could erase—memories of abuse or neglect that have lived inside you for many years. Some of those memories are of things so horrible you may never have told even one other person, and the molester or terrorist or abuser deserves hell, not forgiveness.

The last thing you want to do is walk through some forgiveness process.

I would never suggest that you excuse what happened or that you forget what happened. But I hope that you can begin to work through it with someone else and then let it go. I hate abuse, because when we don't resolve it, we allow the abuser to continue to control our lives. We either do the absurd thing, forgive and move on, or stay stuck in the past, harboring guilt and shame and anger and bitterness.

You may have tried to forgive, but the pain never goes away. If that is the case, I hope you will look back through my story and work through the steps I took. It may take you a year or more to fully reach a point of forgiveness. If that is the case, it is best to start right now. Your hurt could be so deep that it may take five years or more. I understand, and if that is the case, let this be the beginning of that five-year process so that you can live the rest of your life free of the influence of a bad person or a group of bad people. Let this be the day when forgiveness begins.

THE CHOICE TO BE FREE

The choices to grieve and forgive and let go are powerful forces for developing a life that is completely free from the past. They are the stepping-stones out of your old ways and into a future full of all sorts of possibilities and potentials. Often people never experience those possibilities and potentials because they get hung up on certain aspects of the forgiveness process.

One of those is the why of forgiveness. The reason for forgiveness is not to let the other person off the hook; it is to get you unhooked. You forgive so you can move on. Every moment spent in holding a grudge keeps you trapped in the event that took place too long ago for you to be holding on. When you choose to forgive, you are not freeing the other person; you are freeing yourself.

You must also not get hung up on whether or not the person wants to be forgiven or deserves it. If you wait for that individual to want it, you may waste your life waiting for something that will never happen. The hardness of another's heart is not an excuse for you to harden yours. Forgive freely even though the person is unaware that he hurt you. Forgive even though the person denies that it is his problem. Forgive even though the person is continuing to hurt others in his uncaring way. Give him or her forgiveness from your heart so your heart can be free.

Don't think you need to confront the person to be able to forgive. I have avoided telling people to go to someone and tell that person that he or she is forgiven. I think it causes more problems than it solves. It immediately puts the other person on the offensive, or is at least likely to. If you came to me and told me you forgave me, I might be defensive, and I know I would be reluctant—even though I know it would be a healing experience for both of us. I think it is better to just forgive the person. Let it go, and get on with your life. If you need to document that it happened, write it in your Bible or journal that on this day you forgave the person who hurt you, even though he or she did not ask for it, want it, or deserve it.

BIBLICAL MANDATE

Speaking of the Bible, it has a lot to say about our need to forgive others. The ultimate model is Christ forgiving us even though we don't deserve it. He went to the cross for us even though we did not even know we needed Him to. The minute we were born He had provided a way for us to be free of our past because He had already taken action to forgive it, in spite of the rebelliousness we would exhibit or the stubbornness we would display in staying stuck in our sins. He forgave us, and He expects us to forgive others.

A pretty sharp directive is found in Matthew 6:14–15: "If you forgive men when they sin against you, your heavenly Father will also forgive you. But if you do not forgive men their sins, your Father will not forgive your sins" (NIV). It does not get much clearer than that.

That verse can be confusing to some, because we are told in Romans 10:9 that if we confess with our mouths and believe in our hearts that God has raised Christ from the dead, we shall be saved. Matthew 6:14 seems to indicate that it takes more than that. Here is what I believe about that scripture. The only reason you would not forgive someone of his or her sins is that you would not fully grasp what God has done for you or the sins from which He has freed you. If you don't believe you are a sinner in need of forgiveness, then you won't forgive others. If you are grateful that God has forgiven you through Christ, then you will naturally extend to others what has been extended to you. So a lack of forgiveness could be an indication that you have not accepted Christ's sacrifice as the key to your own forgiveness. If you are holding a grudge, I have to ask if you truly believe and trust in Christ.

You might protest that your situation is different. You might demand to be the exception to the rule, but you are not. I was speaking about this need to forgive and accept forgiveness at a "Lose It for Life Institute" this past year. I talked of carrying the guilt of someone else's sin and the need to believe that you are not deserving of shame. I asked those present to think of the child molesters who killed their victims and are now sitting on death row waiting to be executed. I suggested that some of us might say, "Shame on you" to some of them. But shame does not have to be upon them—not even them. Even they can accept Christ's sacrifice for their sins and live free of the guilt. If they are not deserving of the shame, neither is the person you are holding a grudge against. Let that person go with forgiveness, and you free yourself to live a life of healing and hope.

REMBRANDT'S PRODIGAL

Some years back I was in Toronto, Ontario, listening to Henry Nouwen speak. He was quite amazing as he spoke on the prodigal son. Most people know Jesus' parable of the young man who demanded his portion of the inheritance and then squandered it all, only to find himself living among pigs and eating the pigs' diet of husks and other scraps. In a great moment of insight, he realized that his father's servants ate better, so he made his way humbly back home to ask to serve and experience good food and a secure place to live. When he came up over the hill, there was his father, looking off in the distance as if he had been waiting all along. He greeted the boy and welcomed him back into the family by placing a ring on his finger and throwing a major celebration.

It is interesting to note that the boy had already taken his portion of everything. When he came back, his expectations were few, but his father placed a ring on his finger, symbolizing that he was now entitled to his inheritance again. He had been accepted back with full status as son.

No wonder the elder brother was angry. He was now down to less than the original inheritance he could expect. Rather than be grateful for that and the redemption of his brother, he was full of anger and resentment. The story is rich with symbolism and representation. The father represents God's feelings and actions toward us. The prodigal represents all of us who rebel and go our separate ways. The elder brother represents our judgmental ways of dealing with those who have been caught up in sin and find their way back to our churches.

That night Henry Nouwen concluded his talk by handing out prints of a painting by Rembrandt of the moment when the father welcomed the prodigal son back home. It is a painting of the boy on his knees before the father and the father with his arms around the boy, his hands resting on the boy's back. If you look closely at the painting, you see that one of the hands is strong and full of power, obviously painted from the model of a man who was full of power and strength. If you look closely and compare it to the other hand, you discover something quite amazing. The other hand does not match perfectly. It is weaker, softer, and gentler.

Rembrandt used a female to model for the second hand. That soft and gentle second hand represents the gentle grace that God possesses and shares with us. It is the hand of a God so loving that He would send His perfect Son to go suffer and die for all of His prodigal children. When we completely understand the magnitude of that, we are willing to extend that same forgiveness to others. The way I read Matthew 6, not only do our lives here on earth depend on it, but our eternal lives depend on it also.

THE NEW YORK TIMES ON FORGIVENESS

The Bible is not the only place that we find the benefits of forgiveness outlined. Even the New York Times wrote of the power of forgiveness in the "Science Times" section on May 22, 2004. The article by Erica Goode, "To Err May Be Human; To Forgive Is Good for You," focused on Dr. Robert Karen, a psychotherapist. The impetus for the article was Dr. Karen's new book, *The Forgiving Self: The Road from Resentment to Connection.*

In the book and the article, Dr. Karen talked of the damage done when we don't forgive. He said, "If the offense becomes this gnawing resentment that lives with you, then you have never gotten over being a victim. And in that way not forgiving can be a horrible thing for the person who does not forgive." He said he started his study uncomfortably thinking that forgiveness was all about moralistic thinking and religion. What the doctor failed to realize is that the Christian religion is not just a religion; it is a relationship that affects all of life. That is what I love about being a Christian: what I believe has a positive impact on how I live if I fully integrate my faith into how I live. When forgiveness moves from being a religious concept to a way of life, I am free to experience the last word in the doctor's subtitle: *connection.*

Once again I ask the question: Is it always appropriate to forgive? According to Ephesians 4:31–32, forgive for your own sake and for those who live around you: "Get rid of all bitterness, rage and anger, brawling and slander, along with every other form of malice. Be kind and compassionate to one another, forgiving each other, just as in Christ God forgave you" (NIV).

It is always appropriate to forgive and forgive again. Matthew 18:21–22 tells us to forgive seven times seventy times. It was not written to allow a person to hold a grudge upon the 491st infraction. It is there to say we must continue to forgive an infinite number of times, never allowing ourselves to be trapped by resentment or bitterness.

GETTING OVER IT

One of the conferences I produced led me to a woman who was angry, controlling, and bitter. She was plagued by the reality of her situation. She made this statement to me: "Not a day goes by that I don't obsess over my past. No one understands me, because they have not been through what I have been through." I asked her what she had been through, and she said that she was given up by her mother and adopted. Being the father of an adopted daughter, I understand the difficulties adoption presents, but those can and should be worked out before the age of fifty-four. She told me that her whole life had been defined by her adoption; it had defined her life and stolen her joy. She wanted to know what was wrong with her. She had to know why her mother did it. She could not get over the rejection.

I explained to her that she was never rejected. Her parents had no idea who she would grow up to be. They did not know her personality and then reject her. They rejected the concept of having a child, not the actual child. I pointed out to her the huge difference between the two. I asked her to make three healing choices that would change her life.

First, I asked her to embrace her history of adoption. I invited her to connect with others who were adopted rather than reject them as she felt she was rejected. Embracing her history would align her with some very remarkable people who have been adopted, including my daughter.

Second, I asked her to grieve the loss of being in her birth family. I invited her to shed the tears of sorrow so she did not have to bear the burden of bitterness, resentment, and anger. I invited her to free herself from the past and heal her future after all these years.

Third, I invited her to choose forgiveness. Not only forgiveness of her birthparents, but asking for forgiveness from the parents who raised her. She needed to ask them to forgive her for not being grateful for the sacrifices they made to raise her. I suggested that she could trade her resentment for gratitude. You can do the same; you can embrace whatever reality you have. You can grieve all that you have lost, and you can forgive what you cannot undo—when you do, you will be free.

Ephesians 4 tells us to get rid of all bitterness. So take a look at your life and see if there is anything there that is causing you to be bitter. Is a root of bitterness causing all sorts of problems in your relationship with God and others? If so, pull out that root with the tool of forgiveness and in its place grow up tenderheartedness, kindness, and forgiveness that God has given to you.

You May Need It Too

Sometimes it is hard for us to forgive others because we feel so unforgiven ourselves. Sometimes we need to clear up our own irresponsibilities with others to feel the full power of forgiveness. I discovered this during the peak of my wayward lifestyle in college. The process of calling or writing everyone I could remember I had hurt was healing and opened me up to be totally forgiving toward others. Since that time I have had to do the same thing over and over again.

A few years ago, I wrote a letter to a colleague who had been extremely inappropriate with me over lunch. He had just come into new money and was arrogant and angry at the thought that I might do something similar to what he was doing. It was one of those rare times where nothing was going to make the situation better. He even cursed at me at one point. I drove away amazed at the ire I had raised in this man who really needed to take a look at himself and why he was so bothered by my plans that, in reality, would not be competing with what he had done.

As I contemplated the lunch, or more accurately obsessed over it time and time again, I began to look at myself. I began to allow a little bit of light to shine in, and I caught a glimpse of myself in a dark mirror. It was I who had been arrogant. I had not respected his accomplishments, nor had I acknowledged them properly. I had failed to show him the respect that would have softened his heart. So, even though he had his own problems, I needed to take care of mine. I wrote a letter and asked him to forgive me for not being more sensitive to his needs at that lunch. I then acknowledged his great accomplishments.

Several weeks later, he wrote a wonderful letter back to me wanting to renew our relationship. I no longer obsess over that tense lunch. It is not something I even think about anymore unless I am writing a book, looking for a good example of what asking for forgiveness can do for you. This was not a major life crisis, but it was something that was on my mind. And with a simple letter I cleared the air and my own conscience, and I was free from the incident forever. What I experienced over that small lunch dilemma you can experience over the more significant issues that have developed throughout your lifetime.

The Bible says, "Therefore if you bring your gift to the altar, and there remember that your brother has something against you, leave your gift there before the altar, and go your way. First be reconciled to your brother, and then come and offer your gift" (Matthew 5:23–24 NKJV). There is a pretty direct command to take care of personal business before you get on with the spiritual business at hand. If you do, it is a gift to the other person, but it is also a great gift to yourself.

One of our *New Life Live* listeners, Kathleen Parsa, developed some form letters to send to those you need to ask for forgiveness. This is the safest and easiest way to accomplish this. If there is a major offense, and you can meet face-to-face, that is, of course, the best route to take. Second to that would be a phone call. For many people those meetings are just too overwhelming and unpredictable to initiate. If that is true for you, rather than do nothing, you might want to use one of these form letters adapted to your style to take care of some old and troublesome business.

LETTER #1

Dear _____,

It has been a long time.

I am writing because I need to. You are important to me and I have already waited too long. I want to apologize for my past actions. I am sorry for hurting you.

Please forgive me.

Sincerely,

Letter #1 is simple and to the point and gets the job done. It is a bit impersonal, so you might find letter #2 even better for your situation.

LETTER #2

Dear _____,

You are probably surprised to hear from me. It has been a long time.

I am writing because I need to clear my conscience. In the past, when there were situations or conflicts that were hurtful, I would sometimes choose to avoid a person, rather than attempt to resolve the problem.

However, the closer I walk with Jesus, He is showing me that closing doors does not heal relationships. It only temporarily helped me to avoid uncomfortable situations.

Yet, God is good. He has forgiven me for all my shortcomings! Now, out of gratitude to Him, I am apologizing to you for my past actions. I am sorry for hurting you.

Please forgive me.

Sincerely,

These two letters might be too superficial given the gravity of what you have done. If your offense is too grievous to be handled by the first two letters, I want to offer a third option that might work.

LETTER #3

Dear_____,

I have been thinking about you a lot. I have been praying for you and hoping that your life is going well.

The reason I have been thinking about you and praying for you is that I have wanted to confess to you that I was so wrong in what I did. I offer no defense and no excuses or rationalizations. I was wrong, and I have lived with the guilt and shame every day of my life.

I wanted you to know that I did not escape unpunished. I have felt the pain of it almost every day.

I am writing to ask for your forgiveness. I can understand why you would not give it. But I wanted you to know that you mean something to me, and I am so sorry for what I did.

Please forgive me.

I will continue to pray for you and hope for your best.

Sincerely,

Perhaps that will better meet your need if you have deeply wounded someone. If your letters come back unopened, you might want to send a postcard with a simple "I am sorry. Please forgive me" written on it. At least you will feel as if you have gotten through at some level.

I want to beg you to do something in the area of your own need for forgiveness. I am a fellow struggler with you, and I can attest to the great value that comes from a simple letter. It could change your life. It could restore a relationship and bring deep healing to both the other person and you. More than anything, it could reach down deep into your own heart and remove any blockage that is preventing you from forgiving someone else. Even if the person does not forgive you, you will always look back on that time and know that you did what you could to make it right.

THE BIG LIE
"Forgiveness is only for those who deserve it or earn it."

Don't listen to the big lie that forgiveness is only for those who earn it or deserve it. None of us deserve it. It is a gift of grace from

God. God did the unfathomable by taking on our sin and obtaining punishment for it. He did what we do not have to do so we could do what we cannot do. We cannot reach perfection to be worthy to be in His presence, but now we do not have to. He has done it for us. If He has done it for us, we can do it for others. The other party's emotional state or attitude should have nothing to do with our plans to forgive. You never know what a simple request for forgiveness might do for another person.

People's lives have been changed because someone took a risk and asked for forgiveness. The risk becomes the seed of healing in another person's life. Toward the end of the book we will discuss the choice to serve, but it is appropriate to mention it here. Asking someone to forgive you, even if it is for your reaction to the way he or she hurt you, may be the humble act of service needed to initiate healing in another's life.

You may be the most unlikely candidate to help in the process, but God has a history of using very unlikely people to accomplish His goals. Whether you need forgiveness or you need to forgive, making contact and taking a risk will make you a peacemaker and blessed in the eyes of God. Don't wait until someone deserves forgiveness. Forgive anyway, and begin the process right now.

PULLING UP ANCHOR

Resentment, bitterness, and a lack of forgiveness anchor us to a past that cannot be changed. We cannot go back and undo the damage of yesterday, but we can undo the damage it is causing today. We do that with the act of forgiveness. First, we seek God's forgiveness and bathe in its liberating grace. We allow ourselves to be forgiven, and we live as forgiven rather than as guilty and shameful beings. We must clear up our own irresponsibilities by making restitution and seeking to reconcile when it is appropriate. Then we need to offer to others what we have experienced for ourselves. We uproot our own anchors to the past, and we grab on to their chains and help them pull up the anchors of their own.

A few years ago, I was speaking for a wonderful ministry on the West Coast. A brave and courageous woman gave her testimony before I spoke. She said some things that spoke to my heart. She was no longer hiding what she had been through. She was standing up, sharing her story, and at the heart of her story was forgiveness. She was one of those who had been hurt so badly so long ago that forgiveness seemed impossible. She was raped at a young age and had kept it undercover. She said it was hard to heal with her pain undercover. She suffered physical problems and had several addictive behaviors. She trusted no one and lived a pitiful life.

She did all the things those in her church told her to do. She prayed, read the Bible, and went to church, but none of it produced the healing she longed to experience. Finally she heard the voice of God tell her she could remain in her pitiful state or she could develop a powerful life, but she could not do both. She chose a powerful life. She turned to three things to produce the result she wanted: healing.

She turned to God for comfort. She refused to allow her addictions to comfort her anymore. She found her comfort in her relationship with God. She opened herself up to the unconditional love of God and of His followers. She connected with others who could help her, and for the first time, she sought treatment for her pain from the ministry. As she went through treatment, she realized that the only thing more difficult than being healed would be to continue to live unhealed, as she was. It would not be easy, but she could do it.

When she was finished, she was able to experience forgiveness at the heart level for the first time. She said she gave up her own agenda of wanting the man to feel badly about what he had done or recognize the tremendous hurt he had caused. She realized that Christ's death had freed her from the Law, and she could not try to put someone under the Law from which she was freed. Not even the man who raped her. She opened up about her resentment and bitterness, and the sickness and evil power that were there spilled out. She was released from the bondage of those dark secrets.

In the end, she came to be a product of the work of Christ. Her identity became that of a victor, not a victim. She no longer saw herself as a woman who was raped at a young age. She saw herself as a work of God, able to reach out to others and help them walk where she had walked. She used 2 Corinthians 1:3–4 as her guide: "Blessed be the God and Father of our Lord Jesus Christ, the Father of mercies and God of all comfort, who comforts us in all our tribulation, that we may be able to comfort those who are in any trouble, with the comfort with which we ourselves are comforted by God" (NKJV).

With forgiveness finally sinking in at the heart level, she was able to get out of herself and into the lives of others, providing care, comfort, and leadership to those who are hurting. All this from a woman severely hurt so early in life. She ended her presentation with God's Word: "You intended to harm me, but God intended it for good to accomplish what is now being done, the saving of many lives" (Genesis 50:20 NIV). What a message from a woman who has been to the depths of despair and is now seeing that God has brought so much good from it all.

I close this section with a gentle word to those who have been hurt beyond belief. I am not insensitive to your situation. I wish I could help you undo the abuse and years of pain and agony you have experienced. You may be looking at a very long process before you can truly say you have forgiven the person who hurt you. You won't have to end up liking the person or wanting to spend time with that person. I know that if you do the work, however, you can one day forgive and move on with your life. It may take years, so start those years now. I hope and pray you will move out of your bitterness and resentment and move into forgiveness. You cannot do it alone, but with God's help I know you can find the power to forgive.

Healing is a choice. It is God's choice. Sometimes we choose to only ask God to help us heal, but God has provided us with some choices that will usher in healing. The choice to forgive is as big a choice as we can make. It is often the last choice of those who have been hurt badly. No matter what you have done or what was done to you, I hope you will make the healing choice to forgive.

CHAPTER 7 WORKBOOK QUESTIONS

THE SEVENTH CHOICE:
The Choice to Forgive

THE SEVENTH BIG LIE:
"Forgiveness is only for those who deserve it or earn it."

ALEXANDER POPE, THE EIGHTEENTH-CENTURY ENGLISH POET and essayist, penned these words: "To err is human; to forgive, divine."

Read that phrase several times. Read it again. Repeat it aloud. Let it sink deeply into your mind. Ponder its meaning.

Exercise #1: Defining the Phrase

In your own words, describe the meaning of the phrase, "To err is human; to forgive, divine."

_____

_____

_____

_____

_____

_____

_____

Pope realized that all human beings make mistakes and experience failures. It is to be expected. It is the common human experience.

We even have a category for some accidents: "human error." It means an accident was not caused by mechanical or system failure. The person guiding the endeavor caused it. Whatever depends on human beings for control will, at some point, experience a failure due to human error. Why? Because "to err is human."

Pope also realized that without forgiveness, there is no way to deal with human error. Consider a relatively common situation in America. A teenage driver hops into a car and heads for his best friend's house. Driving through a residential area, the young driver diverts his eyes from the road to find his favorite CD. In that instant, he fails to notice the child running into the road to retrieve a ball. Had the teen been focused on the road, he could have stopped in time. Because he looked away, he hit the child, who died on the way to the hospital.

How are human beings able to deal with such tragedy? The young teen may be forever trapped in a dungeon of guilt. In an instant, the child's family is tragically and forever changed. Grief and anger become their constant companions. The teen driver and the child's parents scream out to God, "Why did You let this happen?" But it was not God's fault. It was the result of human error, in this case, a reckless mistake. The young driver took his eyes off the road for one moment and life changed forever. "To err is human." Be it an accident or a choice, we are all prone to err.

We cannot change realities like the one described above. What's done is done. However, we desperately need some way of dealing with human error. How can we live with tragedies of our own making? How can we deal with human error and failure?

This chapter in *Healing Is a Choice* challenges the reader to make choices to forgive. Forgiveness is the most powerful and successful tool we have for dealing with human failure.

The remainder of this lesson is designed to help you make forgiving choices, even in circumstances that seem unforgivable. It is written to show you that forgiveness is the only way to combat the anger, bitterness, and resentment resulting from human failure.

Are you ready? No doubt some of you who are reading this are beginning to feel tense and reluctant to continue. You know you need to forgive someone, or perhaps several people. You think about it often. But you can never quite bring yourself to do it.

This is God's time for you. It is a divine appointment. You are not reading this chapter by accident. Therefore, take a moment to pray before you go farther. Use the prayer below. The next few minutes can be transforming and liberating for you. The Holy Spirit is present. He will help you.

Loving, forgiving Father, I know I am not reading this chapter by accident. You have brought me to this time and place. I need forgiveness, and I need to forgive. I especially need to do this now. I've put it off too long. I need the strength and power of Your Holy Spirit. Please fill me now with His presence and power to do what is clearly Your will. I open my heart and my mind to hear, so please speak to me. I offer my will to obey, so please teach me. I offer my life to You, so please lead me. I trust in the redeeming, forgiving power of Christ my Lord. Amen.

THE MOST DANGEROUS THING ON EARTH: JUSTIFIABLE RESENTMENT

What is the most dangerous thing on earth? A virus? A terrorist? An earthquake? An angry mob? No. The most dangerous thing on earth is a particular attitude we might call "justifiable resentment."

What is resentment? By definition it is "indignation or ill will felt as a result of a real or imagined grievance."[3]

Resentment is a common experience. Far too many people live with it. Some folks are consumed with it. They seem to resent everything, from paying taxes to paying tithes, from the price of gas to the price of groceries, from politicians to preachers. They resent their neighbors and their employers. They may resent their spouses. As their resentment increases, they begin to make negative judgments about those they resent. Eventually, they become negative about everything. Deep resentments sour their lives to the point where no one wants to be with them. The emotional price is too high. Sadly, we all know people like that and we struggle in our relationship with them. In an attempt to help them change, we'll say, "Try not to be so negative," "Look for the good in people and accept them as they are," or "If you'd make a few changes, you'd enjoy life more."

There is a particular kind of resentment that can do irreparable harm. It's a resentment based on a real, horrible event. It is real damage inflicted on a real victim by a real perpetrator. The damage done to the victim is so horrible and painful that it becomes the predominant event in their lives. They experience anger and develop grudges. Because they were victimized, their anger and resentment seem justifiable. In *Healing Is a Choice*, this type of suffering is referred to as "justifiable resentment."

We read stories about such people experiencing justifiable resentment and think, *They have a right to feel as they do,* and *If it were me, I'd feel the same way!* All the evidence supports their anger, bitterness, and unwillingness to forgive. Theirs is not some free-floating resentment. It is resentment for good reason! An event occurred in space and time. It can be documented, and worse, it can be remembered. It was horrible, and the saddest part of it is that it happened to you!

Because you are a victim, your friends, family, and professional caregivers will sympathize with you. No one doubts your story or your feelings. Everyone is very supportive. Some friends will even tell you it's "okay" to feel resentful. Thus, it is easy to embrace and nurture your grudge.

Despite the support you receive from family and friends, justifiable resentment will seriously damage your life. It is as if there is a terrorist inside you trying to blow you apart. It deprives you of joy. It diminishes your life. It hurts your relationship with God. The worst consequence is that it keeps you in bondage to an event. Your life becomes about one thing.

Exercise #2: Exploring Your Resentment

1. Let me ask you to do a brave and personal thing. If there is an event in your life about which you feel justifiable resentment, take a few minutes and do the exercise below. (If you've never experienced such an event, think of a friend or a loved one and write about that person.) Describe the event. What caused your resentment?

_____

_____

_____

_____

2. Explain how you justify your resentment.

_____

_____

_____

_____

We know it is unhealthy and unspiritual to be resentful. Resentment does us great harm and usually hurts us more than those for whom we hold the grudge.

"Justifiable resentment" is an oxymoron (a contradiction in terms). It makes no sense to hold a grudge and justify it at the same time.

In the space below, develop a plan of action that frees you from both the resentment and the temptation to justify it. (Remember, this can only involve your actions. You cannot count on the other person to respond or do the right thing. The issue is what can *you* do?)

_____

_____

_____

_____

Healing Is a Choice encourages us to break free from the bondage of "justifiable resentment." With God's help, you really can let go of it and experience healing. Remember, healing is a choice you make. In this case it is a choice to forgive, let go, and heal.

That brings us back to the second part of Alexander Pope's powerful statement, "to forgive, [is] divine." If you can forgive, you can heal. In fact, if you will forgive, you will wake up one morning and realize that your life has changed. You will realize that you are no longer enslaved by one event in your past. The past will no long terrorize you, as it has most of your life. The healing choice to forgive is yours.

The Physiology of Forgiveness

David wrote, "When I refused to confess my sin, my body wasted away, and I groaned all day long" (Psalm 32:3 NLT). The New International Version is a bit more graphic: "When I kept silent, my bones wasted away through my groaning all day long."

David was expressing what we know to be true about the physiological impact of psychological pressures. Resentment, guilt, repressed feelings, and sin combine to create physical and emotional illnesses in us.

Consider the following report from researchers in Tennessee. They surveyed more than one hundred students who felt they had experienced an incident of serious personal betrayal. The researchers determined which of the students had the most forgiving personalities and which had less-forgiving personalities. Finally, researchers gathered students in a lab, where their vital signs were monitored. The students were asked to recall the incident or incidents of betrayal. Results confirmed that students with forgiving personalities recorded lower blood pressure and heart rate levels than the less-forgiving students. Additionally, signs of sympathetic nervous system arousal (stress response) that elevated during betrayal discussions returned to normal quicker in "forgiving" students than it did in the "less-forgiving types."[4] As a result of their work, they suggested that forgiveness may be not only divine but also a good way to stay healthy.

Physicians and psychologists also confirm reports like the one above. They are substantiating what clergy and people of faith have always intuitively known. Forgiveness is a key to preventing many illnesses and reducing stress. If you can forgive, you can recover, embrace your life, and move confidently into the future.

Holding grudges, being resentful, staying angry, and repeatedly rehearsing past events in your mind are a certain prescription for illness. Your body will suffer the consequences. Your mental health will be impacted. With enough stress, you could even experience chronic disease. You may experience hormonal changes that lead to cardiac disease and impaired immune function. Your heart will suffer. Your misery will increase.

In contrast, forgiveness is a healer. It allows us to deal with our past mistakes and sins by accepting the forgiveness that God offers. It allows us to deal with our present, which is the theme of this chapter. It teaches us that there is no need to hold grudges or nurture resentments. We can release them as we extend forgiveness.

Forgiveness also allows us to deal with our future. Because we have been forgiven, we have hope now and in the future. We can anticipate new friends and more fellowship, because we have learned how to forgive.

The good news is that every one of us has the power to make a free choice to forgive. We don't have to hold on to resentment. We can choose to be forgivers.

Resentment builds walls between people. Forgiveness tears down those walls and unites people.

Take a moment and imagine how dramatically the world would change if people suddenly decided to extend forgiveness to one another. Racial prejudices would fade. Rival African tribal groups would stop killing one another. Irish Protestants and Catholics might learn to live in peace. Arabs and Jews could live together in Palestine. Shiites and Sunnis might discover that they really are brothers. Murder rates would go down. The Chinese and Japanese would give up their ancient rivalries. Families could be reunited and restored. Who knows, Republicans and Democrats might even get along!

THE HARDEST PERSON TO FORGIVE

No discussion of forgiveness would be complete without addressing the subject of forgiving oneself. Thousands of people live in prisons of their own making. How does that happen?

In some families, mothers and fathers had extraordinarily high expectations for their children. Some parents had unreasonable expectations. In such an environment children are almost never able to satisfy their parents. Thus, they often fail. In many cases they are punished for their failures. Being young and naive, the children redouble their efforts to please their parents, only to fail repeatedly. These children grow up wounded and damaged. They take responsibility for never pleasing their unreasonable parents. Deep inside, they resent being raised in such a rigid environment, lacking in affection and patience. They long for someone, anyone, who will show them affection. Thus, they run to the first person who will show them genuine affection, or they will move toward what is familiar, marrying someone like their parents.

In families like the one described, children rarely blame their parents. Rather, they blame themselves. When they grow into adulthood, they have to make a healing choice: Will I continue to accept responsibility for rigid, unaffectionate parents, or will I forgive myself and move on?

You may need to forgive yourself for taking all the blame in your life. You may need to forgive yourself for stuffing away the issues you have with your parents. You may need to forgive yourself for trying to be perfect, rather than normal.

You need to forgive yourself and break free from the emotional prison you inhabit. Forgiving yourself allows you to be a normal person with normal flaws. Remember that God did not create any of us to be perfect. He created us to be His children. God loves us more than our earthly parents or anyone else could ever imagine. "The faithful love of the LORD never ends! His mercies never cease. Great is his faithfulness; his mercies begin afresh each morning" (Lamentations 3:22–23 NLT).

All our stories are different. Some of us lived relatively normal and stable lives. We experienced our parents' affection in a caring environment. However, not everyone was so fortunate. Some of us experienced horrific experiences in life, so traumatic that they cannot be spoken and are never shared with anyone.

The road to freedom and recovery is to make a healing choice to seek help and support. If people do not get appropriate help, they forever allow their past to control them. *Healing Is a Choice* contains so much encouraging information to guide you in the process of working through your past. Use the advice in the book. Consider it God's personal road map to recovery. It is there for you.

TO FORGIVE OR NOT TO FORGIVE, THAT IS THE QUESTION

Not everyone in the world is predisposed toward forgiveness. Certainly, Christians encourage it, and most people embrace forgiveness as a cultural value. But there are countries and cultures in the world that advocate vengeance rather than forgiveness. For them, the goal is not to reconcile or make peace, but to even the score. Ancient Babylonian law taught the same thing. It required "an eye for an eye, and a tooth for a tooth: whatever you did to me, I'll do to you!" One person noted that the only good that comes from such a legal system is a sightless, toothless world!

In cultures where vengeance is accepted, people think, *Why forgive? What good can come from that? The important thing is to get even. Someone killed my son or daughter, so I will kill their son or daughter.* The sad truth in such cultures is that justice is never done. The only result is that two people end up dead rather than one.

However, it is necessary to ask the question, "Why forgive?" The purpose of forgiveness is not just to deal with an offender. Rather, it is also about freeing victims from grudges and resentments that keep them chained to the past. When you choose to forgive, you unlock the chain and set yourself free.

People often say, "I'll be over the pain and abuse when the perpetrator says he's sorry." That dooms the victim to remain in bondage to the past. If the perpetrator never apologizes, then what? Is the victim forever bound? Perhaps. However, by forgiving, you can be free. Lewis Smedes wrote, "When we forgive, we set a prisoner free and discover that the prisoner we set free is us."

Exercise #3: *Forgiving Yourself and Forgiving Others*

Often, the baggage from our past weighs heavily on our minds. You may recall painful encounters and feel guilty as a result. Perhaps you lied to a friend, hurt someone deeply, or ignored a friend who needed you. When you remember these things, you feel guilt and shame. You wish you could correct the damage done, but you don't know how to contact the people. There is a way to deal with such burdens.

In the left column that follows, list the names of the people you would like to contact. In the right column, briefly describe the situation. When your list is complete, pray through the list one at a time. In prayer, describe what happened and why you feel badly about it. Express your sorrow and guilt. Ask God to forgive you, and help the person you're praying for to understand how sorry you feel. Take as long as you need to "talk it out." Finally, ask God to heal your memory of the pain you've carried with regard to these people.

"Forgive us our sins, as we have forgiven those who sin against us" (Matthew 6:12 NLT).

If you are studying in a small group, discuss this exercise and its purpose, but complete it privately.

Name	Situation
1. _____	1. _____
2. _____	2. _____
3. _____	3. _____

BIBLICAL MANDATE

Scripture has much to say about forgiveness, both in instruction and examples. Taste a sample of God's delicious forgiveness in the passages below:

And I will forgive their wickedness, and I will never again remember their sins. (Jeremiah 31:34 NLT)

But if we confess our sins to him, he is faithful and just to forgive us our sins and to cleanse us from all wickedness. (1 John 1:9 NLT)

Instead, be kind to each other, tenderhearted, forgiving one another, just as God through Christ has forgiven you. (Ephesians 4:32 NLT)

Make allowance for each other's faults, and forgive anyone who offends you. Remember, the Lord forgave you, so you must forgive others. (Colossians 3:13 NLT)

We also get biblical examples. For example, Jesus Christ gave His life for the sole purpose of forgiving our sins. His forgiveness was extended to us even before we were aware of the need. It is very clear that He wants us to be forgiving toward everyone we encounter in life. Consider His admonition: "If you forgive those who sin against you, your heavenly Father will forgive you. But if you refuse to forgive others, your Father will not forgive your sins" (Matthew 6:14–15 NLT). What clearer teaching on the necessity of forgiving is there?

Another scriptural example uses math to express the immensity of forgiveness. It is Matthew 18:21–22. In Jesus' story, we are told to forgive seven times seventy times, or 490 times! Think about that. Is 490 the limit of forgiveness? Is that all that is required? Just forgive 490 times, and on the 491st time, we can be unforgiving and hold a grudge? Of course not! Jesus employed hyperbole to make His point. His intent is simple. Forgive 490 times, then another 490, then another; as long as it takes to truly forgive. Do you understand the example? Jesus is telling us to do whatever it takes, as many times as it takes, to ensure that we have forgiven those who harmed us and have let go of our grudges.

Following the Civil War, Robert E. Lee went on a tour of the

South in an attempt to heal the wounds of the Civil War. He encouraged Southerners to forgive and move on with their lives. At one stop in Georgia, he encountered a lady whose plantation home had been burned by the Union army. In front of her home she had a beautiful old tree, more than one hundred years old. As Lee tried to console the woman, she complained angrily about her tree. She spoke venomously of the Union soldiers. Her personal grudge was deeply entrenched, and her anger was overwhelming. Finally, the lady looked straight into Lee's eyes and demanded, "What should I do, sir?" Lee looked back at her and said, "Cut it down, ma'am; cut it down!"

There comes a time to let go of the grudges and unforgiveness. With God's help, we must "cut them down" and set ourselves free.

A Tool for Practical Forgiveness

As we near the end of chapter 7, you may realize that you need to ask for forgiveness or extend it to others. If you feel that tug in your heart, know that it is the Holy Spirit and now is the time to respond.

Reread pages 285–87. There you will find examples of letters that can be used to ask for, or give, forgiveness. Obviously, the best way to seek or give forgiveness is personally, but there are times when distance, emotions, and circumstances prevent personal contact. These letters provide an option. Review the examples and select one or two that feel comfortable. Use them as often as necessary.

The Seventh Big Lie:
"Forgiveness is only for those who deserve it or earn it."

By definition, *deserve* means to "be worthy of." The lie states that we are forgiven because we've earned it. It implies that we've done something to suddenly be worthy of forgiveness. This simply is not true, never has been, and never will be. No human being merits forgiveness. Scripture reminds us that "all have sinned; all fall short of God's glorious standard" (Romans 3:23 NLT). "All" means you and me and everyone else!

We don't deserve what God is willing to give us. This is not something we can earn. It is a free gift of grace from a holy and righteous God, who paid an incredible price to arrange for us to have it.

How should we respond? First, we should receive His grace. Second, we must not keep His grace to ourselves. Forgiveness is not a secret. It's the best news in the world!

Remember that God gave us grace we did not deserve or earn. We can do the same. We can give grace to those who have hurt us. They may not deserve it, and by their actions, they may not have earned it. It doesn't matter, because it doesn't depend on them at all. It depends on us. Like God, we can give grace where it is undeserved. We can forgive though no amends have been made. We have the power to set captives free!

Those who have hurt or abused us are in a prison of our creation. We hold the keys to the prison. The keys we hold are anger, grudges, hatred, ill will, and more. We hold those keys in our hands. We want those who have hurt us to come to us begging forgiveness, but they can't. They are consigned to our prison. We have to unlock the door and let them go. By doing that, we no longer have to attend to or feed them. They are no longer our responsibility.

When we set the captives free, we can move forward into the future without having to take them with us. Here is the wonderful resolution. No one deserved this, but now everyone is free! You are free from grudges and anger that hold you in bondage.

They are free, because they are no longer held in the prisons of your mind. "So if the Son sets you free, you are truly free" (John 8:36 NLT). And if the Son, Jesus Christ, sets us free, we must also set the captives in our prisons free!

There is a holy irony in this. Forgiveness always bears good fruit. When we set captives free, that act of grace becomes the beginning of healing in people's lives.

In the last section of chapter 7, there is a short story about a deeply wounded lady who had been hurt so badly that forgiveness seemed impossible to her. She was raped at a young age and kept it hidden for years. She suffered physical pain and developed addictive behaviors. Finally, she reached a crisis point and made a courageous healing choice to recover her life. She chose to do three powerful things:

1. She turned to God for comfort. Doing that, she stopped allowing addictions to comfort her any longer. Instead, she found her comfort in God and His unconditional love.
2. She connected with people who could help her. We have thoroughly discussed the importance and value of being connected with others.
3. She sought treatment for her pain. She realized that the only thing more difficult than being healed would be to continue to live unhealed.

As a result of her healing choices, she experienced God's forgiveness at deeper levels than she had ever experienced. She began to tell trusted friends about her past. She gradually overcame her bitterness and resentment. She was released from her bondage.

She stopped viewing herself as a victim. The power of forgiveness radically changed her life.

These three steps will work for all who make the choice to be healed. Will you make that choice? Don't hold grudges; it's bad for your health!

JOURNALING

Take a few minutes and review chapter 7. Every chapter in *Healing Is a Choice* is important, but this chapter speaks to one of the most common of human relational needs, so it is especially valuable. As you write, remember times when you have been hurt and have found forgiveness to be difficult. Remember a time when you needed forgiveness. How did that feel? Did you receive it? Think about forgiveness as you write.

PRAYERFUL MEDITATION

As is the custom, find a quiet place where you are relaxed and un-interrupted. Find a comfortable chair or sofa. Take a few minutes and think about the love of God toward you. Ask the Holy Spirit to give you a genuine understanding and appreciation of forgiveness.

Reflect on the forgiveness quotes listed below. Each one provides a slightly different slant to help us better understand forgiveness. Read each one and think about it for a while. Absorb its meaning into your mind and heart.

Forgiveness is the economy of the heart. . . . Forgiveness saves the expense of anger, the cost of hatred, the waste of spirits.

—Hannah More

Any man can seek revenge; it takes a king or a prince to grant a pardon.

—Arthur J. Rehrat

When you forgive, you in no way change the past—but you sure do change the future.

—Bernard Meltzer

When a deep injury is done to us, we never recover until we forgive.

Forgiving isn't forgetting—it's remembering and letting it go.

A good marriage is the union of two forgivers!

I can forgive, but I cannot forget, is only another way of saying, I cannot forgive. Forgiveness ought to be like a canceled note—torn in two and burned up so that it never can be shown against one.

—Henry Ward Beecher

If God were not willing to forgive sin, heaven would be empty.

—German proverb

Forgiveness is almost a selfish act because of its immense benefits to the one who forgives.

—Josh Billings

Forgiveness is setting a prisoner free and then discovering the prisoner was you.

Forgiveness is a choice. It is not a feeling, but an act of the will.

—John Eldredge

Don't wait to forgive until you feel like forgiving; you will never get there. Feelings take time to heal after the choice to forgive is made.

—Neil Anderson

It is by forgiving that one is forgiven.

—Mother Teresa

Think about how forgiveness changes your life and gives you hope. Remember that forgiving is a powerful and divine act. God wants you to experience forgiveness at its deepest levels. Look deep inside yourself and ask, "How am I doing in terms of forgiving others?" Ask the Holy Spirit to help you answer that important question.

PRAYER

Forgiving Father, I admit that I have held and nurtured grudges and hard feelings against a number of people. (Name those people, whether living or dead.) Forgiving these people is very hard, but I acknowledge that it is Your will for me to do that. I do forgive them now. I ask You to heal the wounds and painful memories of my life. I cannot make this choice without Your help. Please send Your Holy Spirit to help seal the choice I have made to forgive and heal. Take from my heart and mind any ill feelings, grudges, resentments, and anger. I acknowledge that these feelings are not Your will for my life. Help me to be as forgiving to others as You are to me. In the name of the One who died to forgive my sins. Amen.

8

The Eighth Choice:
The Choice to Risk Your Life

The Eighth Big Lie:
"I must protect myself from any more pain."

THE PATH OF HEALING TAKES YOU THROUGH THE DEPTHS OF
your feelings, grief, forgiveness, and the embracing of all of your
life. When there are areas that are not healing, you seek out and
obtain the treatment you need. You choose to heal, and with each
choice you allow God's healing grace to replace the sick parts of
your soul. You find your life again, or perhaps for the first time.
As you grow, you reach a point where you either move forward or
you remain stagnant and miss your life. You either cower in fear to
protect yourself, or you take a leap of faith propelled by courage,
and you begin to risk.

If you have suffered a disease, you risk getting another one. If
you have been hurt by a man, you risk by having a relationship with
another one. If you have been so riddled with fear that you have
confined yourself to your neighborhood or house or just your room,
you take a risk and get outside of the walls you have built to protect
yourself. Those walls have not protected you; they have infected

you. They have infected you with soul-rot, because you have ceased to live when you are behind them.

As I have said earlier, I was devastated by my divorce. I was a walking zombie just going from one thing to another. I did not want to be with another woman for fear that I would not measure up and would be rejected and betrayed all over again. I went into hiding or hibernation as I dealt with the wound that I did not want to repeat.

I created a cocoon from my house to work and work to my house. I spun the silk from those two places and ventured out very little other than that; they were the safest places for me. It was the only way I knew to prevent another disaster. I was grieving and I was healing, but I was really going nowhere. As the months went by, it became more and more obvious that I needed to develop a social life again, but I was afraid to risk. I was afraid of one more ounce of pain that could put me over the edge.

Some dear friends of mine suggested that I meet a friend of theirs. Her husband had left her, she was very bright and attractive, and she lived in the next town over. I finally relented and made the call to her. She seemed quite nice on the phone, and we talked a few minutes and decided to meet. It was on a Friday night, and I just wanted to have a cup of coffee with her in a public place, so if it was uncomfortable, the coffee could be consumed quickly and we would be on our way.

I asked her to meet me at the Bombay restaurant, which is not too far from my house. I wanted to meet at seven, but she had a party to attend first, so we decided to meet around nine. Around nine means nine to me; I guess it meant ten to her. After an hour of watching people come in and looking to see if they were unmarried and fit her description, she sauntered up to me and introduced herself. I suggested we get a place to sit closer to a corner so as to avoid what appeared to be a United Nations West gathering of about one hundred people in the lobby, speaking just about every language imaginable—loudly. So much for my plan to meet at a place where conversation would be easy.

I could not hear the woman. We were sitting about one foot apart, and I could not hear her. After about ten minutes of not being able to hear her, I asked if she wanted to go somewhere else where we could talk. I don't know if she was afraid of me or already knew we should make this as brief as possible, but she said she was quite content to talk right there next to the Irish delegation. They must have been elected the loudest country there and were showing off their shouting skills.

There we sat, her saying things I did not hear or understand, and me carrying on a conversation with myself inside my head. I guessed how many words a minute she was speaking and every now and then got in a nod, a grunt, or a "well, there you go." Once I used the "well, there you go" most inappropriately because, rather than saying something that would have fit in front of that, she had actually asked a question. There I was, caught not listening. It wasn't that I did not want to listen; I just could not hear her, and she was not willing to move to a different place.

As the one-way conversation continued, I was allowed to sneak in the fact that I was new at being with someone of the opposite sex, and I was afraid of ending up in the same kind of mess I had been in before. I admitted my inexperience and lack of aptitude at what we were supposed to be doing. She lowered the boom right there on my first outing. She blurted out, "Oh, so that must be why you seem so emotionally unavailable!" That statement pretty much ended any hopes I might have had of her calling the friends who got us together and telling them what a great guy I was.

I thought, *Here I am, a new entrant on the dating scene, and this is my first time out. She is representing all of the female gender to me; she holds my future in her hands* (or at least I thought she did). *How this goes will determine whether or not I ever venture out again, and she can't be nice and polite for a mere twenty-minute cup of coffee.*

All the inferiority and inadequacy I had felt through the years came tumbling down into my lap, and I was ready for this evening to be over. I was not a happy man, because my fear had come true. I had been afraid of rejection and humiliation, and it was exactly what I got. *Retreat from the dating scene* was all I could think of. I wanted a copy of Josh Harris's book *I Kissed Dating Goodbye.* I could not tell her good-bye soon enough. I did not call the next day, but I did call my friends to let them know there would not be any future meetings between Miss Mean and me.

I had taken a risk, and it had stung a little. I realized I was going to have to take another risk if I was going to have a new life full of fun and interesting people, but it was quite a while before I was willing to risk again. I tell you this so you know that I have been where you are if you are having a hard time with this choice. I know the comfort that comes when you wall off every possible hurt in order to protect yourself. I know what it is like to think you will collapse if you feel one more ounce of pain. I also know what it is like to work through fear and begin to risk your life in order to find it.

I am convinced that life without risk is not much of a life. I know young men who inherited a lot of money and had all the comforts and securities you could possibly ask for. They had it all and lived with no fire in the belly, because there was nothing to burn. Their lives were risk free, and they had missed becoming the men they could have been because it was all so predictable and comfortable.

Predictability really can chain us to old things and prevent us from moving toward the new. Comfort can encase us in a womb we should have outgrown but still retreat into. We must give up the chains of predictability and the womb of comfort and jump out there and take a risk if we are to truly live.

Risk is a choice to heal, because it stretches some of the scar tissue and prevents us from being restrained by the energy. Just like a burn patient who must painfully move the scarred limbs to stretch the skin, we must do the same with our souls. We must stretch into what is not comfortable so that we do not confine ourselves to what is comfortable. That stretching comes from risk.

We risk connecting, because if we don't, a part of us will die in isolation. We must risk loving again, because if we don't, we will become bitter and isolated. We risk succeeding, knowing that it might prove to be a failure and we might look inadequate. If we do not risk, however, we will live horrible lives of boredom and loneliness, convincing ourselves we are okay as we mark time toward a miserable end. It does not have to be that way if we will choose to take a risk.

REAL RISK

Some people are so afraid of not making a difference that risk does not seem much of a factor to them. At the time I am writing this, Iraq is not a very safe place to be; it is full of risk. In the past couple of weeks, fifty of our troops have been killed in taking back the city of Fallujah. The July 8, 2004, edition of the *Orange County Register* told the story of a risk taker on the front page. It was the story of Talib Alhamdani of Irvine. The reporter, Vik Jolly, told about Talib's family life in sunny Southern California. They loved the Cheesecake Factory and "driving down open roads on starry nights." He loved his life, but he loved his people back in Iraq more. So in the midst of explosions and battles, he left his comfortable home to go back to Iraq and teach his people the principles of democracy.

In the past, his typical day had included lunch with buddies, poring over websites for news of Iraq. Now his typical day is in the thick of Iraq, meeting with Iraqi staff to arrange town hall civic dialogues, planning lectures, writing reports, and living in the midst of his country's systemic overhaul. He said this about his new life in which bombs have exploded two hundred meters away: "I am very happy with the decision I made. I wish I had made it much earlier. I am very happy to be part of history, and it's a dream for a political scientist to live in an era when political and social change is going on. I expect a bright future for Iraq."

Those are the words of a man whose life is not ruled by fear. Risk is part of the fabric of all of our lives, but Alhamdani has wrapped it around his life. He is an example of being able to make a difference once you work through your fears and move out into an unsafe world full of risk. When you are able to navigate life with a healthy awareness of danger, but willing to take risks to make a difference, you begin to live life in a new dimension.

WHAT ARE YOU MISSING?

Have you stopped to think of what you might be missing because you are unwilling to risk? Perhaps it is a relationship with an amazing person. Perhaps it is being on a mission trip where lives are changed forever. Maybe it is being in a group where you share your life and find hope and encouragement. There are so many things you might miss if you are unwilling to take a risk. I understand the security that comes from everything remaining the same, but predictability can become a god. You may be living your life more toward making it predictable than toward finding what God would have you to do. There may be a new life out there waiting for you if you are willing to take a risk.

> *I understand the security that comes from everything remaining the same, but predictability can become a god.*

The January 2004 edition of *Smithsonian Magazine* contained an amazing article about a family who knew what it was like to risk. It was the story of Hassan Lamungu of Somalia. This man was part of the Bantu tribe, the lowest of the lowest tribes from that country, and Hassan was about as low as you could get when it came to material things. He did not even have one chicken, and in his country even the poorest had a chicken. He did not speak any language other than his own and knew only the skill of hard labor in whatever form it came, but he wanted something better for his family.

Hassan signed up for the lottery to immigrate to America. He had heard of the good life here and of all the danger too. He knew that people like him were exploited every day, but he wanted to try to make a life for his family and himself. Year after year he waited for the lottery to choose him to come to America. When it finally did, he picked up his family, traveled halfway around the world, and started a new life so he could make something of himself and make some money to send home to other family members.

Hassan is making it. One day at a time he is making it in a land where he does not know the language or the customs. His children are full of delight and wonder, and his wife admires his courage and willingness to take a risk. I have to wonder how many of us are not living where we could, doing what we could, because we are so averse to risk. There may be a whole other life as different as America is from Africa, but we will never experience it if we are not willing to take a risk.

THE BUDDY SYSTEM

If you are thinking that you just do not have it in you to take a risk, think again. You may be paralyzed by fear, and your past might justify such fear. But you don't have to stay in the riskless world just because someone caused so much damage that you cannot imagine venturing out into the waters where it could happen again. Indeed, you on your own may not have what it takes, but you and a buddy might. The buddy system has been working for centuries as two people team up to keep each other safe in dangerous territory.

I was burned one time by having a horrible buddy to team with. He deserted me and then just laughed it off as if I were a spineless wimp. It happened when I went diving with some friends off of Dr. Henry Cloud's boat. I have been diving since I was forty, but I had never taken a dip off the coast of Newport Beach. There was a reason for that—the water is very cold. I learned to dive in Honduras, where the water was eighty-six degrees on a cool day. Newport Beach water is in the fifties and sixties and will jump over seventy a few days in August or during El Niño, so I had resisted Henry's many invitations to dive off his boat.

One day we were out and I was feeling quite game and ready for a day of shivering and cold. I suited up and was assigned to someone who was supposed to be my buddy. He was about half my age and had been marketed to me as an experienced diver. I needed someone with experience, because I figured that I would be in such a state of cold that I might lose touch with reality. So down we went into the icy waters. Much to my horror, the visibility was only about five feet, and it was colder than I had expected, but I did not want to appear to be a wimp, and I went on down with the pack.

Increasing my horror as I sank down in my much-too-thin rubber suit, my buddy shot out of sight. I looked over at him, and all I saw were flippers moving off into the murk. I was startled—I was buddyless. I started looking around and found Henry just barely in my sight. Then, *shrrrooomm*, the prodigal bud of mine came flipping by and then went off into the murk in the other direction.

I waited for his return, and sure enough, he came by again. When he did, I reached out and grabbed him, looked him in the eye, pointed to him and then to myself, and then pushed my two index fingers together, indicating that he and I had been selected as buddies. I did not have an acceptable underwater gesture that would indicate to him that his greatly annoying actions were destroying my spirituality at forty feet below sea level. Our new relationship lasted about two minutes as we all headed the same direction. We headed the same direction until "Flipper" darted out in front of everyone and out of sight, leaving me to feel as I had felt before. I did what you may have to do to start to risk again.

The safest—or at least the easiest—thing for me to do was to surface, but what would come of that? Only missed opportunities to tell tales later and connect over the chilliest of all adventures I have taken. So I did what I needed to do—I got a different buddy. I stayed with Henry and his buddy until the dive was complete. I no longer counted on someone who was not worth counting on. I did what I needed to do to protect myself while still enjoying life. In Henry and his buddy, I found the perfect buddies.

If you are so out of your comfort zone you think you might not ever be able to risk again, you need to get a buddy. You need to find someone who has been through what you have been through and made it out the other side. You can bolster your own confidence by relying on the strength of two rather than one. Think about who you know that could help you by going to a meeting with you or even going on a date. Think of different areas where a buddy might help you live again, and write them down. If you don't know of anyone, you might be able to find someone through your pastor or a recovery group. It might be a little embarrassing to ask for someone to help you get out of your comfort zone, but the world you are going to live in is worth the risk—and so is the reward.

It might be a little embarrassing to ask for someone to help you get out of your comfort zone, but the world you are going to live in is worth the risk—and so is the reward.

Madeline and I experienced this just the other day at Knotts Berry Farm. It was the day before Thanksgiving, and she had the day off. After I did one live *New Life Live* and recorded another, we took off for Knotts, determined to ride as many roller coasters as possible.

Madeline has always had a love-hate relationship with the beasts, sometimes wanting to ride and other times leaving the park, waiting for courage on another day. A friend of hers had been to Knotts, and I think she wanted to be sure that she could hold her ground with her friend. As we made our way toward the roller coasters, there, rising above us, was the ultimate challenge. When Madeline saw it, she said her stomach dropped. It was the Accelerator.

The Accelerator was in a league of its own. It shot you out of the hangar to a speed of eighty miles an hour in less than two seconds. Botox could not come close to smoothing out the lines of the faces of those poor people strapped in those cars of doom. Then, once you hit eighty, you literally were shot straight up toward the clouds, did a loop over the top and then straight down, completing the journey with a few loops and upside down rolls. We took a closer look and decided we would have to try a few others before we would even consider going on that one.

We rode a few other roller coasters that by Accelerator standards were quite lame. Then we moseyed over to the Accelerator entrance and made our way into line. There were two lines, and we stood in the shorter one hoping to get it over with sooner. Madeline had gone from "no way" to "willing to give it a try." I was so impressed that, even though she was very afraid, she wanted to do it. I think bragging rights meant something to her. It was not long before we noticed that although our line was shorter, it was not moving as quickly as the other one. When we got up to the ride, we realized we were standing in the line waiting for the front car. Madeline's eyes got a little red around the edges, as they are prone to do, but she said she wanted to stay in that line. So stay we did.

When it was our turn, we took the front seat in the front car. So there we were, going from fear of even riding the thing to riding it in the front row, shivering as we waited for it to boost us down the track. I looked at Madeline, and through the fear there was a grin of anticipation, but I could tell she was really worried.

They counted down with lights, and when the last light came on we shot out of the stall like a cannon. I have never been so afraid in my life. My cheeks must have been pulled back to plug up my ears, because I don't remember hearing a thing. Then after we hit eighty miles per hour, we went straight up. It felt like being on the tip of a rocket's nose cone. Then came the loop over the top and straight down. I thought I was going to fall out, but as we leveled off at the end of the drop, my fists went up, and I looked at Madeline, and she was beaming.

We finished the rest of the rollovers with ease and then came in for a smooth stop, me yelling at the top of my lungs, "We did it! We did it! Whoohooo, we did it!" Whereupon I think she said, "Dad," requesting that I hold it down a bit as we pulled back into the starting stall.

It really was the scariest thing I have ever done, and it was the same for her, but it was also the most exciting ride of my life. We both took a risk, and as a result we have a bond. We connected at one thousand feet in a way we would not have if our feet had remained flat on the ground. We experienced exhilaration and excitement and even adrenaline-induced euphoria because we risked feeling out of control and took the ride of our lives. It was much more challenging for Madeline. She did not have the lifetime of information that I have. She did not know just how safe it really was; she was not aware of all the testing that goes on before a ride like that can operate.

Madeline was the one really facing her fears, moving forward in courage rather than sitting in the grip of fear. I was so proud of her to go from "no way" to all the way to the front car of the roller coaster. In this case, like so many, risk led to a great reward for both of us. We used the buddy system to get us both on the machine that gave us a thrill we will never stop talking about. You have to risk if you are going to live life to the fullest.

RISK WITH LIMITS

My story with Madeline was one of risk, but it was one of reasonable risk. I did not tell you that we sneaked into the park at night, broke into the ride, and then rode it without supervision, a seat belt, or a restraining bar. That would have been unreasonable risk. Sometimes people equate all risk with unreasonable risk, and it is not true. No one is asking you to go out on a rotten limb but to pick a strong one and get out there. If you catastrophize every risk, you will never take the ones that are reasonable. Only you can set up the limits between reasonable and unreasonable. Air travel is a good analogy. If you are afraid of flying, I would not recommend you volunteer to be shot out of a cannon the next time the circus comes to town. That, in my mind, is high-risk flight, even with a pretty strong net. I could recommend, however, that you sail through the sky at more than five hundred miles per hour with no net—if you are in an airplane. I know that is safe because of the thousands and thousands of flights every day that take off and land as predicted.

I have seen the statistics that prove that it is far more dangerous to take a trip in a car than in a plane. I know that fewer people die or are hurt in air travel than in automobiles. So airplane travel is a reasonable risk to take. The boundaries and the limits you place on your risk taking can give you the freedom to take them without overwhelming fear.

If you have been burned in a relationship, meeting someone in a singles bar and hoping to not get burned again is a bit foolish. That is risk beyond what you should take. Hanging out with a group of singles at Starbucks after church, however, is filled with little risk other than burning your tongue. You might not have set limits and boundaries in the past, and that is why you have a hard time with risk. But a life of reasonable risk could help you find and live the life you have always been looking for.

If you have been burned in a relationship,
meeting someone in a singles bar and hoping
to not get burned again is a bit foolish.

TEDDY KNEW

One of my favorite quotes of all time will most likely be familiar to you. It is from a speech by Theodore Roosevelt. It remains one of the greatest motivational speeches ever written. Here is how he addressed the issue of risk and choosing to live a life that is too safe:

The credit belongs to the man who is actually in the arena; whose face is marred by dust and sweat and blood; who strives valiantly; who errs and comes up short again and again; who knows the great enthusiasms, the great devotions, and spends himself in a worthy cause; who at the best knows in the end the triumph of high achievement; and who, at the worst, if he fails, at least fails while daring greatly, so that his place shall never be with those cold and timid souls who know neither victory nor defeat.

I love those words, and they inspire me to move forward in spite of my fears. The worst that can happen to me is that I might lose, but if I lose, God is there for me, loving me as He always does. One of the reasons you may not be willing to risk has to do with your concept of God and His love. His love allows us to go beyond our fears even to the point of failing over and over again. If we are not willing to risk and willing to fail as we learn from failing, then we may have a problem in the area of our love relationship with God.

"There is no fear in love. But perfect love drives out fear, because fear has to do with punishment. The one who fears is not made perfect in love" (1 John 4:18 NIV). If you have a riskless nature, it may be because you have a loveless nature. Your love relationship with God might be all messed up. You might be so afraid that He will punish you that you are unwilling to step out and enjoy your life by living it to the fullest and using it to serve others. If you live in fear of punishment rather than in the confidence of God's love, it is no wonder that you don't want to risk. You must have God's love, God's Spirit, and God's power if you are to conquer your fears and move into risking your life.

"God did not give us a spirit of timidity, but a spirit of power, of love and of self-discipline" (2 Timothy 1:7 NIV). If you are living in fear, you are not living as God intended; He wants you free from fear. He wants to help you move from fear to fearless, willing to take risks with your life so you can feel what life can become. His love is so powerful that if you work through whatever keeps you from experiencing it, you can feel the safety you have been longing for and trying to create in your attempts to avoid risk.

In God's love we are free to love and to love again. We are free to give all of ourselves to another person, knowing that we might experience rejection all over again. In God's love we can fail, because we know that He will take that failure and make something spectacular from it. Knowing that, we ease off building our protective barriers and begin to live life a little more freely and fully.

If you are holding on way too tight, I am writing to encourage you to let go. I am hopeful that you can release your grip and allow God to guide you into some situations that are scary for you, but for the two of you hold no downside at all. God said, "Never will I leave you, never will I forsake you!" (Hebrews 13:5 NIV). I am going to ask you to stop right now and just meditate a moment on that passage.

God will never forsake you. There is nothing you can do to run God off. He will never leave you. God will always be there for you. God is the best thing you have going for you. God loves you and will be there to help you pick up the pieces and put them back together again in the form of something far more beautiful than the original. God created you and will always be there for you. If God is for you in that way, who could possibly be against you and win? Who could harm you if God is always there waiting to pick you up? God loves you. God is there for you, and you need have no fear of today or what tomorrow might bring.

REASONS TO RISK

There are many excuses you may have used to play it safe. They have worked well for you in your goal to avoid risk, but they have not worked well for you in living a great life. To live a great life you must have risk. You cannot love unless you risk. You cannot even care about someone unless you risk. There is always the chance that you will be rejected when you put a part of yourself or all of yourself out there. You cannot connect without risk. Loving, caring, and connecting—those vital elements of life that give it meaning and purpose—are great reasons to risk.

You can't serve without risking either. But when you serve, you serve Christ. You do to Christ what you do for another. That is worth risking even if all you do is get rejected and have it thrown back in your face. When you serve and are not loved for it but instead are rejected, you end up sharing in the sufferings of Jesus. You fellowship with Christ through your rejection, since almost all of His life was filled with rejection. That fellowship with Christ is a powerful healer that cannot be experienced unless you are willing to take some risks.

You cannot make your world small enough to be risk free.

THE HEALING POWER OF RISK

Risk is a healer. It demands faith and trust. It eliminates a lifestyle of self-preservation. Self-preservation and protection ignore the power of God, because you cannot be healed and still be living under your own power. Those who are healed live by the grace of God and in God's power. Each time you step out under God's power, you heal a little of the fear that developed from your troubled past. You have to fully trust God and walk in His power before that last ounce of soul sickness is healed.

You can't allow yourself to be healed if you are holding back and trying to protect yourself from what cannot be prevented—trials and sorrows. You are going to have them, and when you take a risk and move into them under God's power rather than defend against them under your own power, you are choosing to heal.

The great preacher Charles Haddon Spurgeon said, "Anxiety does not empty tomorrow of its sorrows but only empties today of its strength." You cannot lead a healed life in anxiety. It will rob you of the strength you need today. It will steal from you the tomorrow you were born to enjoy.

The answer for those who need healing from a risk-adverse life is found in 1 Peter 5:7: "Cast all your anxiety on him because he cares for you" (NIV). Do that right now. You can trust God that He cares for you. It is worth the risk to say to God that you give Him all your fears, and you are ready to ride out your life on the front seat of the first car, healed in excited anticipation of what might be around the next turn.

"Peace I leave with you; my peace I give you. I do not give to you as the world gives. Do not let your hearts be troubled and do not be afraid" (John 14:27 NIV). My prayer for you is to feel God's healing love. I pray that you would write down what it is you are afraid of. Write out what you have held on to for yourself and what you need to do to give all your life to God. What needs to take place to feel the peace God has given you and then the courage to go out and live life even though you might be hurt again?

THE BIG LIE
"I must protect myself from any more pain."

This big lie is a really big one. It tells you that you have to protect yourself from any more pain. If you have tried to live your life that way, I have a question for you. How is it going so far? What kind of life is a life of defense, always looking for the next bad thing to deflect away? I would say that is no life at all. Protect yourself, be a wise steward of what God has given you, but don't allow fears and hardships to keep you from moving forward.

You are going to be hurt and you cannot do anything to prevent it, but what you *can* do is trust God each time a hurt comes along. Trust that while you don't have the power to protect yourself, He has the power to turn every hurt into something that improves who you are and glorifies Him. You will never protect yourself from all the hurt, but you will protect yourself from missing the life God intended when you make the choice to risk.

Healing is a choice. It is God's choice, but many times we stand in the way of what God wants for us. Our stubbornness often prevents us from looking at the reality of our lives, but God challenges us to make choices that heal. There is not one choice more difficult than the choice to risk. My hat is off to all of you who will make that choice on this day. Blessings of God be upon you for your amazing courage.

CHAPTER 8 WORKBOOK QUESTIONS

THE EIGHTH CHOICE:
The Choice to Risk Your Life

THE EIGHTH BIG LIE:
"I must protect myself from any more pain."

TWENTY YEARS FROM NOW YOU WILL BE MORE DISAPPOINTED by the things that you didn't do than by the ones you did do. So throw off the bowlines. Sail away from the safe harbor. Catch the trade winds in your sails. Explore. Dream. Discover." Mark Twain wrote those words. Could he be right?

Will we sit down at some point in the future and realize that we missed great opportunities that would have enriched our lives? Will we approach the end of our lives filled with regrets and missed opportunities? From a more positive perspective, how can we live life to its fullest?

One thing is certain. We will never live a full life without being willing to take some risks. Choosing to risk your life is the theme of chapter 8.

Simply reading the opening paragraph may cause you to feel anxious. Risk is hard for you. You don't consider yourself to be brave. You get tense around risk takers. You panic when someone challenges you to take a risk. Even now, you're thinking, *This is a really good book. Why did it have to be ruined by including this chapter?*

Please don't stop reading. The discussion about risk is not as threatening as you might fear. It is very important and involves another choice to heal. By the way, you won't be asked to sail across the ocean alone, or hang-glide in the Rocky Mountains. Nor will we ask you to do anything reckless.

Before we tackle this important subject, let's look at where we've been:

- In chapter 1, we discussed the critical need to connect with other people who can help and support us in our time of need.
- Chapter 2 encouraged us to really feel our lives, instead of denying or running from them. Pain lets us know that we are ill and need to make a choice to heal.
- The next chapter challenged us to investigate our lives. If we are going to make healing choices, we need to identify the places that need correction and improvement.
- Chapter 4 encouraged us to heal our future. The challenge was to acknowledge our losses, grieve them, and make healing choices that propel us into the future.
- Chapter 5 taught us to heal our lives by making the choice to heal. Acknowledging our need to help our lives motivates us to put away the false hope of self-help and consider seeking professionals who can assist us in the healing process.
- Chapter 6 introduced us to the wonderful power of redemption, which changes our lives and gives us hope.

It deals with our sins and motivates us to seek the healing we need.

- Chapter 7 introduced one of the most important points in the book, the power of forgiveness, which is the only reliable means to combat the anger, bitterness, and resentment resulting from human failure.

We have come a long way on the journey to be healed. Hopefully, you noticed that each lesson connects with the previous one to strengthen and guide us toward healing.

When we complete the study, you will have vital information necessary to embrace and heal your life. However, the choice is up to you. Healing is a choice. It is God's choice, but you can, and should, join the effort. God wants to heal you. He asks you to participate with Him in that process. Chapter 8 calls you to become boldly involved in the healing effort.

THE EIGHTH CHOICE:
The Choice to Risk Your Life

A POINT OF DECISION

You have reached an important juncture in this study. Now you are faced with two choices. The first and best choice is to keep making healing choices and move forward. The second choice is to remain where you are. If you take the second choice, you will most likely get "stuck" and miss the opportunity to heal your life.

Why would anyone take the second option? Why bring your life to a halt and never move on?

On the surface, that question sounds absurd. Of course people will choose to move on! But that is not the case. Some decide to stay where they are because they are afraid. The present is familiar to them. Their predictable routines are comfortable and serve as protective walls keeping them sequestered. Within their walls, they are safe and protected from pain. In contrast, the future is unknown and unpredictable. Moving forward feels dangerous. Fear immobilizes them and they get "stuck." Their protective walls have infected them with what *Healing Is a Choice* describes as "soul-rot."

For these folks, the decision to move ahead reduces to one important personal question: "Am I willing to take risks?"

Everyone must wrestle with the reality of risk, because we cannot live without encountering it.

What is the definition of *risk*? It has two prominent meanings:

- The possibility of suffering harm or loss; danger
- A factor, thing, element, or course involving uncertain danger

The definition assumes we will take risks, and it assumes the possibility of some danger. So, we must consider how much risk to take and when it is or is not appropriate.

Exercise #1: How Much Risk Will I Tolerate?

By yourself or in a small group, answer and discuss the following questions.

1. In your own words, describe what you think the term *soul-rot* means.

_____

_____

_____

2. If you are studying in a small group, take a few minutes to share your definitions. Discuss the dangers of "soul-rot."

_____

_____

_____

3. How might a person catch the "soul-rot" disease?

_____

_____

_____

4. List some ways to combat the dangers of "soul-rot."

_____

_____

5. Complete a personal "risk appraisal." Follow these instructions:

(a) For each statement below, answer yes or no by checking the appropriate line.

(b) On the lines below each statement, explain why you answered yes or no.

1. I never take risks!   Yes   No
                                       ☐   ☐

_____

_____

2. I enjoy taking risks, and am a risk taker   Yes   No
   by nature.   ☐   ☐

_____

3. I take risks occasionally, only when   Yes   No
   absolutely necessary.   ☐   ☐

_____

_____

4. I believe it is important to take risks   Yes   No
   on a regular basis.   ☐   ☐

_____

5. I have often failed when taking risks.   Yes   No
                                       ☐   ☐

_____

6. I have been successful when taking   Yes   No
   risks.   ☐   ☐

_____

_____

When you have completed this exercise, ask a trusted friend to sit with you and discuss your responses. Some thoughtful discussion questions include:

- Do I avoid risks?
- Why am I reluctant to take risks?
- Can I live a full life without any risks?
- Am I harming my life by being reluctant to take risks?
- How can I begin taking some risks that will build up my confidence and strength?

RISK IS INEVITABLE

Some people believe they can avoid taking risks. However, that is not reality. It is magical thinking.

Helen Keller said, "Security is mostly a superstition. It does not exist in nature, nor do the children of men as a whole experience it. Avoiding danger is no safer in the long run than outright exposure. Life is either a daring adventure or nothing."

If anyone was ever entitled to build walls of protection and live in isolation, it was Keller. Yet her life was one of the most meaningful and important in United States history. Keller took a risk every time she took a step.

Scripture warns us that life is filled with risks. "When you work in a quarry, stones might fall and crush you. When you chop wood, there is danger with each stroke of your ax" (Ecclesiastes 10:9 NLT).

The result of taking no risks is not safety and security. The result of taking no risks is withdrawal, isolation, and even dishonesty.

Why is it dishonest? If you believe you can avoid risks, you are mistaken. No one lives life without risks. It is a lie to believe otherwise. Each of us runs the risk of contracting disease, being hurt by friends, or injuring ourselves. Even if we locked ourselves in a room alone, bolted the doors, and nailed the windows shut, we would still face some risks.

You cannot protect yourself from pain. You are subject to the human condition. By trying to avoid risks, you will harm yourself, becoming disconnected from the friends and family you need. You will become isolated and preoccupied with your safety. You may experience "soul-rot."

The simple truth is that life without risk is not much of a life, or, to take it one step further, "Life without risks is not life at all."

Ouch! Life without risks is not life at all? That is true because life is filled with risks of various kinds. If you are going to live, you will face risks. Life requires it!

BARRIERS TO RISK

Risk has some natural enemies. Two of them are predictability and comfort.

Predictability is like a straitjacket, keeping us wrapped tightly, unable to move about, and stuck in one environment. It prevents us from growing and exploring the wonders of life. Many people put themselves in psychological and emotional straitjackets or predictability. Thus, they are immobilized. To be sure, there is some security that results from things remaining the same. The danger comes from maintaining predictability at the expense of what God wants you to do with your life. His will is not our predictability, but our willingness to join the grand adventure of introducing Jesus Christ to the world!

A second enemy of risk is comfort. It drains the joy out of life. Comfort is a dream killer! There are people who will not join a mission team to a foreign country because they will not have a comfortable bed to sleep on or a warm shower at the end of the workday. They value comfort more than Christian service. Sadly, they will never experience the utter exhilaration of building a church, running a medical clinic, teaching uneducated children, feeding the hungry, or giving water to the thirsty.

In this matter, we should learn from Jesus, who said,

"Foxes have dens to live in, and birds have nests, but the Son of Man has no place even to lay his head." He said to another person, "Come, follow me." The man agreed, but he said, "Lord, first let me return home and bury my father." But Jesus told him, "Let the spiritually dead bury their own dead! Your duty is to go and preach about the coming of the Kingdom of God." Another said, "Yes, Lord, I will follow you, but first let me say good-bye to my family." But Jesus told him, "Anyone who puts a hand to the plow and then looks back is not fit for the Kingdom of God." (Luke 9:58–62 NLT)

Imagine you live in the early part of the first century AD. You are a disciple of Jesus Christ, who was recently crucified and then, to everyone's amazement, resurrected to life. You follow the risen Christ to Galilee. Now, with some friends, you've gathered on a mountain to hear Him preach. To your surprise, He does not offer a sermon. Instead, He utters four sentences that will change the course of world history.

Listen to Him: "I have been given all authority in heaven and on earth. Therefore, go and make disciples of all the nations, baptizing them in the name of the Father and the Son and the Holy Spirit. Teach these new disciples to obey all the commands I have given you. And be sure of this: I am with you always, even to the end of the age" (Matthew 28:18–20 NLT).

Think about those precious words. Who would have thought that such brief and beautiful words would contain within them such tremendous risks?

In subsequent years, Jesus' followers took incredible risks for His sake. They were rejected, repudiated, beaten, whipped, tortured, burned, thrown to animals, hanged, imprisoned, and more. Through the centuries, Christians became acquainted with every known instrument of torture.

Yet the world today is predominantly Christian due to the fact that a handful of believers were willing to accept the risks in order to obey Christ.

Would anyone suggest that risks taken for Jesus' sake were not worth it? No! Every risk taken to spread the gospel was, and is, worth any consequence. Yet some people, bound tightly by predictability and comfort, will not risk stepping out of their routines for Jesus' sake!

This chapter calls risk a healing choice. At first that sounds strange, like a contradiction in terms. However, a little thought confirms the truth of the statement. Risk tears the cocoon that binds us right off our bodies. Risk sets us free to be really alive. It forces us to connect with people and experience the thrill of being alive.

If we do not take risks, our lives will be horribly boring and lonely. They will be unexamined lives, devoid of purpose.

Healing Is a Choice teaches that accepting risks is a decision to heal. It forces us to experience life in ways we've never before known. We begin to live as Jesus wants us to, connected to one another; working, growing, and living together for common purposes. Getting to that place may sometimes be painful, but it is well worth it!

Exercise #2: One Man's Example

Look back through chapter 8 and reread pages 317–18 under the heading "Real Risk." Answer the following questions. If you are studying in a small group, discuss the questions aloud.

1. What was the true risk that Talib Alhamdani faced? Was it returning to a hostile and dangerous environment? Was it the fear of not helping his people? Or, was it what *Healing Is a Choice* states on page 317: "Some people are so afraid of not making a difference that risk does not seem much of a factor to them"? Could that have been the motivation that propelled Talib to take such a great risk? Discuss.

_____

_____

_____

2. Each of us can make a real difference in some area of life. True or false? How?

_____

_____

_____

3. In order to make a difference in life, we must be willing to work through our fears and venture into the world with all its risks. We must accept the reality of risk and live with it, rather than cowering in fear. Ask yourself, *Can I do that? Am I willing to take some risks to achieve the will of God in my life?*

_____

_____

_____

4. Paragraph three on page 318 states: "When you are able to navigate life with a healthy awareness of danger, but willing to take risks to make a difference, you begin to live life in a new dimension." Discuss that statement in your small group, focusing on the twin goals of

(a) healthy awareness of danger

(b) (being) willing to take risks to make a difference.

How do those two goals work together in our lives?

_____

_____

_____

WHAT ARE YOU MISSING?

We must face an important truth. If we choose a predictable and comfortable life without any risks, we will certainly miss many wonderful things.

A very famous poem, most often attributed to poet laureate Alfred Lord Tennyson, says:

> *I hold it true, whate'er befall;*
> *I feel it, when I sorrow most;*
> *'Tis better to have loved and lost*
> *Than never to have loved at all.*

His point is simple. It is better to take a risk for a good reason and fail, than never to try. The joy and meaning come to us in the process more than the outcome. It's the endeavor that counts most.

Classical Latin vocabulary includes the word *praxis*. It is the root of our English word *practice*. Praxis roughly means "the meaning of something comes in the doing of it." Thus, if you want to be a great tennis player, you must play a lot of tennis. The meaning of tennis to you and how proficient you become are the result of constant practice and improvement. If you want to be a great teacher, you must practice. If you want to be adept at risk taking, you must practice. You must experience some risks in order to manage it well. The good news is, you can do it! Praxis makes perfect!

If you are unwilling to take a risk, you may miss a relationship with a fabulous person. You might miss seeing people's lives dramatically changed because you were not part of a mission team. Perhaps the greatest loss will be the opportunity to become the person God planned you to be!

By now, you might be thinking, *I understand. It makes sense, but risk is dangerous. I will get hurt.* The truth is that you may experience some hurt, but the pain of not taking a risk is ultimately greater and more injurious to our psyches than any pain we'd feel in the risk.

A wise man once wrote, "A ship in its harbor is safe, but that is not what ships are for!" Ships were meant to sail!

Furthermore, it is important to realize that risk does not mean running headlong into harm's way.

There is a business science called "risk management" that seeks to measure the degree of danger or threat in a given risk. To some extent, we all do some risk management.

Jesus was using risk management at the wedding in Cana in John 2:

The next day there was a wedding celebration in the village of Cana in Galilee. Jesus' mother was there, and Jesus and his disciples were also invited to the celebration. The wine supply ran out during the festivities, so Jesus' mother told him, "They have no more wine." "Dear woman, that's not our problem," Jesus replied. "My time has not yet come." (vv. 1–4 NLT)

Jesus' mother asked Him to solve an embarrassing situation. To do it required a miracle. Jesus weighed the risk. If He performed the miracle, word would spread quickly and a confrontation with His enemies might occur before He was ready to reveal Himself publicly. That is what Jesus meant when He said, "My time has not yet come." Still, He considered His mother's request, and He cared about the wedding and guests. Ultimately, He weighed the risk and performed the miracle.

Some people will take greater risks than others. That is natural. What is not natural is to take no risks. Risks are necessary to live a full life. It may even be painful at times, but it is the pain that lets you know you are alive!

Life without any risks is no life at all! It's existence, but it's not life.

PICK A BUDDY

One way to manage risk is to employ a "buddy system." Some people never take risks, because of pain and injury sustained early in life. They cannot envision taking a risk of any kind, especially alone. However, with a friend, they might be persuaded. With a buddy, there is enough security to take a risk or two.

Jesus understood that principle and dispatched His disciples in a buddy system. "And he called his twelve disciples together and began sending them out two by two, giving them authority to cast out evil spirits" (Mark 6:7 NLT).

The buddy system has worked for centuries throughout the world and is an effective way to turn a risk avoider into a risk taker.

Consider selecting a "buddy." Is there a person or two in your life who could become a buddy and help you learn to take some risks? Think carefully about this choice.

1. List several potential buddies on the lines below in order of your preference.

_____

_____

2. Contact the first person on your list. Explain that you want to be a bit bolder and take a few risks (nothing dramatic, just small steps). Ask the person to join you for support and fellowship. Give them permission to push you a bit. Pick a challenge together. Be sure it is manageable, but also be sure there is some degree of risk involved. When you conquer your first challenge, move ahead to a new one and conquer it too! Ask

your buddy how you're doing. Accept his or her encouragement and support. Together, you can conquer your fear and build a track record of success and confidence. Your life will change! You will feel the confidence build inside. You will feel an urge to do more.

3. If your first selection for a buddy does not work out, contact the second person on your list and try again. Above all, do not give up. Push through your fear. Throw away the ways that you are set in.

Exercise #3: The Courage to Take Risks

Ralph Waldo Emerson wrote, "Whatever you do, you need courage. Whatever course you set, there is always someone to tell you that you are wrong. There are always difficulties arising that tempt you to believe your critics are right. To map out a course of action and follow it to an end requires some of the same courage that a soldier needs. Peace has its victories, but it takes brave men and women to win them."

Perhaps it's been a while since you've taken a risk. Here is an exercise to use as you venture into the world of risk taking. None of these things are threatening or dangerous, but doing them will build your confidence. Completing them in sequence will make it easier. It will take some time to accomplish these things. Don't be pressured by time, but don't put them off. Doing them will help you become comfortable with risks and will invest you in self-improvement and the Lord's work.

Check each one as you complete it.

1. _____ Phone a friend you haven't heard from in a while and get reacquainted.
2. _____ If you haven't been out of your house or apartment for a while, go to lunch at a new restaurant, or go see a movie.

3. _____ Call your church and volunteer to help with an outreach ministry such as inner-city feeding, a homeless shelter, or a literacy program.

4. _____ Bake cookies or a casserole and take it to your neighbor. If invited, stay and visit for a while.

5. _____ Invite a friend or a relative to an amusement park. Ride a roller coaster.

6. _____ Call your pastor and ask if you can share your testimony in a midweek service, small group, or Sunday school class. Prior to sharing, write your testimony and rehearse it several times, so you will be comfortable and natural as you tell your story.

7. _____ Join a team that provides worship services for senior citizens. Involve yourself in the worship.

8. _____ Contact someone with whom you have been estranged. Make a committed effort to reconcile with that person.

9. _____ Join a small group at your church and faithfully attend the meetings. Get to know the other participants. Get involved in the Bible studies and sharing.

10. _____ Plan a minivacation out of town. Visit a location you've long wanted to see. Create an itinerary, make housing reservations, have your car serviced, and enjoy yourself.

Each time you accomplish one of the risk-challenges listed above, you will grow stronger and more confident. You will feel energy gathering inside you.

Taking risks requires courage. That point is made vividly in Frank Baum's story *The Wonderful Wizard of Oz.*[1] Most people have read the book or seen the 1939 movie. It's a great story about taking risks.

348

Dorothy was caught in a storm and mysteriously arrived in the land of Oz. Her only way home was to move forward and find the Wizard of Oz, who supposedly had the power to transport her home. Along the journey to Oz, Dorothy made three friends— the Scarecrow, the Tin Woodsman, and the Cowardly Lion—all struggling with their own weaknesses and liabilities. Each was afraid and embarrassed by his own deficiency. Like Dorothy, they needed to take the risk of finding Oz. The journey was long and dangerous. They forced themselves to move forward, battling and overcoming, always staying on the yellow brick road. The journey to Oz changed each of them. When they finally arrived at Oz, they were shocked. The powerful Wizard of Oz was no wizard at all. Rather, he was a mere mortal. He was incapable of performing the magic that would send Dorothy home, give the Cowardly Lion a heart, put a brain in the Scarecrow, or place a heart in the Tin Woodsman.

But wait! They suddenly realized that the journey had changed each of them. Dorothy found her way home. Suddenly, the Cowardly Lion was courageous. The Tin Woodsman felt emotions. The Scarecrow was smart.

The Wizard of Oz is a story about risk, growth, and maturity. Each character began the journey handicapped. Dorothy was lost and displaced. The Cowardly Lion was bound by fear. The Scarecrow suffered from the bondage of inferiority. The Tin Woodsman had lost touch with his feelings.

Yet they all realized that their only hope was to move ahead. They had no real choice but to take the risks.

Notice the important fact that they took the journey together. They connected with one another and found mutual support and, ultimately, love. Each of them mustered up what little courage they could find, headed down the yellow brick road as a team, and completed their quest confident and strong.

The Wizard of Oz is a metaphor for everyone who is immobilized and unwilling to take risks.

Here is a simple fact of life: We all must take risks in life. They are inevitable. The worst that can happen is that we might fail, but if we do, God is there with us, loving, nudging, and pushing us to try again. His love allows us to move beyond our fears. Taking a risk to move boldly into the future is a healing choice, and a prelude to leaving the past behind.

"One does not discover new lands without consenting to lose sight of the shore for a very long time" (Andre Gide, twentieth-century French writer, 1947 Nobel Prize winner).

Scripture reminds us that God's "love has no fear because perfect love expels all fear. If we are afraid, it is for fear of punishment, and this shows that we have not fully experienced his perfect love" (1 John 4:18 NLT).

"For God has not given us a spirit of fear and timidity, but of power, love, and self-discipline" (2 Timothy 1:7 NLT).

Healing Is a Choice makes an emphatic point: "If you are living in fear, you are not living as God intended; He wants you free from fear."

THE EIGHTH BIG LIE:
"I must protect myself from any more pain."

We called chapter 6's big lie a whopper. This chapter's lie is the Mt. Everest of lies! People are not capable of protecting themselves from pain.

Trying to protect yourself from pain only makes your life more miserable. If you are in a defensive mode, you will be preoccupied with pain. You will worry about your body. You will probably develop psychosomatic symptoms because you are so worried. Anxiety and fear will grow stronger in you.

At some time in your life, you are going to be hurt, and there's nothing you can do about it. That's life. It will probably happen more than once. However, you can be sure that Jesus will never leave or forsake you. You can be fortified by that truth and draw strength from it.

As repeated a number of times within, you must make a decision to be healed. Healing is God's choice, but we must cooperate with Him and not resist what He is doing in our lives. The choice to heal by taking risks is one of the most powerful decisions you will make. Be not afraid! It was Will Rogers who said, "Don't be afraid to go out on a limb. That's where the fruit is."

JOURNALING

The book reminds us that risk is a healer. Risk demands faith and trust. It forbids us from living a life of self-preservation. Are you ready to take some risks? What are the things that continue to stand in your way, blocking your path?

Remember that the powerful Holy Spirit is standing with you. He is your champion, and you can draw courage and strength from Him. This is the day to put away all the old, stifling patterns of your life. This is the day that all things become new! Spend time processing these thoughts and record your feelings as you journal.

PRAYERFUL MEDITATION

Chapter 8 asks us to meditate on Deuteronomy 31:6: "Be strong and courageous! Do not be afraid and do not panic before them. The LORD your God will personally go ahead of you. He will neither fail you nor forsake you" (NLT).

You will find these words on page 328: "God will never forsake you. There is nothing you can do to run God off. He will never leave you. God will always be there for you. . . . God created you and will always be there for you. If God is for you in that way, who could possibly be against you and win? God loves you. God is there for you, and you need have no fear of today or what tomorrow might bring."

PRAYER

God of Power and Might, I confess my fears and my reluctance to take risks. I've become very familiar with the ruts in which I live. The truth is that they are very uncomfortable and constricting. I often dream of reaching out, being brave and bold. I am ready for change. Please help me. Help me risk connecting, so I don't die in isolation. Help me risk loving again, so I won't become bitter and isolated. Help me risk succeeding, knowing I could fail. Spare me from a horrible life of boredom and loneliness. Send Your Holy Spirit to give me courage. Help me not to be dissuaded. Block me from retreating back into my ruts. I want my life to count for You and for me. Heal my fear. Give me strength today to make the healing choice to take some risks for Your kingdom's sake, through Christ, my Champion, amen.

9

THE NINTH CHOICE:
The Choice to Serve

THE NINTH BIG LIE:
"Until I am completely healed and strong, there is no place for me to serve God."

A MAN NAMED GIDEON

IN THE BOOK OF JUDGES IS A WONDERFUL STORY MOST PEOPLE are familiar with. It is the story of a man named Gideon. There are two things that are well-known about the story. One is his use of a fleece to see if God was really with him. One night, Gideon wanted God to soak a wool fleece while the ground around it would remain dry. On the next night, he wanted God to make the ground all around the fleece wet while the fleece remained dry. God did just as Gideon had asked, and Gideon knew that God was with him.

When I heard that story as a young man in love with Patricia down the street, I repeated Gideon's request. I put a ball of cotton out on the lawn and asked God to reveal to me whether or not Patricia loved me by making the cotton dry while the dew surrounded it. Well, my young love must not have been meant to be, because the cotton was just as wet as the ground around it. Of course it was a silly thing to do, but people still do it, not recognizing that the fleece was a unique experience designed just for Gideon. Seeing the odds Gideon was up against, it is no wonder God allowed him to know for sure He was with Gideon.

The other very familiar part of Gideon's story is his great battle victory against what seemed to be insurmountable odds. If I had been taking 300 men into battle against 135,000 well-armed troops, I would have wanted a direct sign from God that He was definitely with my men and me. Most of us are familiar with the story out of the sixth chapter of Judges in which the 135,000 became so confused that they started fighting one another and either killed each other or fled in fear to distant lands. It is a great story of a man who wanted to serve God, did not think he was capable, was full of doubt, needed reassurance, moved forward anyway, and won the victory. What a great story of God working in a person's life in a mighty way.

That great victory, however, is not the highlight of the story for me. That God played the fleece game with Gideon is not the highlight of the story either. That is interesting, but it is not the best part of the story for me. The best part of the story for me is found in Judges 6:11–16 (MSG):

One day the angel of GOD came and sat down under the oak in Ophrah that belonged to Joash the Abiezrite, whose son Gideon was threshing wheat in the winepress, out of sight of the Midianites. The angel of GOD appeared to him and said, "GOD is with you, O mighty warrior!"

Gideon replied, "With *me*, my master? If GOD is with us, why has all this happened to us? Where are all the miracle-wonders our parents and grandparents told us about, telling us, 'Didn't GOD deliver us from Egypt?' The fact is, GOD has nothing to do with us—he has turned us over to Midian."

But GOD faced him directly: "Go in this strength that is yours. Save Israel from Midian. Haven't I just sent you?"

Gideon said to him, "*Me*, my master? How and with what could I ever save Israel? Look at me. My clan's the weakest in Manasseh and I'm the runt of the litter."

GOD said to him, "I'll be with you. Believe me, you'll defeat Midian as one man."

When I discovered this part of the story, it meant so much to me. Even if Gideon had been a horrible warrior, I would have still loved this story. It points out two amazing things about God. First, Gideon had his doubts about God because of the circumstances around him. He and his people were not having a great life because of the Midianites. The Midianites were mistreating the Israelites, and Gideon was not happy about it, but the mistreatment was the consequence of Israel's doing evil things in the eyes of the Lord. When God came to Gideon, Gideon wasn't much of a believer. He had heard what God had done in the past, but he had seen nothing like the miracles that freed the Israelites from Egypt. If he would just do as he was told and serve God in the way God needed him to serve, however, he would become part of one of the greatest miracles ever told.

You—right now, in the midst of your difficult circumstances— might doubt whether or not God exists or is involved in your life. It might feel as if God is either not in heaven or does not care about you. You might feel so weak that you cannot relate to a powerful God who does not seem to be doing anything in your life. But just as God was with Gideon, even though Gideon was not aware of God or could not feel God's presence, God is with you and wants to use you.

That may sound absurd if you are facing a divorce or recovering from one. If you are still struggling from something that happened in your childhood, you may not believe that God was for you then or is for you now, but God is for you. God is with you, and you are going to have to do something that Gideon did. You have to trust in God if you are going to become part of a miracle that may be just as astounding as the miracle of Gideon and 300 men defeating an army of 135,000.

God wants you to serve Him. God has chosen a purpose for your life. God wants you to go after that purpose and be used by Him for the benefit of His kingdom. God will take you and use you even if you get up and go along with Him, kicking and screaming like a big baby. Kick and scream, but move toward the place God wants you. Doubt God's presence, but risk enough to trust in what you do not see. At the height of your pain or abuse or neglect, it may not have seemed that God was there or involved. It sure did not seem that way to Gideon, but God was there and was planning all along to use Gideon, just as God has planned all along to use you, if you will let Him.

This story of Gideon means so much to me because of Gideon's response in the fifteenth verse. Look at it closely with me, because it is often overlooked, yet it is the most significant part of the story. In that verse Gideon points out that God is calling him to serve, and to Gideon it looks like a huge mistake. God has chosen a man from the weakest family, clan, or tribe in all of Manasseh. They were the poorest of the poor, and God chose to raise up a leader right out of the middle of these poor and weak people. But of all the people in that family, there was one who was weaker than all the rest. That was Gideon. Gideon was the weakest of this weak family. He was the least of the least, and God chose him to serve as a mighty warrior.

I am sure you get my point here. God did not go throughout the land and find the most experienced warrior to bring a victory to His people. He chose the least of the least. He chose the person least likely to win the battle. It was just like choosing Moses to speak to Pharoah for Him. Moses had a speech impediment, yet God chose him as His voice. He was as unlikely a candidate to serve as God's voice as Gideon was to serve as God's warrior, but that is who God chose. Because God chose Gideon rather than some giant, God gets all the glory for the victory, while Gideon gets to become part of a miracle that people still talk and write about thousands of years later.

NO EXCUSES

One of the things I learned early in my life is that there is no excuse good enough to miss out on the life that God has chosen for me. Gideon's story reinforces that point. Gideon was the least of the least to pull off one of God's greatest victories. That is how I see myself, as embarrassing as it is.

I don't have a PhD, yet I get to work with some of the best. I did not marry the woman I met in Sunday school and stay married for the rest of my life, yet I work with some men and women who have the strongest marriages possible. I did not study broadcasting or broadcast journalism, yet I have a radio show that station managers say brings more new listeners to their stations than any other program. I wish I had more strengths, and I wish my life had worked out more perfectly, but it did not. God has used me anyway, in spite of me.

There are so many excuses I could have used to stay back and not serve God. Any of them would have been good enough for me to stay in my comfort zone, but none of them good enough to miss God's best. Just the fact that I paid for an abortion could have kept me on the sidelines rather than preach God's truth. In spite of that horrific ordeal, God has allowed me to speak at Crisis Pregnancy centers and help them raise millions of dollars during the past ten years. What a blessing it has been for me to be used in that way. Because I have failed in so many ways, God gets all the glory for anything and everything that has come out of my life that is worth mentioning. So no matter what befalls me, if God can still use me, as embarrassing as it might be and humbling as it might be, I want to be used for Him. I want the same for you.

No matter what befalls me, if God can still use me, as embarrassing as it might be and humbling as it might be, I want to be used for Him. I want the same for you.

WHAT'S YOUR EXCUSE?

If you believe the Bible to be true, the story of Gideon has to have an impact on your life. If you believe God speaks to us through His Word, surely you believe He has used this story to help you over-come any excuse you might have for not serving Him. Gideon's story is God taking a weak man from a weak clan leading a weak army to defeat a mighty foe. What is your story? If, one day, there was to be a Third Testament written, and your story was in it, what would it say? Would it be a great story of victory against the greatest of odds? Would it be a story of how you responded to God and served Him even though you doubted and were afraid? Would it be a story of how you refused to allow any excuse to keep you from living out your purpose and calling from God? I pray that as you read this, you will choose to remove any excuse from your life that keeps you from serving God.

What have you been using as an excuse not to serve God? Are you weak? Perfect. When lives are changed and people are transformed, God will get double glory because of the result and because He used you to bring about the miracle. Are you wounded? Perfect. When God uses a wounded person to heal someone else, not only will He get the glory for the result in the life of the sick, but He will also be glorified when people see how your assistance of others began a healing process in you. Are you untalented? Perfect. God does not need talent. All God needs is willingness, and He takes that willingness and weaves it into a miracle that your family may be talking about for years to come.

Right now I am inviting you to give up your excuses and serve God. Your situation could not be any worse than Gideon's, and your miracle will be no less if you move out and into God's purpose for you. Give up any excuse that keeps you stagnant and self-absorbed, and pick up your life and serve. When you do, you will be astounded at the healing that will come into your life.

COME ALIVE

I am sorry to say that I don't know who Harold Whitman is. He may be Walt Whitman's grandson for all I know, but he was quoted in the July–August 2004 *Relevant* magazine. This quote was sprawled across the page, and I tore it out to save it and share it with you. He said, "Don't ask yourself what the world needs; ask yourself what makes you come alive and then go do that, because the world needs people who have come alive."

When you pick up your life and serve, you find a new life. You come alive in a way you never dreamed. Your eyes sparkle with the delight of having made a difference. Your soul stirs in anticipation of God using you the next time you are in His service. Serving is a choice to heal and come alive. It is the act of getting out of yourself and into others. It is the evidence that you "get it" when it comes to understanding how God works. He does not work because of our strength, but in spite of our weakness. He does not wait until we are strong to help the weak. He takes us in our weaknesses, connects us with other weak people, and does a mighty work to heal them as He continues to heal us.

Have you made every healing choice except for the one choice to serve God? If so, you are not fully aware of what your life can be. You should be excited about that. If you have ever been so dull and dead that you wondered, *Is this all there is?* be encouraged. It is not all there is. This life is not just about how hurt you feel about how badly you have been treated. This life is about how God uses bad people—who feel bad because they have been treated badly—to do good things for Him. All of the previous choices are there to bring you here, a place of service. All the choices are weak and shallow if they do not lead you to this place and motivate you to reach out to others to do what little you can. All He asks is that you give a little to others of what He has given to you.

GIVING BACK

Serving others really is as simple as giving back. God provides you with some money, and He expects you to give some back. Often it is the little that the poor person gives that God uses in a mightier way than the portion that comes from a rich person. It is not just money, however, that God wants us to give back. Surely He wants us to give back some money, but more important, He wants us to give back a portion of our lives.

The ultimate verse that lays out this principle is 2 Corinthians 1:4: "He comforts us in all our troubles so that we can comfort others. When they are troubled, we will be able to give them the same comfort God has given us" (NLT).

Now you might be thinking you have not been given enough comfort yet. You might tell yourself and tell God that you want to serve, but it just does not feel right because you don't feel right. You may tell yourself that until the day you die. I am giving you a personal invitation to throw that excuse away. Take whatever comfort God has given you and use it. If you were abused and you made it through the trauma of being the victim of someone else's sin, use what you learned about survival and recovery to help someone who is having a tougher time than you did. You may not have much insight into it, but there are those that have none. Use what little you have to reach out and help others.

SECRET POWERS

Most of what I have presented is the concept of serving out of weakness or using our own wounds to heal others. It has been about

God not wasting anything, even your hurts and betrayals, if you are willing to serve Him. It has been about getting out of your own self-obsession with your problems and moving into the dynamic life of helping others and comforting others as you have been comforted. It has been about transforming your pain into a new purpose, allowing your misery to develop into a new mission or ministry. It has also been about creating something good out of something evil that Satan wanted to use to destroy us. That kind of service is important, and it should encourage all of us that no matter how weak or broken, God has a place and a purpose for us.

There is another kind of service at the other end of the spectrum. It is not allowing God to take our deficits and defects and turn them into platforms of service; it is taking our strengths and offering them up to God for the good of His kingdom. It has always been fascinating to me that God has put supernatural evidence of Himself into every person. Within every person God has placed some secret powers that give individuals supernatural abilities to do things better and more effectively than others. When you discover it about yourself or even see it in others, it is quite astounding—especially when it is a power you did not know you had or were using.

Just this past month I discovered I had two supernatural abilities I was unaware of. I have been writing about secret powers of God for some time. I helped develop a project for young women to discover those secret powers. So you might think that I would be going through life aware of my strengths and gifts that came directly from God. Here are my latest discoveries, and you might find out you have the same powers.

First is a rather strange and quirky little power that had to be pointed out to me. I have been having meetings at my house for the management team of New Life ministries. When they come over, I have the house looking spotless, flowers in vases on the mantel, and I cook breakfast. Why do I do these things? They just come naturally to me. I want to make people feel welcome and at home. It is a small way of serving the people I love, because as I just discovered, I have the gift of hospitality. It is a secret power that God uses for His service.

I have always been this way. When I had guests spend the night, I went out and purchased a little bedside pitcher for water and placed candies by the side of their bed. When couples have stayed, I have made sure they had candles in the bedroom in case they wanted a little romance during the evening. I have made sure they knew where the fresh towels were and have taken care of the details of their stay so they would feel at home. After doing this for years, three people in the past few months have asked me about or commented on my gift of hospitality.

For a man that might not be the most desired power, strength, or gift. I am glad it is not the only one God has given me, but it is obvious as I look back on my life that I have that gift. It is a gift that people have used in churches to make people feel comfortable in a setting that can be quite challenging. Some use the gift to create homes for the homeless and safe houses for the abused. There are all sorts of ways God uses this simple little gift when it is dedicated to Him. You might be thinking that you have the gift of hospitality. Have you ever used it for God? Have you ever dedicated this secret power and supernatural ability to His service? If not, you can choose to do so right now.

I have used this gift in some small ways to make people more comfortable in my home. I have seen others use it in a grand way to minister to hundreds of thousands of people. Mary Graham, the president of Women of Faith, has used this gift more effectively than anyone I know. I love going over to her house in Frisco. The moment you walk in, you sense and feel all the love you can imagine. It is warm and inviting and just makes you want to stick around for an extra hour or an extra month. If anyone has this gift, it is Mary, and it shows up not only in her home but also in her ministry.

I have watched her make a cold and cavernous sports arena feel like home to thousands of women, because she has this gift. Because of her style and touch and charm, I have watched her use this super-natural power from the platform to make twenty thousand women at a time feel as if she is talking to each one individually. The warmth and hospitality she shows from the stage produce the same feeling when you enter her home. It is nothing short of miraculous how she does it. She does it because she has a supernatural power from God called the gift of hospitality.

If you cannot relate to the gift of hospitality, you are not alone. It is a quirky little gift that a lot of people just do not have, but if you study the Scriptures and examine your life, you will find that you have some other gifts you are not aware of. When I discovered this hospitality gift that had been hidden so long, I wondered if there was another secret power lying hidden inside. I did a little survey of myself that I will ask you to do also. When I did it, I found a gift that I am so grateful God gave me. But sadly, it is a gift I have used too little. I plan to make up for some lost time now that I know I have it.

When I was asked to speak at Promise Keepers in Winnipeg last year and give the altar call, hundreds of men came to the front. They were weeping and confessing and making decisions of surren-der. There were so many that we had to ask pastors to come down to the front and help us. When I spoke again on a Friday night in

Manitoba, the same thing happened. Hundreds of men poured into the aisles, and we had to ask for additional help from pastors again. It was a supernatural outpouring of God's Spirit moving these men to change their lives. He had used me, the least of the least, to be part of it.

Then, a couple of weeks ago, I was the last speaker at one of New Life's conferences. At the end, I asked those who were there to surrender all of their lives or a portion of their lives. In record numbers it seemed that almost everyone got up and came down to the front to make a decision for Christ. They were putting a stake in the ground in Bensalem, Pennsylvania, that their lives would never be the same again.

The pastor of the church came to me and told me how much that moment meant to him. Then my good friend John said something to me. He said that he had gone back to his agency and told them he had attended the conference. He told them he had watched me offer that invitation. His comments were, "It was as powerful as anything I have ever seen Billy Graham do." Now, he was not saying I was as good a preacher as Billy Graham; he was just commenting on the power of the moment when people were asked to respond and they did.

I had just taken Madeline to hear Billy Graham in Los Angeles at one of his last crusades. At the end we watched people fill the field as they decided to change their lives forever. Billy Graham obviously has the gift of evangelism. With John's comment, my experiences in Canada, at New Life, and at the Billy Graham crusade, I realized at the age of fifty-one that I had the gift of evangelism and had rarely used it.

This is not bragging in any way, because this supernatural gift is not something of me. It is not something I worked hard for. It is a supernatural gift from God, and I am so grateful I have it. Discovering it has pushed me deeper into healing, motivating me even more to be all I can be for God. Discovering your gifts and secret powers will do the same for you.

WHAT IS YOUR SECRET POWER?

I have written way too much about my own secret powers. I want you to discover yours. You have one or two that you may or may not be aware of. These gifts are there, ready to be used in service to God. When you use them, you will feel complete and healed. You will feel connected to God, because you realize that unless He put them there, they would never have been developed within you. They are the things you did not have to take a class to understand even though you might have studied to learn how to use them better. They are innate and within the very fabric of who you are. You may have one or two or you may have many, but if you will begin to look for them, you will find them.

Romans 12 is one place we learn about the spiritual gifts that I call secret powers. We learn that some people have a gift to declare God's truth in such a way that people turn from their old ways and start a new life. Some are called to serve others with all of their lives, such as being an assistant to a missionary or building houses for the homeless. You might have the gift of teaching and are able to organize and present your thoughts in such a way that people truly learn God's Word and His principles. You might be an encourager and always seem to have the words that will cheer someone up or point out the best in the worst of situations.

There are those who have the gift of giving. They are so successful and have such a heart for others that they spend much of their time figuring out how to give to others. It is the ultimate fulfilling act of service to them. There is also the gift of mercy that leads a person to help those who have hurt themselves. Without blame and judgment, the person with the gift of mercy sees mistakes as part of life and moves to help those who are in trouble. There are so many gifts and unique combinations of gifts.

Other gifts are outlined in 1 Corinthians 12, such as the gift of giving wise advice and the supernatural ability to know what God would say to a person. There is the gift of speaking in another language and the ability to interpret what was said. Healing is a gift, as well as administration. The gift of discernment is an unusual gift whereby you can see below the surface and make good decisions based on more than what is presented on the surface. When all of these gifts are put into use, the church becomes a dynamic place where lives are transformed and God's kingdom is built. There are other places outside the church that these gifts can be used.

For Dr. Robert del Junco, healing is truly a choice. It is a choice he makes to heal others. He uses his gifts to heal and asks other doctors to come along. Recently he and six other surgeons and eighty hospital staff members worked together to perform surgeries on thirty-one children in Orange County, California, at St. Joseph Hospital. These were children who needed the help but had fallen through the cracks of the health care system. They did not have money or insurance, so Dr. Del Junco organized the healing Saturday just as he had done in Northern California the past three years. He is an example of how our choice to heal may not always just focus on ourselves. We may find the way to get out of ourselves, use what gifts we have been given, and choose to heal others.[1]

SURVEY YOURSELF

Maybe it is time you take a survey of yourself. Perhaps you have felt a nudge here or there that makes you think you could do more or that you should do more. Maybe you have never taken the time to examine your life, and now is the time to do that. If you do, you may come up with some areas of talents, skills, and gifts that could really benefit others. Here is a guide to start you thinking about what you may have that could be used to serve other people:

1. Do you have a talent that is appealing to others, such as not being the world's greatest piano player, but being willing to teach others how to play? Or admitting that you are the world's greatest piano player and teaching others to play?

2. Do you have a strength that stands out? You might be able to account for things, budget better, or even train people to get in shape. Whatever that unique strength is, you can use it to help others develop the same strength.

3. Do you have an interest that is unique? You might be an amateur astronomer, and you could introduce others to the world up and beyond out there.

4. Do you have a personality trait that stands out? You might be a person who is able to listen better than anyone else. You might be someone whom people come to for advice. All you need is a place to volunteer, and you can use your talent to lead others to make good decisions and not give up hope.

5. Is there something you do that is outstanding? Even if it is growing the world's largest pumpkin, that outstanding feat can be used to encourage and teach others.

6. Is there a desire to do something that has stayed with you for years? You might have always wanted to work with inner-city kids, or kids whose parents have died from AIDS. This could mean there is an ability within you that has never been developed or utilized. When you see people doing certain things for others, such as building homes for the homeless, do you react differently than to other charitable acts? Have you wanted to join in, but just did not know how to get involved?

7. Do you have more of something than most people? It could be money, time, patience, or even a collection of valuable things. These could be the result of special skills and talents that you could share with others.

8. Is there an area of your life you feel is wasted? Is there something you can do but you don't feel as if anyone has put it to good use?

9. Is there someone in your life who continues to ask you about getting involved in helping others because you have an expertise or a resource he or she could use?

10. Have you experienced something that would be devastating for others? Have you come through it and have wisdom you could share that would help others go through it better?

All of these could be indicators that you have some special gifts and abilities that could be used to help others, heal others, and heal yourself. All or a few of them may be pointing toward your need to step out and finally use what you have to help others. Ask God to speak to you and give you a nudge toward serving and then the courage to follow up on that nudge and do something about it. If you do nothing else, a phone call to your pastor could set you on the course of serving.

Ask your pastor how you could use what you have to reach out to others. It could bring healing to many people, including you.

MAKING SENSE OF IT ALL

When you look back at your life, it might seem like a fragmented jangle of shattered pieces that are hanging together by a slender thread of your awareness. Other than knowing what happened in your life, you might find it difficult to make any sense of it. You see the pain and heartache and still feel the sting to some degree. You lived through the difficulties that others caused for you or that you caused yourself. You even know the gifts and strengths that you have, but when you look back, it makes no sense to you. There is no reason for it all. You lack a unifying understanding of why all these unrelated pieces are hanging together in your life. If so, the choice to serve may be the choice that puts it all together for you.

We wander through this world with our collection of strengths and weaknesses, doing the best we can to survive. It all seems so meaningless unless we have committed it to God for His use. When we commit our lives for service, we take everything we have and begin to use it for something far greater than our own little lives. Then it makes sense. Then we see God's hand in it and take His hand and allow Him to lead us into a life of purpose.

It is the selfless life and the other-centered perspective that brings it all together. Romans 15:2 reminds us that we are called to serve others: "Each one of us needs to look after the good of the people around us, asking ourselves, 'How can I help?'" (MSG). You are not truly healed until you are using what you have to heal others.

Alcoholics Anonymous has focused on this from the very beginning.

AA takes a self-obsessed drunk, who is only interested in the next drink or the next moment of relief, and assists in the total transformation of that person. The transformation of a person who thinks nothing of lying and covering up, into a person who just wants to do the next right thing and live in honest humility, is a complete and miraculous transformation. It does not end there, however. The transformation is only complete when the recovering alcoholic is moving through the twelfth step and carrying the message to others. No one in AA would take that step unless he felt he had experienced something worth sharing and had desire to use his own plight to relieve the heartache of another.

The same is true for all of us who have been saved by the sacrifice of Jesus Christ. After trying so hard to be good enough, we find great comfort in knowing that we don't have to, because Jesus has paid the price. We have eternal, life-saving knowledge that is worth sharing. We serve others when we respond to the Great Commission that Christ gave us to share the truth with others all over this world. If we truly understand the gift that has been given, we will want to serve by sharing it.

You have life-changing knowledge that may change others if you will enter into the humble service of sharing it with them. It may be the discovery of how to survive a divorce. You may have even discovered how to keep a marriage together because yours fell apart. You may have learned how to forgive yourself after a life of bungling mistakes. There may be a supernatural gift that you have learned to use in a unique way. You might have discovered how to emerge from fear to courage, or from anger to forgiveness. If you have a pulse, there is something you have experienced or learned that would benefit another if you choose to share your life through serving.

The serving life is the best life. It is the life God has called you to live. It is the life Christ modeled while here on earth. Do not let this world keep marching on while you sit in a lounge chair, killing time and destroying your opportunity to truly live. Right now you can begin to find that life by making the choice to serve. Tell God that on this day it all changes. Commit that you will use what you have to reach out to others, and then find a place where God can use you. If you don't have a great idea about how to serve, use someone else's idea.

I often go to Saddleback Church, pastored by Rick Warren, and am amazed at the ministries of service that have started out of that church. If someone approaches Rick and says there is a need for single moms to have an oil change and car repair, Rick encourages that person to start the ministry. One man decided that there were many years of wear remaining on most discarded tennis shoes, so he started collecting them and taking them to Mexico to give to those who had no shoes. Ministries to the homeless, elderly, men, women, and special-needs kids have all emerged from an attitude of "share your life by serving others."

THE BIG LIE
"Until I am completely healed and strong, there is no place for me to serve God."

When I was working in alcohol and drug treatment centers, it was a frequent occurrence for some folks to be completely hopeless one month and then to feel so good that they knew they were called to be an alcohol and drug counselor. Rather than work on their own healing, they got involved prematurely with others. They didn't know that what they were doing was harmful and a way of not looking at their own stuff. Some were so serious about it that they quit their jobs and started training before the dust had settled on their drinking or drugging. Their counseling usually did not last long. They often relapsed back into their addiction, because they started working on others and stopped working on themselves. No one should get involved in helping others too soon.

By the same token, no one should wait too long to help others either. So rather than attempting to become an instant alcohol abuse counselor, you could help by going to a meeting early and making the coffee. You might not be ready to help other cancer survivors, but you could put up posters that notify others of the next meeting. You might not be able to get out of bed to drive someone to a doctor's appointment, but you could call to encourage that person. Helping too early produces an unhealthy focus on others and takes it off of you, but waiting to choose to serve may prevent you from experiencing the final stages of healing.

Satan is your enemy, and he does not want you to heal. He certainly does not want you going around helping build the kingdom of the God he rebelled against. He will trap you in the lie that you are not ready. If he has his way, you will never be ready and you will never feel ready and you will never do anything helpful or unselfish with your life. He will get you to believe the big lie: "Until I am completely healed and strong, there is no place for me to serve God."

He will add some little lies to that big lie as well. He will get you to believe that you don't have anything to give anyway. If you believe your gifts and talents are not strong enough or good enough, then Satan has you right where he wants you. If you think the mistakes you made disqualify you from helping others who have made them or from helping with the prevention of those same mistakes, then your stagnant life will glorify Satan.

Do not listen to the lies that rob you of your life. Make the healing choice to reach out and discover how God can use you to serve other people.

SERVING CHRIST HIMSELF

In the twenty-fifth chapter of Matthew is a fascinating passage that expresses the heart of God when it comes to the issue of service and using what we have to do the best we can do. If you read the entire chapter, you plainly see that God expects those who have been given a lot of talents to use them. God also expects those who don't have many to use what they have. He expects us to use what we have in the best way possible. Christ laid out the importance of what we do and the hidden meaning behind our acts of service:

> But when the Son of Man comes in His glory, and all the angels with Him, then He will sit on His glorious throne. And all the nations will be gathered before Him; and He will separate them from one another, as the shepherd separates the sheep from the goats; and He will put the sheep on His right, and the goats on the left. Then the King will say to those on His right, "Come, you who are blessed of My Father, inherit the kingdom prepared for you from the foundation of the world. For I was hungry, and you gave Me something to eat; I was thirsty, and you gave Me drink; I was a stranger, and you invited Me in; naked, and you clothed Me; I was sick, and you visited Me; I was in prison, and you came to Me."
>
> Then the righteous will answer Him, saying, "Lord, when did we

see You hungry, and feed You, or thirsty, and give You drink? And when did we see You a stranger, and invite You in, or naked, and clothe You? And when did we see You sick, or in prison, and come to You?"

And the King will answer and say to them, "Truly I say to you, to the extent that you did it to one of these brothers of Mine, even the least of them, you did it to Me."

Then He will also say to those on His left, "Depart from Me, accursed ones, into the eternal fire which has been prepared for the devil and his angels; for I was hungry, and you gave Me nothing to eat; I was thirsty, and you gave Me nothing to drink; I was a stranger, and you did not invite Me in; naked, and you did not clothe Me; sick, and in prison, and you did not visit Me."

Then they themselves also will answer, saying, "Lord, when did we see You hungry, or thirsty, or a stranger, or naked, or sick, or in prison, and did not take care of You?"

Then He will answer them, saying, "Truly I say to you, to the extent that you did not do it to one of the least of these, you did not do it to Me."

And these will go away into eternal punishment, but the righteous into eternal life. (Matthew 25:31–46 NASB)

I think it is really clear that we need to be in the flock of sheep at the end of this passage, rather than in a herd of goats. Our acts of service mean something to Christ. When we truly appreciate His humble gift of life, we are compelled to humbly go out and serve others. When we get out of our lives and share our lives, we are serving Christ. When we meet the need of a struggling stranger who does not count by most standards of this world, we are actually serving

Christ. To withhold your life from others and not serve others is essentially the same as refusing to give Christ a cup of water as He dragged His cross up Golgotha to die for you.

Healing is a choice. It is God's choice. But we can stand in the way of healing if we don't use what we have to serve others. God calls us to serve. He delivers deeper healing into our souls when we get out of the way and move toward others in humble service. He wants our lives to be inconvenienced for others. He wants our days to be cluttered with untidy people who could use our gifts. He wants us to go without so others can have. God is interested in our sharing our lives in humble service. When we do, we discover what we are here for. We find fulfillment when we live out that calling and purpose.

CHAPTER 9 WORKBOOK QUESTIONS

THE NINTH CHOICE:
The Choice to Serve

THE NINTH BIG LIE:
"Until I am completely healed and strong, there is no place for me to serve God."

He appeared at the door of the plane, saluted smartly, and then made his way carefully down the steep steps. Stopping in front of the microphone, his rugged face haggard yet calm, he said, "We are honored to have served our country under difficult circumstances." America watched, moved by the sight of this man just released from years of captivity in North Vietnam as he expressed his gratitude and ended unforgettably with, "God bless America!"

The man was Captain Jeremiah Denton. The date was February 11, 1973.

Those words, "We are honored . . . ," have clung hauntingly to my mind down through the years. They were underscored in February ten years later, when the film clip was again aired on national television accompanied in person by Jeremiah Denton, then a US senator.

All this is a prelude to one thought: Is this how the believer will feel when he stands one day before God? Liberated from this earth and its struggles, will we say, "We are honored to have served . . . under difficult circumstances"?[2]

Have you had an opportunity to say that? Has there been a time in your life when you were able to serve God, even under difficult circumstances? Or are you still waiting for an opportunity?

THE NINTH CHOICE:
The Choice to Serve

Judges 6 records the story of God offering Gideon the opportunity for meaningful service:

> Then the angel of the LORD came and sat beneath the oak tree at Ophrah, which belonged to Joash of the clan of Abiezer. Gideon son of Joash had been threshing wheat at the bottom of a winepress to hide the grain from the Midianites. The angel of the LORD appeared to him and said, "Mighty hero, the LORD is with you!"
>
> "Sir," Gideon replied, "if the LORD is with us, why has all this happened to us? And where are all the miracles our ancestors told us about? Didn't they say, 'The LORD brought us up out of Egypt'? But now the LORD has abandoned us and handed us over to the Midianites."
>
> Then the LORD turned to him and said, "Go with the strength you have and rescue Israel from the Midianites. I am sending you!"
>
> "But Lord," Gideon replied, "how can I rescue Israel? My clan is the weakest in the whole tribe of Manasseh, and I am the least in my entire family!"

The LORD said to him, "I will be with you. And you will destroy the Midianites as if you were fighting against one man." (vv. 11–16 NLT)

Gideon was skeptical, a tough sell! He had heard many accounts of the wonderful things God had done for Israel in the past, but he had not seen anything like that in his lifetime. Further, he pointed out that his tribe, Manasseh, was the weakest clan in Israel, and among them, he was the weakest person.

Gideon felt insecure and unprepared, the weakest member of a weak family. He was the most unlikely candidate to be commander in chief of the Israeli army. However, it didn't matter, because God was with him and Gideon did lead Israel to victory against the Midianites.

Just as God was with Gideon, He is with us. You may not feel qualified. Neither did Gideon. You may feel weak and inadequate. So did Gideon. You may feel you have no apparent skills or qualifications. That's just how Gideon felt. You might say to yourself, *I am not wise. I don't know where or how to begin.* Listen to what God says to that:

This foolish plan of God is wiser than the wisest of human plans, and God's weakness is stronger than the greatest of human strength.

Remember, dear brothers and sisters, that few of you were wise in the world's eyes or powerful or wealthy when God called you. Instead, God chose things the world considers foolish in order to shame those who think they are wise. And he chose things that are powerless to shame those who are powerful. God chose things despised by the world, things counted as nothing at all, and used them to bring to nothing what the world considers important. As a result, no one can ever boast in the presence of God.

God has united you with Christ Jesus. For our benefit God made him to be wisdom itself. Christ made us right with God; he made us pure and holy, and he freed us from sin. Therefore, as the Scriptures say, "If you want to boast, boast only about the LORD." (1 Corinthians 1:25–31 NLT)

GOD IS CALLING YOU INTO SERVICE

The person who feels most inadequate and unprepared is often the one God uses. That teaching is prominent throughout Scripture, yet people will argue every day that they are not capable, worthy, or prepared to serve the kingdom of God. Who is right, God or us? God is right, of course! His track record proves it! He consistently chooses the least likely people to do the most incredible things. The good news is that you can be one of them!

We should not resist God's call into service. Rather, we should be thrilled that He has chosen to use us. In fact, Romans 12:1–2 infers that God would love for us to volunteer rather than wait to be drafted:

And so, dear brothers and sisters, I plead with you to give your bodies to God because of all he has done for you. Let them be a living and holy sacrifice—the kind he will find acceptable. This is truly the way to worship him. Don't copy the behavior and customs of this world, but let God transform you into a new person by changing the way you think. Then you will learn to know God's will for you, which is good and pleasing and perfect. (NLT)

Our daily prayer should be, Lord, how may I serve You?

Exercise #1: *What's Your Excuse?*

1. **What prevents you from serving God? Circle any of the things listed below that keep you from serving. Use the lines at the end of the list to write in things not listed.**

Family demands	Work responsibilities	Financial concerns
Feel unworthy	Illness / health	Feel inadequate
Don't know people	Don't know what to do	No available time
Too shy to volunteer	Embarrassed	Not talented
Not spiritual enough	Not connected to church	No commitment

_____

_____

_____

_____

2. **List the five most serious objections from your list on the left line below.**

3. **In the spaces to the right, list three ways you can overcome your objections.**

#1 _____   _____

   _____

#2 _____   _____

   _____

#3 _____   _____

   _____

   _____

#4 _____   _____

_____

_____

#5 _____   _____

_____

_____

4. **Having completed the exercise, ask this important question: Is there a good reason not to offer yourself for service in God's work? Are you holding on to excuses to keep from serving?**

The decision to serve is not so much about your feelings (i.e., "Do you feel like serving or not?"). Rather, it is a very objective decision. This may sound irreligious, but the decision to serve God does not require hours of prayer. Why? The answer is simple. Scripture is very forthright about the expectation of serving. Paul reminds us that God created us to serve, specifically to do the good things He planned for us before we were born. Our prayers should be directed toward where, when, and how we will serve, but never *if* we will serve.

"God saved you by his grace when you believed. And you can't take credit for this; it is a gift from God. Salvation is not a reward for the good things we have done, so none of us can boast about it. For we are God's masterpiece. He has created us anew in Christ Jesus, so that we can do the good things he planned for us long ago" (Ephesians 2:8–10 NLT).

I hope these exercises have made an impact on you. Serving is not an option. It is an integral part of a believer's life, as much a part of our lives as the blood that flows through our veins. Serving is not a choice to be made. Rather, it is a manifestation of what it means to be alive.

Jesus said, "For even the Son of Man came not to be served but to serve others, and to give his life as a ransom for many" (Mark 10:45 NLT).

Jesus came to serve, and we are supposed to be like Him, so we must serve!

COME ALIVE

When you make the decision to serve, you experience a brand-new way of life. You come alive as never before. One of the most important benefits of serving is that your life suddenly has meaning. In serving, you develop a sense of purpose, a reason for being. As a result, you feel purposeful and motivated. It excites your life!

Typically, when people join a foreign or home mission trip, they change. Perhaps they've built a church or a school. Maybe they've helped run a medical clinic. Whatever the mission, the payoff comes at the end as team members reflect in awe and say things like, "Did I really help do this?" "What a miracle!" or "I would never have imagined I could be part of something like this!" The feeling of having accomplished something remarkable for others is overwhelming.

Richard Foster expressed that feeling in his book *Celebration of Discipline*. He wrote, "When we set out on a consciously chosen course of action that accents the good of others and is for the most part a hidden work, a deep change occurs in our spirit."[3]

When people give themselves in service to the kingdom of God, they acquire a deep sense of knowing they are doing exactly what Jesus asked them to do. They find themselves in the very center of

God's will. In that moment of realization, they discover who they have truly become.

Like Jesus, we are on this planet not to be served but to pour our lives out in service to others.

Exercise #2: Giving Back

The healing choice to serve is one of the most impacting decisions you will ever make. The previous healing choices you've made all combine for this moment when you give yourself back to others, so that they also can make healing choices.

1. The notion of giving back is based on the premise that God has blessed us, so that we can become conduits through whom He can bless others.

(a) To reinforce this point, do the following exercise.

(b) Read the two passages below. After each, paraphrase the verse using your own words and thoughts.

"He comforts us in all our troubles so that we can comfort others. When they are troubled, we will be able to give them the same comfort God has given us" (2 Corinthians 1:4 NLT).

_____

_____

_____

384

"When someone has been given much, much will be required in return; and when someone has been entrusted with much, even more will be required" (Luke 12:48 NLT).

---

2. In your own words, and as fully as you can, describe what the previous texts mean to you.

Here is an important caveat. It may be that you do not feel sufficiently healed to be serving. You may be thinking, *I'm not ready yet*, or *I'm still battling with choices I need to make or lies I need to overcome*. Be very careful. You could hold on to that argument forever and never make any progress.

The fact is that we all are in process. We can serve, though we are still wounded.

Henri Nouwen wrote a book titled *The Wounded Healer*.[4] His premise was that we all could help one another in the healing process, just as we are, wounded and broken. Nouwen said that in order to help those who are suffering, the helper must first recognize his own pain. It is the servant's personal pain that allows him or her to empathize with other needy people to genuinely help them heal.

If you had no pain of your own, how could you understand the pain of others?

Remember that the chapter 8 workbook questions introduced us to the Latin word *praxis*. Praxis teaches us that the meaning of things comes in the doing of them.

It is as you are serving that you become a servant. You don't have to be ever preparing to become a servant. If that were true, most of us would never serve. You can serve as a wounded person who becomes a wounded healer! Gideon overcame his weaknesses. So can you.

Remember the truth in the previous exercise. God comforts us in our troubles so that we can comfort others. Healing is a choice.

The decision to begin serving, even while working through personal issues and struggles, is a healing choice. Yes, you may still be working through pain and grief. You may be working hard to investigate your life and make corrections. You may be experiencing redemption for the first time or working very hard on forgiveness.

Here is an interesting irony. The fact that you are still struggling with issues does not disqualify you from service. Rather, it empowers you. You can draw from the help God's Holy Spirit is giving you in order to help others.

If you were abused or hurt and have begun to recover from those scars, you can use what you have learned about surviving and overcoming to help others. You can empathize with their pain. You know what they are thinking and how it impacts their lives.

Be encouraged! Jump into the healing struggle. Take what is a noble title and use it; you can be a wounded healer as you serve others.

GOD GIVES YOU SECRET POWER

We have been discussing the fact that God wants you to serve, even though you may still feel wounded and inadequate. We reinforced the idea that He can use you when you are still struggling and wounded. You can be a wounded healer.

However, you might wonder where the strength comes from to serve, even while you are still struggling with issues and pain.

The answer is what *Healing Is a Choice* calls "secret powers." Secret powers are supernatural strengths and gifts that God's Holy Spirit gives us to help us serve. God gives gifts to all His children. He personally selects the gifts you receive.

Scripture teaches us that the Holy Spirit disburses a variety of spiritual gifts among believers. Most relevant to our discussion are two categories of gifts mentioned in 1 Corinthians 12:4, 9. Paul wrote that there are "different kinds of service" and "gifts of healing."

Clearly God gives us the ability to serve, and in a wide variety of venues and opportunities. In a sense, He individualizes our service. By creating so many service opportunities in the world, we can move toward those that best suit our gifts, talents, and skills. So serving God can occur in a limitless way. Wherever people need help, believers can respond.

In addition, God gives "gifts of healing." Aren't you glad? Isn't it encouraging to know that healing is available from the Great Physician?

Here are two important truths to understand. First, the fact that God gives "gifts of healing" implies that there is much sickness and pain in the world. We wouldn't need healing if everyone was well.

Second, Scripture teaches that God's response to illness and pain is to give us a wide variety of healing options.

At times, we may need medical science to help us heal. God gives doctors and nurses great knowledge and skill to perform their tasks. He gives physicians some of His "gifts of healing."

At other times, we don't need doctors or medication as much as we need love and support. In those situations, God gives other "gifts of healings" that are expressed in human kindness and understanding, support and encouragement.

Spiritual gifts come from God, thus they are, indeed, secret powers. Human beings don't always know how God's gifts of healing work, but there are people who benefit from them every day.

WHAT IS YOUR SECRET POWER?

Healing Is a Choice offers ten guiding questions to get you started on the path toward discovering your secret powers. Answering the survey questions will point you in the direction of your spiritual gifts. This exercise asks you to do three things. It will take a while and require some Bible study. Please take time to complete the exercise. What you will discover about yourself may change your life forever and ignite your service with the Holy Spirit's power. Before you start, offer this prayer:

Father of all good gifts, thank You for guiding me to this exercise.
I realize Your Holy Spirit is speaking to me through this process, so
I open my heart and mind to hear. As I read and think and make
discoveries in the next few minutes, make Your will clear to me. I
know I am not perfect, but I am in the process of growing, thanks to
You. I truly want to be a faithful servant, so please speak to me in this
exercise. My life belongs to You, Lord. Use it as You have planned.
Trusting Christ, who orders my steps, amen.

1. Familiarize yourself with biblical texts related to spiritual gifts by reading the passages listed. After each passage, list the spiritual gifts mentioned in the passage. Note gifts that are mentioned more than once.

(a) Romans 12:1–8

(b) Ephesians 4:11–13

(c) 1 Peter 4:9–11

(d) 1 Corinthians 12:7–10

2. Read the passages listed below. In the space provided, describe in your own words how they relate to spiritual gifts.

(a) 1 Corinthians 12:4–6

(b) 1 Corinthians 12:11

3. What is the purpose of spiritual gifts? To answer this question, refer to the passages listed below. Then describe the stated purpose of spiritual gifts mentioned in each text.

(a) Romans 12:5

_____

(b) 1 Corinthians 12:7

_____

(c) 1 Corinthians 12:18

_____

(d) 1 Corinthians 12:20–27

_____

(e) 1 Peter 4:10

_____

4. Respond to each of the ten questions mentioned in chapter 9 under the heading "Survey Yourself" (pp. 368–69). Use a piece of paper to record your responses, or write them in the margin next to each question.

5. When you have completed the exercise, take a few minutes to think about what you have read and studied. Think about the ten questions you answered. Based on that, write the spiritual gifts you believe you have in the spaces below.

_____

_____

_____

6. There are four ways in which you can test your results.

(a) Ask a close Christian friend to respond to your gifts. Do they see those gifts in you? Can they confirm that the gift is working in you?

(b) Schedule an appointment with your pastor. Explain the process you've been through as you've explored spiritual gifts. Ask him to confirm that the gifts identified are working in you.

(c) Is it clear to you that the gifts you identified are being expressed in your life?

(d) Spend time in focused prayer, asking God either to confirm the gifts you've identified or to lead you to the correct ones.

This important exercise will get you started on the road to identifying your gifts.

Being aware of your gifts is crucial as you serve, because the gifts given to you by the Holy Spirit are the ones God wants you to use as you serve. You may be surprised to discover that as you serve others, you are experiencing more healing in your own life.

Healing Is a Choice reminds us that making decisions to help others also heals us. The powerful choice to serve does a remarkable thing. It immediately changes your focus. Alone and unconnected to people, we become self-absorbed quickly. Our problems are always on our minds. Our focus on pain makes it more acute. Our loneliness makes us sour and selfish. Thus, our illness becomes worse.

However, the moment we make a healing choice to serve, our entire perspective changes from ourselves to others. Connected to people, we feel less alone. Our problems diminish as we focus on the trouble others are enduring. We feel less personal pain as we focus on relieving the pain of others. Our loneliness diminishes as we encourage and make ourselves available to others. Thus, our pain improves.

When you serve, you bring far more to the effort than you realize. You have your experience. You have the wisdom you have gained as you walked through your own struggles. You have solutions you learned in the school of hard knocks that others have not yet experienced. You have victories, great and small, that others are desperately hoping to experience. Will you help those who need you? Will you offer yourself in service? You may be the only person some people will hear. Yours may be the only perspective they see as related to them. You may be their only help!

The Ninth Big Lie:
"Until I am completely healed and strong, there is no place for me to serve God."

Scripture makes it very plain that God uses broken and damaged people before they are healed. In fact, Scripture assumes our brokenness and struggles. To some extent we are all strugglers in this world, experiencing failures more than we'd prefer.

Actually, Scripture is filled with examples of God's good people who experienced huge failures. For example, Cain murdered his brother. Rebekah and Jacob conspired against Isaac and Esau to swindle an inheritance. Moses smote the rock. Eli was a terrible father whose children brought a reproach on the nation. Saul turned into a ruthless despot. David lied to God on three separate occasions.

Those lies were so serious that the entire nation of Israel suffered thousands of deaths as a consequence.

Many of Israel's kings led the people into idolatry more than toward God. Prophets sometimes prophesied contrary to God's will, because they were afraid for their lives. Elijah endured a deep, dark depression, because the queen had threatened his life. When God called Jonah to go to Nineveh, the prophet went in exactly the opposite direction. Even after he finally did what God called him to do, he griped and complained.

Peter betrayed Christ. John Mark was such a problem for Barnabas that he was sent home. These are just a few examples.

The Bible is clear about the failures of its characters. It does not withhold the truth.

The irony is that many of the "failures" mentioned above were powerfully used by God to do great things. These were people filled with human foibles, yet God used them. Few of them were completely perfect or healed of their problems when God used them.

The ninth lie is particularly dangerous, because it holds out an impossible expectation and forever leaves people under God's judgment rather than His grace.

Let me explain. The impossible expectation is that I can be completely healed and strong.

It will never happen. As long as we are encumbered in human flesh, we will be susceptible to failure, defeat, illness, and human problems. As long as we are human beings, we will struggle with our pain, disconnectedness, fear of investigating our lives, and unwillingness to serve.

The good news is, God uses fallible humans. It is fortunate that He doesn't use just "completely healed and strong" people, because there would not be any at His disposal. We can be thankful He uses people like us.

The ninth lie holds people under God's judgment because it says, "There is no place for me to serve God." Please understand that God is not placing these folks under His judgment. No, it's the people who have placed themselves under His judgment. God has not condemned them. They have condemned themselves ("There is no place for *me* to serve . . ."). The individual has decided he or she cannot serve.

This lie is particularly destructive. It kills hope. It alienates people from God. If we tolerate this dangerous lie, we function in outright contradiction to the will of God.

Here is the good news. You can serve God now, with your faults, failures, weaknesses, pains, and problems. Despite all that and more, God can use you. He takes broken people and enables them to do great things. He takes people's pain and turns it into a positive, productive force.

As *Healing Is a Choice* reminds us, there is a time to serve. No one should serve before he or she is able. If you are deeply addicted and have relapsed repeatedly, it might not be the time to serve.

On the other hand, no one should wait too long to serve. As soon as you feel some ego-strength, do something for God's sake. You may not be ready to teach Sunday school, but you could mow the church lawn or drive someone to a doctor's appointment.

Serving is a path to healing, so the longer we put off serving, the slower we will heal.

Matthew 25 teaches us that God expects people to use their talents and abilities for His sake. Those who have more talents and abilities have more responsibility. Those with fewer talents must use what they have. Our acts of service mean something important to Christ. They must also mean something important to us.

When we share our lives with others, we are serving Jesus Christ. As a result, when we serve others, God provides more healing for our growth and development, so that we can serve more people, and receive more healing, and serve more until He comes!

JOURNALING

What is the degree and quality of my service for Christ? Am I serving? Is my life making a difference for Jesus' sake? Do I know what my spiritual gifts are? Am I cultivating them for God's purposes on earth? Do I want to be useful in the kingdom of God? These are guiding questions as you begin journaling in response to chapter 9. Take some time to think about the questions and record your thoughts below.

PRAYERFUL MEDITATION

"I have given you an example to follow. Do as I have done to you. I tell you the truth, slaves are not greater than their master. Nor is the messenger more important than the one who sends the message. Now that you know these things, God will bless you for doing them" (John 13:15–17 NLT).

Think about this text. Are you following Jesus' example of servanthood? Is there any reason why you are not? If so, pray about it. Jesus didn't leave us any choice in the matter. He emphatically called us to serve. Therefore, we must get ourselves into the service mode, active and impacting. At the end of the passage, Jesus said, "God will bless you for doing them." The Greek word for blessed, *makarios*, roughly means deep spiritual meaning and fulfillment. Isn't that what we all crave? It can be ours if we will serve.

Clearly, the road to deep meaning and spiritual fulfillment is serving.

PRAYER

Merciful, loving Father, I confess my reluctance to serve. Often, I'm consumed with my own needs and desires. I'm battling my own pain and failures. It's hard for me to believe I can serve anyone in a way that would help him or her. However, I do believe that through Your power and guidance, I can do all things. But I need Your help so much! I don't know where to begin or what to do. Please direct me in the right direction. Today, in this moment of prayer, I give my life to You as a humble servant. Order my steps and guide my efforts. Take me to the people and places where I am most needed. I'm not sure where all this is going, but I absolutely trust You to be with me. Through Christ, my strength, amen.

IO

THE TENTH CHOICE:
The Choice to Persevere

THE TENTH BIG LIE:
"There is no hope for me."

WHEN HEALING IS DELAYED

HEALING IS GOD'S CHOICE AS WELL AS THE TIMING OF THAT choice and the method of the healing. When we are struggling with something or have some major defect or disease, we want God to choose "now" as the timing and "instant and easy" as the method. It is only natural and human to want to be healed right now. We want it not only to relieve whatever it is that is hurting us, but also to have proof that we are special in the eyes of God. We would know beyond a shadow of a doubt He loves us, cares for us, and is intimately involved in our lives if He healed us. The instant type of healing does not come often, however, and when it does it is called a miracle. If it happened frequently, it would not be called a miracle. It would be called an everyday occurrence. We all want an instant miracle, and we don't ever need to feel badly about asking for one.

The reality for many who have physical deformities, birth defects, and serious diseases is that their healing is not going to be instant. Most likely their healing is going to have to wait until heaven. If it comes before that, it will truly be a miracle. If you are in one of those situations, hope in God and pray for the physical healing. As you pray, be aware that God has chosen not to intervene in history and perform many miracles. He still does it, but not often, so pray for the miracle, but be realistic about your expectations or you will be disappointed with all of your life rather than finding areas where you can be grateful.

I spoke with a lady who had been blind most of her life. She had prayed and prayed for years that God would choose to perform a miracle and restore her sight; those who loved her had prayed the same prayer. Then one Sunday in church, everything changed; the lights began to come back on, and her sight started coming back. By evening she could see again. The blind woman could not see on Sunday, and by Thursday of the same week she had a driver's license.

That was a miracle, but we don't know what kind of miracle it was. It could have been God's direct intervention or it could have been the result of a natural healing process that had been going on for years. It could have even been an accidental bump of the head that jarred a nerve or light receptor, or a hormonal change and an altered body chemistry that changed her sight. Whatever the method, the result was a miracle.

I don't know why God chooses a miraculous healing for someone like her and does not choose it for someone like you. You may be like me and have had to work through the feelings of abandonment when your miracle did not come. I wanted my marriage to experience a miraculous transformation. I have talked to hundreds of couples who are living happily ever after because of a major breakthrough and a supernatural restoration. I wanted that for us. I wanted it but did not just sit around and hope God would deliver it. I was in counseling for myself, I was in support groups with other men, and we were in marriage counseling. The miracle never came.

I don't know why God chooses a miraculous healing for someone like her and does not choose it for someone like you. You may be like me and have had to work through the feelings of abandonment when your miracle did not come.

THE MIRACLE OF THE SOUL

Many of us are left with broken bodies, broken relationships, and broken futures. We pray and pray and nothing changes to indicate that God is doing a work. And in the struggle and the pain, God asks us to not give up and to persevere no matter what. That was the path that James Hall took when at age forty his life took a sudden dark turn.

James was diagnosed with diabetes, asthma, and high blood pressure. He was the picture of poor and deteriorating health. As things got worse for him, he suffered a head injury that left him with a vision disorder. If that was not bad enough, his immune system developed a deficiency that caused repeated viral and bacterial infections that left him with constant illnesses. He stayed so ill that he could not drive or work. Just about everything in his life changed for the worse.

As James tells the story, he talks of some friends who were encouraging to him. They hoped for the best and prayed for the best but were prepared for the worse. He also had some friends who were very unhealthy for him and produced much discouragement. They said things like:

- "You are worse than an infidel because you can't work." (I find it amazing that James would call anyone who would say something like that a friend. Friends don't talk to sick people that way. Nor do those who are living and walking in the Spirit.)
- "You have major unconfessed sin." (Even though Scripture is very specific about this not always being the case, it is often thrown at people. When Jesus was confronted with a blind man and asked whose sin caused the blindness, Jesus was very clear that the blindness was not the result of anyone's sin [John 9:1–3]. The blindness was there so that the world could see what a powerful God could do with blindness.)

James's "friends" reprimanded him for not repeating enough Scripture out loud and not doing all the other formulaic procedures that are supposed to produce instant healing. They were nothing but hurtful and caused James's struggle to be much more difficult than it needed to be. Because of their harshness, the healing that did take place in James was much deeper and purer. The healing that he experienced was not in his body but in his soul.

After years of the struggle, never giving up, always looking for one more day, James said, "I have learned that God is always faithful and willing to help even in the darkest hours." I know that what is true for James is true for you and me. God is always faithful, and no matter how difficult the circumstance, He wants us to hang on one more day and persevere through the pain, no matter what.

JUST ONE MORE DAY

Today I was in Bensalem, Pennsylvania, speaking with Dr. Henry Cloud, Dr. John Townsend, and Dr. Jill Hubbard. We were part of a very moving conference with many people making commitments to change their lives and surrender parts of their lives that they had previously refused to give up. At the close of our time, hundreds of people walked down the aisles to place a symbolic stake in the ground that this was going to be the beginning of a new life for them. I was in tears as I watched people make a healing choice to get up out of their seats and make a public statement that their lives would never be the same again. For many it was the beginning of a new life.

When it was over, a line of people formed to speak with me. There were very moving stories and expressions of gratitude. I was so glad my flight allowed me to stay and connect with the people.

One lady came up with her boyfriend to speak with me. They seemed to be a happily connected couple interested in the same things, and many of those things were spiritual. She told me that she had once reached a point in her life where she no longer felt she could go on. She was depressed and alone and felt she could not endure the misery any longer. She placed a bottle of pills up to her mouth, but before she downed them she turned on her radio one last time. Our show was being broadcast, and she heard me give out our phone number, asking people to call if they needed help. Hearing the number, she felt it was a divine intervention, put down the pills, picked up the phone, and made the call.

The phone counselor who answered was loving and kind and had the right words for the despair she was feeling. She asked her not to kill herself on that night. She asked her to hold on for one more day to see what that day might bring. This woman knew she could not make it through the night and allowed the counselor to call for help. The counselor actually had someone else call for help while she stayed on the line until help arrived. The woman was admitted to a local hospital, was put on medication, and is alive today because she just held on one more day. That is what perseverance is—it is holding on for just one more day.

THE TOUGHEST CHOICE

You may be at the end of your rope. You may have been living in a deep, dark cavern of hopelessness with no apparent way out. The future may seem to be an impossible place to reach, but all you have to do to get there is to make one final choice—the choice to persevere. You may be ready to give up because you have attempted every other choice, but nothing has changed. You may be lifeless and stagnant because you seem to be the exception to every rule. What other people try just does not seem to work for you. You thought you were connected and feeling and grieving, but you are still in the middle of your stuck life. If there is a new life for you, you are not able to find it. If that is you, you have one more choice to make and that is the choice to persevere.

Holding on is never pleasant, but it protects you from a messy, premature end that flings turmoil all over everyone who felt they were close to you. There are some very important reasons to hold on when you don't feel that you can. The most important reason is that God loves you greatly and wants the very best possible for you.

You are a valuable person to Him, and He wants you to persevere. To God, one day is worth a thousand years. Think about that. The Creator of infinite time, who has all the time in the world, values every minute of time you continue to live.

Sometimes we think so small; we think in terms of what is before us on this earth. We can only understand the tangible, but there are some intangible dimensions of time that we are not aware of. Somehow the impact of one person remaining alive for one more day has an eternal value that equals one thousand years. I don't know how that works, but I believe it, because God's Word says it.

By the same token, if you end your life too soon, one day can have the impact of one thousand negative and destructive years. There are many things we do not understand perfectly, and time is one of them. It is a complex dimension that we must never underestimate. You have a final decision to make: the decision to hold on and not do the easy thing of ending your life. Today must not be the day when you give up on the time that has been allotted you. In the midst of despair and hopelessness, you can decide to give your life one more day.

You can make this decision that will prevent your time from being ended prematurely. You can make this final decision that just may be the first decision that will heal your life. Whether it is the first or the final decision, it is certainly the toughest one, because it is made at the greatest point of hopelessness. Make it, right now, no matter how tough it is.

THE VALUE OF LIFE

Another reason to hang on is the high value God places on all of life, especially your life. You have been fearfully and wonderfully made, according to Psalm 139:14 (NIV). Your life is full of wonder and meaning and value placed there by God. Any feeling otherwise is implanted in you by the evil one. John 10:10 clearly lays out what Satan has done to you and what Christ wants to do for you: "The thief comes only to steal, and kill, and destroy; I came that they may have life, and might have it abundantly" (NASB). I read this to mean:

You are feeling very badly about your life and all that has happened to you and all of the trouble you are in right now, because Satan wanted you to feel that way. Satan wanted to rob you of your hope and everything else he can steal from you. The reason you would like to end it all is because he wants to kill you and destroy you. Satan wants to steal from you the life God has given you. It is no wonder you want to die, because there is such a powerful enemy of yours and God's that would like for you to die, right now, and if you did, there would be rejoicing in hell that another life was wasted.

But in the midst of all of Satan's lies and his attempts to destroy you, Christ has come into your life to give you real life, and not just a way to survive. Christ wants to give you a great life here. It will be so great and so much better than what you have experienced that it is impossible for you to imagine it being so great. In fact, it is far beyond anything you could have dreamed of even on your best days. And this life that you can have right here won't just end here. It will continue right on into all of eternity, and it is for all of eternity that God wants you to be in heaven with Him—but not today. Someday—but not this day.

So you can listen to the sad and depressing voice of Satan telling you to give up and give in and end this whole thing right now. Or you can trust there is a God who is more powerful than Satan and who can help you out of your despair and lead you to the life that you always wanted to live. And to do that, all you have to do is persevere and hold on for one more day.

That is my interpretation of that verse. It is a verse of truth that gives insight as to how you got to be where you are. It is a verse of insight that tells you there is no need to give up. You can have a different life if you just persevere. Hebrews 10:36 says, "You need to persevere so that when you have done the will of God, you will receive what he has promised" (NIV). Another translation says that what He has promised is the crown of life. Notice that the verse does not say that you need to be perfect; you just need to hold on and persevere. You can do that right now, and if you need some help doing it, you can call 1-800-New-Life.

Another reason that I hope you will decide to persevere is so that you can see all of the wonder that God can bring from your life. Your desperate situation shows that you do not have it in you to make the changes you need to make. The God who made you does, so surrender to God and allow God to do what only He can do. Ask God to come alongside you and help you in ways you never dreamed you could be helped. Stay alive to watch Him unfold an amazing display of His power that will more than compensate for your weaknesses.

TOUGH REALITY

You may not be thinking of ending your life, but you might be thinking of running from your life. You have blended a quagmire of consequences, and you have no idea how to find freedom from what you have helped create. You are discovering that there is no quick fix and no instant solution. You don't talk or think about suicide, but you sure would like to run. You might like to run into the arms of someone who could give you instant affirmation and affection, or you might want to run into the world of drugs and alcohol-induced euphoria. God does not want you to run. God wants you to stay right where you are. He wants to work with you one day at a time to change your tough reality into a future of hope, healing, and purpose.

If you study the Scriptures, you find person after person and people after people making crummy decisions that end in death and destruction. You are not alone. God is used to people like you if you are the one who has masterminded what looks and feels like complete failure in your life. If that is the case, God knows your heart. He knows how you got yourself into that situation, and He knows how to get you out. Most likely there will be no quick fix, and in some cases there will be no fix. If you are in jail for mass murder, there is little chance that part of the fix is going to result in your walking the streets again. Within that jail, however, your healed soul can make a huge difference, and you can live with joy and peace.

There is most likely not going to be an instant solution. For many there may be no solution. Be realistic about what you expect to happen. If you spent years beating your wife, and she finally sought help and developed strength enough to leave you, there may be little chance that your marriage is going to survive. Be realistic about that as you humble yourself to do whatever you can to reestablish connection with her and assist her in healing her own heart. Pray for the miracle, but be realistic. God knows you and loves you in spite of the difficult circumstances you have created for yourself. He can help you in them, but be realistic about whether or not the circumstances will change. Then work on your soul so that it heals no matter what the circumstances.

The more realistic your expectations are about your tough reality, the easier it will be to develop a life that is fulfilling as you walk out of your destructive ways and into the healing ways of God. Don't let unrealistic expectations cause you added frustrations that lead to giving up. Do not give up. God is with you and wants to grow your character. The quick fix or instant solution does not do that. It takes work and time to heal your soul from the inside out. Character is never instant, and God often uses our circumstances to build it within us. Too often, just before the evidence of God's work shows up, the person has already given up. Don't let that be you. Continue to persevere—no matter how tough a bind you are in. Do not ever give up. No matter what, let this be the day you decide to continue one more day.

Too often, just before the evidence of God's work shows up,
the person has already given up. Don't let that be you.

A MATTER OF TRUST

As you look at your life, it may not make a lot of sense. You have some ideas about how it could all work so much better, but God does not seem to be viewing your plans or wanting to implement them either. When things seem so clear to you, it is hard to sit back and allow God to work in your life, but that is exactly what God wants you to do. Your way of doing things is not His way. What looks perfectly right and normal to you is anything but that to Him.

What God unfolds and the way He does it may seem foolish and even ridiculous to you, but I want to encourage you to trust God even though it does not seem to make sense to do so.

First Corinthians 1:26–29 gives some insight into this. God's "foolish" plan is far wiser that the wisest of human plans, and God's weakness is far stronger than the greatest of human strength:

> Remember, dear brothers and sisters, that few of you were wise in the world's eyes or powerful or wealthy when God called you. Instead, God chose things the world considers foolish in order to shame those who think they are wise. And he chose things that are powerless to shame those who are powerful. God chose things despised by the world, things counted as nothing at all, and used them to bring to nothing what the world considers important. As a result, no one can ever boast in the presence of God. (NLT)

So what does this mean to you? It means that if your circumstances make no sense to you or to those around you, perfect. If you cannot see any way out of your mess under your own power, perfect. If what looks wise and smart to you is not exactly what God seems to be doing, perfect. God has been making foolish things work for His good since the beginning of time. So don't give in to hopelessness; give in to God's miraculous plan and allow Him to unfold that plan right before your eyes.

So my question to you is one of trust. Will you trust Him? Will you trust Him enough to hang on one more day? Will you trust Him enough to make your foolish circumstances an example of how He can make the best of the worst situations? Will you trust Him enough to make the healing choice to persevere? Will you trust Him enough to live for Him even when healing is delayed? Will you trust Him enough to promote the healing of others while you make choices for your own healing? Before you can heal, you have to answer the question of trust.

I beg you to trust Him enough to persevere.

NOT ALONE IN DOUBTS

You may think God hates you or does not love you because of your doubts about His power or your doubts about whether He is really working in your life. You are not alone in those doubts. God is used to people with doubts. I sure had them. When I started walking around as a single divorced guy, full of pain and humiliation, I could not feel God's presence. I knew He was there, but it was a faint knowledge, and I landed in the middle of a huge faith crisis. The crisis was not about whether or not God existed, and the crisis was not about whether or not Jesus died on the cross to save me from my sin. The crisis was about whether God was involved in my life the way I had believed He was.

Every time something great happened to me or for me, I praised God and thanked Him. Women of Faith is a traveling conference I created to encourage women. They go to almost thirty cities every year. Over three million women have attended that conference. When Women of Faith succeeded and we passed the one million mark of women in attendance, I was so grateful. When the *Every Man's Battle* series took off and won awards, I felt God there and thanked Him. Almost every day as I appreciated the wonder of who Madeline was, I thanked Him. But in the center of the storm of divorce, I had a hard time believing He was there for me. He had done good things for me, and great things for me—why had He not prevented the bad? It was a real crisis, but I was not alone.

BACK TO GIDEON

Earlier in the chapter on serving I presented Gideon, the least likely candidate to be used by God. He was part of God's plan to bring down 135,000 warriors with only 300 men. But there is another part of the story that shows that Gideon is like you and me. He had his doubts also, and he shared them out loud. In the book of Judges, in the sixth chapter, an angel of the Lord comes to Gideon and tells him that the Lord is with him. In the thirteenth verse, Gideon makes this response: "Sir, if the LORD is with us, why has all this happened to us? And where are all the miracles our ancestors told us about?" (NLT).

It seems that Gideon had plenty of doubts, just like you and me. In the good times it was easier to believe. But when the miracles stop and all you have is the faint memories of good things, the faith and trust change. They did for Gideon and they did for me and they do for you. But as you know, the end of that story is one of great victory for Gideon. Even though he doubted, he kept on moving forward and had a willingness that brought him victory in the end.

God can handle your doubts in the bad times. He knows you and He knows human nature at large. Your doubts are not unexpected, so doubt, and share your doubts with Him. Doubt all you want, but don't give up. Question everything about your faith, but don't stop moving toward God while the questions are being answered. Persevere. Carry on. Move forward. Do all this as you continue to move toward a closer relationship with God.

The reality is, this is a tough world. Some very crummy things are going to happen that will cause you to question whether or not there is a God. From that first eating problem in the Garden until today, we have been living in a fallen world full of trouble. It is going to come. It is a reality you cannot shed or run from. Satan is in this fallen world, and it seems that the more you do for God, the more Satan would like to kill you and claim a great victory for the evil kingdom. His deceptions are amazing, and no one is immune to his influence.

Then there is this loving God who tests us and tempers us. God disciplines us as we discipline our children, because we love them and want a few negative consequences to shape and mold their behavior. He loves us too much to leave us alone, so He does not. He comes after us with things that make us tougher and gentler at the same time. He transforms the warrior into a great lover. He moves us, and many times that movement is tough, hard, and painful, because it is discipline intended to change our lives.

The other reason it is hard for us to live in this world is because we make mistakes that hurt others and ourselves. Sometimes we don't even know we are doing it. When it comes to the world's pain bank, we are frequent donors. If that is not bad enough, there are those who also make mistakes, but those mistakes hurt us and abuse us and neglect us. These individuals infect our minds with evil and invite us to resent them and question the existence of God. With all of these horrible things happening around us, it is no wonder we question if God exists and if He is involved with our lives while the horrible details of the real world mount up. So we doubt, but we are not alone.

Thomas was a doubter. A man who walked in the presence of Jesus and heard Him teach still doubted His existence after the resurrection. Peter was a doubter also. If he had not been, he would never have denied that he knew Jesus the first through the third times. These were men who walked with Jesus. There were others, and their decision to turn from Jesus is found in John 6:66. Don't you like the number combination? That verse says, "Many of his disciples turned away and deserted him" (NLT). They did not persevere.

Can you imagine being in the presence of Jesus and doubting and turning away? Would you have done the same thing? Even after watching thousands of people fed from a little boy's lunch of fish and bread, they still doubted. They witnessed a blind man see for the first time, but they doubted. They watched Lazarus get up and walk after being dead, and saw a small girl brought back to life. They watched Jesus walk on water, but they still doubted. If they could have done it while He walked the face of the earth, it is no wonder that we do it—we who have never seen Him. So—doubt. Doubt and question and search for the truth, but don't give up. Don't allow any influence from any source to keep you from doing the one thing you need to do for at least one more day—persevere.

Life is not easy. It is hard, and God knows it. He hurts with you and weeps with you. Hold on to Him, because He is holding on to you. Don't let your doubts rob you of His love. Don't let your questions destroy your relationship with the God of the universe. He can handle the questions and the doubts. Just don't use questions and doubts as an excuse to stop persevering.

IT REALLY WILL BE OKAY

When I am under severe stress or have just received bad news, I say to myself over and over again that it will all be okay. And I know that it will. I may not be able to pay my bills next month, but it will be okay. I may have a hard time with a new illness next month, but it will be okay. I may lose it all, but it will be okay. Knowing this and telling myself this helps me to persevere through all sorts of difficulties.

No matter what you are going through, it is going to be okay. In fact, it is going to be more than okay. If you persevere with God, through God's power He will make it more than okay and make it good for you.

Thomas Watson lived in the 1600s. Watson was a pastor who lived and ministered in London and was well respected by the great preacher Spurgeon. In the book *A Divine Cordial*, published in 1663, Watson wrote about bad things happening to good people.

Most of us realize that for a field to bring forth a bountiful harvest, the sod must be broken and the fields plowed up. The painful process of breaking up leads to life. Without the crumbling of the clods into fine rich soil, it would not yield much of a crop. We have no problem with understanding that there is a breaking that leads to the fulfillment of that field.

Yet we fight accepting that for ourselves. We are a field, and God needs to do some plowing there. If we allow Him, He will take the breaking of one lowly substance and transform it into the making of a great life for you—full of wisdom and understanding of others. Romans 8:28 tells us that "everything works together for the good of those who love the Lord and are called according to His name" (my paraphrase). If that is true, how does it happen?

The following are some thoughts from Thomas Watson that might help us understand how it happens. He called the negative stuff "affliction." He said that when we experience affliction, we come to understand what sin really is. We hear about sin and how horrible it is, but we do not fear it. So from time to time God will let loose affliction, and we will then be able to feel sin and know that it is horrible. A sick person lying on his or her back often learns more than someone listening to a sermon. As C. S. Lewis said, "Pain is at times God's megaphone to get through to us when other ways would do no good." When we are in pain, it helps to remember that it will all be okay. It will be, but it is going to hurt quite a bit in the meantime.

Bad times teach us about ourselves in ways that we would not know if times were only good. When times are good, we sail along, developing without our insight. With success and good things running through our minds, we seldom take the time to stop and evaluate ourselves. It is in the tough times that we come to know ourselves. The good and the bad and the ugly are revealed when we experience affliction and hard times.

When we are hurting and afflicted, we become more like Christ as we run out of all the other options other than the option to conform to the likeness of Christ. God's rod is not a metal beam. It is instead a pencil that He uses to draw a more lifelike image of Christ upon us. When we persevere through all of the heartache and pain, we become more like Him every day. We hate our pain and wish it was not there, but if we are to be like Christ, we will have to suffer as He did. His crown had thorns in it; all we want is roses. It is good for us to be like Christ, even though it hurts badly when we are suffering.

Afflictions actually become healing agents for us. They destroy the sin within us if we allow them to. Heat removes the dross from gold and the fiery darts of affliction heat up our souls and allow the bad and the sin to be poured away. They also heal us, because they get us unplugged and uprooted from this world. When we are in pain, we turn on what got us there. Just as you dig away the soil from the roots of a tree you would like to transplant, God digs away at our earthly comforts that keep us rooted in sin, disease, and the past.

Many times we harden our hearts to God and to others. Pain and suffering clear the way for comfort to come to us. John 16:20 says that our grief will turn to joy. God will take the dirty water of your life and turn it into a delicious wine. When we are without hope or out of our own power, we finally look up to God and receive His comfort and His healing balm. Paul sang from the heart while in prison. Watson said that God's rod had honey on the end of it. If we were to fly high all the time and never have to deal with pain and suffering to some degree, we would never soften and experience the comfort that only God can give.

Hard times and affliction work for our good because they amplify our work, publicize it, and magnify it. The world only looks briefly at those for whom everything has wonderfully worked out better than expected. It is those for whom things are not going so well who draw us in. We wonder what it must be like and we wonder what the outcome will be. The trauma of a person's life turns up the volume of it, and the obscure become the focus of attention.

We can also feel bigger than life because when we are struggling, God lowers Himself way down to notice us and help us. It magnifies us and helps us move on for one more day, knowing that God is paying attention, even though we are mere dust and ashes to Him.

Another reason to persevere in the midst of adversity and affliction is that they eventually will make us happy if we will stay grounded in God's Word and do the next right thing. Job 5:17 says,

"Blessed is the man whom God corrects" (NIV). These difficult times, and the discipline on top of them, bring us down to a lowly, humble state. We experience sanctification through them, and that brings us closer to God. In the good times we don't think we need anyone, and we don't act like it either. When we hit the wall of affliction, however, we come running back to God. The prodigal son did it and was happy to find that he was accepted back in, and even honored, after being so dishonorable. We wonder if God is with us, but in the depth of our grief and despair, we can feel noticed by God because we can feel God's comfort upon us.

Finally, these tough times make way for God's glory. When you persevere through them, you allow God to be glorified as people see God work in your life in spite of the hardship. And when you hang on to God through the tough times, you are able to testify that it is by God's power that you survived, persevered, and came out victorious on the other side.

> For momentary, light affliction is producing for us an eternal weight of glory far beyond all comparison. (2 Corinthians 4:17 NASB)

> These hard times are small potatoes compared to the coming good times, the lavish celebration prepared for us. (2 Corinthians 4:17 MSG)

God lays a dark background, and then, just when it can be made no darker, there is a stroke of light. A brushstroke of gold or silver covers the darkness and brings glory to God. You may be in the darkest part of your life, but do not despair. God is about to unleash His light upon it, and you will see His glory in it all. All of your sorrow and struggle and pain will be used for your good and

His glory. He will not waste a thing. So don't give up on God. Give up on some of your old ways, but do not give up on God.

GIVING UP THE OLD WAYS

Randall is an example of what it means to give up the old ways that have produced hopelessness and start to see and do things from an entirely different perspective. He described how he made a choice that led him out of hopelessness:

I had been married for more than twenty-two years, and for most of that time I had a lot of trouble pleasing my wife. No matter what I did, it seemed to be wrong. I tried to be apathetic, but deep down it hurt every time an action that was intended to please went ignored, or even worse, was met with contempt. The pain turned to anger, and I spent many nights alone in the church sanctuary arguing with God about why He would put me with a woman who seemed to care very little about me.

It was during one of these exchanges that I realized that I had been trying to please the wrong person. God needed to have total control of my life in order to heal me. Instead of trying to please God by doing whatever He wanted, I tried only to please my wife, who was always upset with me.

I was on my knees when I told God that I would do anything He wanted, no matter what it might be. If You want me to be a missionary to Africa, or to go into the slums to help the underprivileged, I will do it, is what I told Him. It was amazing how He took me at my word, and the Spirit began to change and heal me. The first thing I needed to focus on was not pleasing my wife, but pleasing Him by becoming the man He wanted me to be. That meant focusing on how to please Him.

At that time, I felt a leading to do everything I could to save the marriage and to begin by changing myself. All sorts of areas of my life began to crop up in my mind as areas that needed work. Although I felt bad about the sin in my life, I felt like God did not have contempt for me over it, but just wanted me to know that these areas needed work. I really felt His forgiveness, so much so that I was able to objectively look at myself and where I needed to change. It was amazing what a peace this brought to me, even though my wife was talking about divorce and how she never loved me.

Although these words hurt, I knew God loved me and had plans for me and that was all I needed. Somehow, through all this, she seemed more pleased with me even though that was not my aim. For a time, my marriage was reconciled. It was during this time while I focused on pleasing the Lord that God prepared and healed me. When my wife eventually divorced me, I was unhappy, but I knew I had done exactly what God wanted me to do. There was nothing more I could have done. There was a great feeling of peace in that, and I knew I had pleased God.

That may not sound like much of a success story because it all ended up in divorce. It is a success story because even in divorce Randall was hopeful, because he knew God was with him. Have you just been divorced? There is hope. Have you been diagnosed with a terminal illness? There is hope. Have you failed again to be successful over that addiction? There is hope. Turn your life over to God. Surrender to His power. Lie back in His arms and you will experience hope.

THE BIG LIE
"There is no hope for me."

The big lie you may have told yourself is that there is no hope for you or for change in the difficult relationship you find yourself in. The lie tells you that you have done everything possible you can do and it is time to throw in the towel and give up. If you were to back away and look at your situation from a different perspective, you might see things differently. What you have attempted to do may have produced little or no results and left you in this hopeless state, but what you have done may have been the opposite of what you need to do.

Your life is like a river, full of mystery and wonder, power and movement. It looks predictable and tame, but below the surface there are wild currents that can take you places you may not want to go. You may be out there on that river, paddling with all your might upstream. You have exhausted all your earthly power to fight the current to get someplace just up ahead that you have always wanted to go, someplace you believed held the key to your happiness and security. You have paddled and paddled out on that stream, and you have done it all alone. Others could have picked up an oar and helped out, but they did not. You have done it all yourself. After all that exhausting work, you are no closer to that place just up ahead and around the bend that could give you peace and happiness and the life you have always wanted.

In real life this paddling is what we call trying harder. Against all odds you have used every ounce of your strength to change your life and make things better. You have exerted more effort than you even imagined you could. No one could say that you have not worked on yourself or your relationship—you have given it all you've got. When it comes to paddling, you have become a world-class rower, but you are about to give up. The current is starting to win. It is stronger than ever, and your strength is starting to wane. Well, you can give up. In fact, the best thing you could do is give up. But how you give up and to whom you give up has a lot to do with whether or not you ever find the life you were called to live.

You see, as you were paddling upstream with that very strong current coming at you, you thought you were doing that noble and right thing. Your efforts looked good, and you had your sights on that place that you knew had everything you needed and wanted. That may not be true, however, and you may not ever know it unless you give up all that hard work. I invite you to do that and see what God has for you downstream.

I ask you to consider going with the flow. Stop the paddling that saps you of your strength and proves that you do not have it in you to fix your life. Instead, use your strength to guide the oar as a rudder. Use your power to find your place in the river as you travel to a spot downstream you never dreamed was where you needed to be. Give up and start to move with God's power and strength, and you may find there is tremendous hope. You may find that there is tremendous power you never knew existed, but it is all downstream, and you get to it by working with the river of life, the giver of life, rather than against.

Do not destroy your life over a big lie. You feel hopeless because you have been using your own power, not because there is no hope. You feel hopeless because you have been headed the wrong direction, not because there is no hope. You feel hopeless because you have cut yourself off from others who could help you and guide you, not because there is no hope. You feel hopeless because you have tried hard and tried even harder under your own power. You are not hopeless because there is no hope. There is hope for you, if you will just persevere long enough to find it.

TRYING HARDER

If you are tired of trying and want to give up, it makes perfect sense. Trying harder does not help a situation. If it did, you would have helped yourself long ago. Under your own power you cannot continue to run your life with efforts that never seem to work out or improve your situation, but you can persevere under the power of God. You have to surrender to Him for you to be able to experience that power.

Surrender to God; let Him do for you what you cannot do for yourself. Give up your ways and invite His ways. Ask for His strength and power, and He will gladly give it to you. Fall back into His arms. Fully give your life to Him. Trust that He is real, and watch Him show you that He is. Watch Him do through you and your pain things that would never have been accomplished otherwise. Do not give up in the midst of the suffering.

Two famous French painters, Renoir and Matisse, were quite good friends and spent time together sharing a portion of their lives with each other. They enjoyed each other's company, as they had the common bond of love of color, beauty, and painting. While Matisse painted freely with minimal health concerns, Renoir developed a very serious case of arthritis. It was so debilitating as it progressed that he was almost completely paralyzed by it. No matter how severe the pain, no matter how difficult that stroke, he continued to paint. Each brushstroke sent a streak of pain through him. He would wince and jerk as he applied the color to the canvas.

Matisse watched his friend with great concern and passion. He was mystified by the dedication and commitment that led to creating at such a painful level of personal sacrifice. One day he asked Renoir why he continued to paint with such distressing effort. Renoir replied, "Because the beauty remains: the pain passes." What a beautiful picture to all of us who are struggling in painful times.

I believe that God will create beauty from your ashes. There will be something of great value that will emerge out of your pain. And one day that pain is going to go away for good. You won't feel the pain, but you will be able to look back on your life and know you made a difference. You will no longer feel as you feel today. Replacing that pain will be a sense of fulfillment and purpose. Do not give up today. Allow God time to bring the beauty that only He can bring from a troubled and difficult life. Do not give up. There is beauty to be created from the painful episodes of your life.

If your life is riddled with pain, suffering, and struggle, please do not give up. Surrender and persevere. Let go while you hang on. Don't give up. Never stop believing. Do this one thing. Hang on to your God. Hang on to your faith, and hang on to your life. Do not throw it away. Make the healing choice to persevere and to do whatever you have to do to hang on one more day.

Healing is a choice. It is God's choice, but we have to continue to make healing choices if we are to experience the gifts that God has for us. The choice to persevere is never an easy one; it is only made by those who are tired of living life as before and finally want things to be different. Make a choice today to heal your life. Choose to persevere and never look back.

CHAPTER 10 WORKBOOK QUESTIONS

THE TENTH CHOICE:
The Choice to Persevere

THE TENTH BIG LIE:
"There is no hope for me."

DR. NORMAN VINCENT PEALE, IN A SERMON TITLED "Problems Are Good for You," told the following story.

A young woman stood before a crowd of thousands, watching in disbelief as Queen Elizabeth II approached to crown her the tennis champion of the world. It all seemed so unreal.

The young lady was born to a poor family. She lived on a ramshackle farm outside New York City and was very ill most of her early years. Her family survived on welfare. She had trouble in school and frequently ran away from home.

"But she had a persevering mother," said Peale, "who one day said to her, 'There's a stone down by the barn. Can you see it, dear?' Peering from the porch, the child recognized the potato-shaped stone. 'I want you to go down there,' her mother went on, 'and bring that stone up here so we can use it as a step by the kitchen door.'"

Sobbing, the child protested, "Mommy, I'm so weak I can hardly walk down there. I can't move the stone alone!" But her mother persevered. "You go down there, child, and if necessary, move it only half an inch at a time, but move it."

Inch by inch over the following days, the little girl did as she was asked, often with tears. It took her two months to do what normally healthy children her age could have done in fifteen minutes. But as she struggled with that stone, she lost her weakness and grew stronger. A few years later she took up tennis. It was a natural fit for her and she began winning tournaments. In time, she became a professional and played her way to the Wimbledon tennis courts, where in 1957, she became the first African-American woman to win both the singles and doubles championships there.

When she returned home to New York City, a ticker-tape parade was held in her honor. The once weak and troubled little girl was applauded by thousands of people standing on the streets to see her, Althea Gibson, one of the greatest tennis players of all time.[1]

Through perseverance and determination, Althea overcame a poor family environment, bad health, welfare, and prejudice. Her story is a testimony to the incredible power of perseverance.

THE TENTH CHOICE:
The Choice to Persevere

Wait. Be patient. Give it time. Persevere. These are words that frustrate more than encourage us. We live in a culture where things are expected to happen quickly. We want quick food, quick service, and quick healing.

Healing is a choice. It is God's choice. He chooses when and how quickly we will be healed. That fact flies in the face of our impatience.

More than anything, we want God to heal us now. We think, *If He would heal me right now, my pain would stop, and that would prove how much He cares for me. Others can have progressive healing; I want a miracle!*

Miracles are by definition rare, yet they do happen. We have every right to pray for miracles, but we must remember they are not the norm. Therefore, most people who suffer are not going to be healed miraculously. They may need medical treatment, medications, counseling, even hospitalization. It may require time and effort for them to be well. If the illness is chronic, they need to have a very large dose of perseverance.

THE TOUGHEST CHOICE

Perseverance is extraordinarily difficult to manage. It doesn't heal us. It just says, "Hang on," "Wait," and "Be patient." Persevering often feels as if nothing positive is happening. That's frustrating, because we crave instant healing.

We feel stuck in our illness. We're still not connected to others. We're grieving and still having trouble forgiving people.

But God is in the persevering. He is doing a healing work. We cannot heal ourselves, but we can make the healing choice to cooperate with God as He heals us. He asks us to have faith and not give up while healing is occurring.

Persevering is tough, but it is also beneficial. You may not enjoy the process, but it produces good fruit in our lives.

We wish we could avoid perseverance. But something marvelous happens to us during the process.

1. Read the text below:

We can rejoice, too, when we run into problems and trials, for we know that they help us develop endurance. And endurance develops strength of character, and character strengthens our confident hope of salvation. (Romans 5:3–4 NLT)

2. Paraphrase the text in your own words.

_____

_____

_____

_____

_____

_____

_____

_____

3. If you are studying in a small group, discuss your individual paraphrases together.

4. According to the earlier verse, what are the positive benefits of persevering?

_____

_____

_____

You can see that persevering is an important healing choice.

THE VALUE OF OUR LIVES TO GOD

You may think that your life is not worth much. Your self-esteem was damaged long ago and has not yet been rebuilt. You are persevering, but it's difficult to see any progress. You're tempted to think God has abandoned you.

It's important to remember that your feelings can tell you a direct lie. Human feelings are both fickle and very subjective, causing you to feel great one day and depressed the next. If you live each day based on how you feel, you may crash.

Feelings do not define you, nor should you allow them to control your life. What is necessary is to live life based on God's truth. What is God's truth about you?

Let's explore that.

1. We know God loves us and values our lives, but to what extent? Find Psalm 139:1–24 in your Bible and read it carefully. You may want to read it several times.

2. Identify the key statements in the chapter. These statements tell us something about how God relates to us.

3. Read the key statements below taken from Psalm 139. Think about each one. Meditate on its meaning for a few moments.

"You know everything about me."

"You know my every thought when far away."

"Every moment you know where I am."

"You know what I am going to say even before I say it."

"You place your hand of blessing on my head."

"I can never escape from your spirit!"

"Your strength will support me."

"You made all the delicate, inner parts of my body."

"Thank you for making me so wonderfully complex!"

"Your workmanship is marvelous."

"You watched me as I was being formed."

"Every day of my life was recorded in your book."

"How precious are your thoughts about me, O God."

"When I wake up in the morning, you are still with me."

"Search me, O God, and know my heart; test me and know my thoughts."

"Point out anything in me that offends you, and lead me along the path of everlasting life."

4. **In the spaces below, describe in your own words how these key statements speak to you about your value to God.**

_____

_____

_____

_____

5. **Take some time to offer a prayer of thanksgiving for the astonishing love and commitment God extends to you.**

All the wonderful things God said about you in Psalm 139 are exactly how He feels about you now, even while you are in the process of persevering. If you feel anxious and impatient while waiting for your healing, remember that He loves you very much, and never leaves or forsakes you. Persevere. He is with you.

Because God loves you, He doesn't just want you to survive; He wants you to experience the joy of living! God's prophet Isaiah said it this way: "To all who mourn in Israel, he will give a crown of beauty for ashes, a joyous blessing instead of mourning, festive praise instead of despair. In their righteousness, they will be like great oaks that the LORD planted has planted for his own glory" (Isaiah 61:3 NLT).

TOUGH REALITY

There are times, when persevering, that you get discouraged. You are only human. It feels like you can't take any more. You've waited and waited. You finally take two steps forward, only to take three steps back.

One day you sense that you might be healing, only to experience two days of misery. Healing seems like a distant promise.

You're losing confidence in persevering and wondering if other options might work quicker. There are plenty of false options awaiting you: drugs, illicit relationships, gambling, codependent friends, and more. However, you know that is not the answer.

All this is made worse because you feel a sense of guilt. Did you bring all this on yourself? Will you ever recover? How long can you persevere? Can you possibly heal?

Then reality hits you hard. There are no quick fixes or easy solutions. You can't take a shortcut. You would never consider taking your life, but you are very tempted to run for your life!

Will you run? Will you give up the healing process and succumb to some easy solution—one that will make you sicker?

No! You will face your tough reality and plow through it! God will give you the necessary strength. Jesus will persevere with you, because He promised never to leave or forsake you. The Holy Spirit will guide you, so make the tough choice to persevere. Now is not the time to run! If you run now, you run away from God's will. Instead, take the practical advice of Scripture, "Those who endure to the end will be saved" (Matthew 24:13 NLT). You have come too far in your healing to give up now. Christianity is a distance run, not a sprint. It takes patience and perseverance.

Confucius once told his students something very important. He said, "It does not matter how slowly you go, so long as you do not stop."

A MATTER OF TRUST

There is a human trait in us that begins working when we face problems and crises. That trait is the tendency to solve our own problems. We are wired to fix what isn't working properly. We're natural problem solvers. To be sure, some folks have not nurtured that trait as well as others, but it's still there in us.

Our problem-solving capacity is often hindered by our arrogance and naiveté. Problems arise and we think, *I'll take care of this. No problem!* In short order, we realize that we're in over our heads, and failing in our efforts to solve the problem.

At other times, problems arise and we think, *This is easy. Anybody could solve this!* Later, we find ourselves baffled by the perplexity of it.

We repeatedly fail at problem solving, yet we still hold to the notion that we can handle whatever challenges us!

We move stubbornly through life thinking we're in control and can manage our own lives, when most of the time we have very little control.

However, if *Healing Is a Choice* teaches us anything, it is that we don't manage our lives very well. We damage one another. We experience considerable failure. We tolerate lifelong pain with no real plan for recovery. Our problem-solving ability is not as good as we imagined.

The apostle Paul spoke to this issue in 1 Corinthians. Using paradoxical language, he quickly catches our attention. Let's look at the text in several translations:

1. **Read 1 Corinthians 1:25–29 in two or three translations of your choice. Include the New International Version.**

2. **Now, read the New Living Translation printed below:**

Remember, dear brothers and sisters, that few of you were wise in the world's eyes or powerful or wealthy when God called you. Instead, God chose things the world considers foolish in order to shame those who think they are wise. And he chose things that are powerless to shame those who are powerful. God chose things despised by the world, things counted as nothing at all, and used them to bring to nothing what the world considers important. As a result, no one can ever boast in the presence of God. (1 Corinthians 1:26–29)

Reading several translations gives you a good sense of the paradox Paul describes.

We imagine ourselves to be great problem solvers. We think we are smart, but what we consider smart, God often views as foolish. What God considers wise, we often view as foolish.

As mentioned in the introduction, a good biblical example is Naaman (2 Kings 5:1–14). He was a decent man who had been stricken with leprosy. King Aram loved him and sought help from the Israelite prophet Elisha. The prophet sent word to Naaman, instructing him to do something unexpected and seemingly foolish. Elisha's message was, "Go wash yourself seven times in the Jordan River, and you will be healed." Initially, Naaman was offended. It made no sense to him. Why bathe in the muddy Jordan, when two other beautiful rivers were accessible to him? It must have felt like an insult to a man of Naaman's stature.

However, God's ways are paradoxical and unexpected. When we think we're being smart, God says it's foolish. Naaman thought the instructions were foolish. God called it wisdom. Naaman swallowed his pride and dunked himself in the muddy little river, seven times!

It must have wounded his pride. How would his fellow soldiers and servants react? What would happen to his reputation when word reached home regarding this indignity?

Naaman thought it through very carefully. What if the prophet was right? What if he could be healed? Was Elisha's God that powerful? What if he bathed in the river and nothing happened?

In the end, Naaman made a powerful healing decision. He admitted to those around him, but mostly to himself, that he was ill and could not heal himself. He persevered. He didn't run for his horse and ride away angry. He may not have been thrilled with the prescription Elisha gave him, but he slowly squatted, lower and lower, until he was underwater. He came up. No change! He persevered. One down, six to go!

The seventh time up, he was healed. He rose above his pride and persevered.

Naaman's choice to trust Elisha's God was a bold step for a pagan soldier. He realized he was not in control of his life. His only option was to trust, risk, and persevere.

Healing is also a matter of trust for us. Like Naaman, we want it on our terms, but that is not likely to be the way we will be healed. Our healing will be on God's terms. It may not make sense to you. It may even seem foolish, but it will be genuine healing. Sometimes, it takes a great deal of perseverance to reach the place where God can heal us. As we said earlier, God is in the persevering. He is working all things out for your good. Will you trust Him, or will you struggle to work out your own solutions?

NOT ALONE IN DOUBTS

Some years ago, Os Guinness wrote a wonderful and challenging book titled *In Two Minds*.[2] The subject of the book was doubt.

Too many well-meaning Christians have been taught that doubt is synonymous with unbelief. Nothing could be further from the truth. Such teaching is particularly destructive to those struggling with healing.

God is never surprised or particularly offended by our doubts. Guinness suggested that doubt is the beginning of true faith. He also wrote, "In no way is the fact that we doubt a negative reflection on our faith."

He explained a great truth about doubt: "Doubt is not so much our problem as everybody's problem. It is not primarily a Christian problem, but a human problem."

The truth is that we all struggle with doubt, and God understands that struggle. To have doubt is not synonymous with denying our faith, but it is to acknowledge our humanity.

Many people in the Bible struggled with doubts of various kinds, but God did not reject them. Most of us struggle with doubt, and, thankfully, God does not reject us.

Remember the story of Gideon in chapter 9. Gideon was demoralized and asked the angel of the Lord, "If the Lord is with us, why has all this happened to us?" and, "Where are the miracles our ancestors told us about?" It would not be surprising to discover that most Christians have asked those two questions at some point in their lives. Many of the people mentioned in this book wrestle with those questions every day! "Why has this happened to me?" and, "Where are the miracles that could end my suffering?" In the absence of an answer, doubt is a normal human response.

Gideon had plenty of doubts, and probably a good supply of fears, but he went to battle. The point is that Gideon was not disqualified by God simply because he had some doubts. God is not afraid of our doubts. He is patient and understanding of our human struggles. As a result, we can persevere!

A wise person once offered this observation: "Show me a person with no doubts, and I will show you a person drowning in denial!" That is not great oratory, but it is great truth. To be human is to struggle with doubt to some degree.

The notion that doubt is "un-Christian" is particularly destructive, and even cruel for those who suffer.

Frankly, those who say they have no doubts are being arrogant. It is important to remember that Thomas, the disciple, was a doubter.

He spent three years in the presence of the Son of God, but after the Crucifixion, he doubted the resurrection.

Scripture reminds us that many of the disciples deserted Jesus. From our perspective, that's hard to imagine. We judge those men and think, *How could they?* Didn't they remember the miracles? Didn't they recall His words? How could they doubt? The truth is, they did just what you and I have done. They doubted!

Here is an important truth. The problem with doubt is not that we waver in our Christian fidelity. The problem is that it attacks our ability to persevere. Doubt is like a roadblock, stopping us smack in the middle of the road! It diverts our attention and hinders our progress.

Our goal is not to deny that we have doubts. Rather, it is to deal with them directly. We must acknowledge that we have doubt. The truth is that everybody has doubts of some sort, especially in times of weakness and pain. Having doubts is not an insurmountable barrier. Take the power out of doubts by diminishing them. Acknowledge it and move on. At all costs, persevere.

Please understand that your relationship with God is not predicated on doubts you may have. On the contrary, it is based entirely on the work of Jesus Christ on the cross for you!

The truth is graceful. You can trust in Christ even as you wrestle with doubts of various kinds, and that is not a contradiction in terms!

IT REALLY WILL BE OKAY

Life is sometimes a very difficult taskmaster. Consider what happens when there are problems or crises in our lives. Some event occurs, often a painful one. There is an outcome on the horizon. What we have to endure is the awful period between the event and the outcome. That period can be an excruciating, painful, anxiety-ridden time. We desperately yearn for resolution, but it is not to be. Each crisis has its own timeline.

We cannot speed it up or slow it down. So we wait and wring our hands worrying. We pace the floor. Then in its own good time the resolution comes. We breathe a sigh of relief. It's over. And, the best part is that it worked out okay. Everything is going to be all right.

How many hours do we spend worrying about things that work out fine in the end? Part of our pain and worry results from trying to figure things out ourselves. We want to control the outcome, but that will not happen. We lack that control.

On the other hand, the apostle Paul offered a way of dealing with these tough moments: "And we know that God causes everything to work together for the good of those who love God and are called according to his purpose for them" (Romans 8:28 NLT).

Between the events and the outcomes of life, we can trust that God is at work on our behalf. He is orchestrating the affairs of our lives so the outcomes will be for our good.

A believer's life does not unfold in a random way. It unfolds according to God's purposes. That is one of the most comforting truths in our lives. We are not alone. We are connected to Christ. He knows our pain, helps us face it, and is instrumental in our healing. He searches our hearts and helps us investigate our lives. He stands with us in our grief and strengthens us to make healing choices. He redeems our failures and gives us hope and the power to forgive.

Because God is attached to us, we know that regardless of what we face, everything really will be okay.

Even our pain and suffering are important, because they push us toward being okay. *Healing Is a Choice* reminds us: "Tough times make way for God's glory."

We all experience trouble, more often than we prefer. We worry about outcomes that result from the events in our lives. We hate the long, painful time between events and outcomes. But we know that God is with us, and "our present troubles are quite small and won't last very long. Yet they produce for us an immeasurably great glory that will last forever!" (2 Corinthians 4:17 NLT).

Our response is simple. We must persevere! Never give up! Never, never give up.

Keep trusting! Keep believing! Keep enduring! Keep persevering!

THE TENTH BIG LIE:
"There is no hope for me."

King David had the perfect response to the tenth big lie. He wrote, "But as for me, I will always have hope; I will praise you more and more" (Psalm 71:14 NIV).

The theme of this chapter is the choice to persevere. Our perseverance needs motivation to keep us moving forward. Hope motivates us to persevere. Hope inspires us to keep making healing choices.

The tenth lie is vicious and cruel. It says, "You're worthless." "You're not worth God's time or attention." "Give up; you'll never heal." "Don't pay any attention to this book; it's all a pipe dream." "You're being set up!"

That lie tempts you to give up and settle for a life of pain and defeat. If you believe the lie, you will lose ground you fought long and hard to gain. This lie will add more pain and misery to your life. Even if you are struggling to maintain hope, remember that God has confidence in you. Please, at all costs, reject this lie!

REVIEW AND ACTION PLAN

You made an important decision to read *Healing Is a Choice*. You have gained the information necessary for your growth and healing. However, you need to stay invested in the healing process. This last exercise asks you to evaluate where you are now and create an action plan to guide you in the months ahead.

THE FIRST CHOICE
The Choice to Connect Your Life

Check the one area below that best identifies where you are in the healing process now.

Still Struggling ____   Experiencing Success ____

Making Progress ____   Feeling the Healing ____

ACTION

During the next six months, I will connect with more people by:

a. _____

b. _____

c. _____

THE BIG LIE:
"All I need to heal is just God and me."

Explain why this is a lie.

_____

_____

_____

THE SECOND CHOICE
The Choice to Feel Your Life

Check the one area below that best identifies where you are in the healing process now.

Still Struggling ____   Experiencing Success ____

Making Progress ____   Feeling the Healing ____

ACTION

During the next six months, I will face the pains in my life, examine them, and deal with them by:

a. _____

b. _____

c. _____

THE BIG LIE:
"Real Christians should have a real peace in all circumstances."

Explain why this is a lie.

_____

_____

_____

THE THIRD CHOICE
The Choice to Investigate Your Life in Search of Truth

Check the one area below that best identifies where you are in the
healing process now.

Still Struggling ____   Experiencing Success ____

Making Progress ____   Feeling the Healing ____

ACTION

During the next six months, I will continue to investigate my life by:

a. _____

b. _____

c. _____

THE BIG LIE:
"It does no good to look back or look inside."

Explain why this is a lie.

_____

_____

_____

THE FOURTH CHOICE
The Choice to Heal Your Future

Check the one area below that best identifies where you are in the
healing process now.

Still Struggling ____   Experiencing Success ____

Making Progress ____   Feeling the Healing ____

ACTION

During the next six months, I will grieve the losses in my life, so that I can move boldly into the future by:

a. _____

b. _____

c. _____

THE BIG LIE:
"Time heals all wounds."

Explain why this is a lie.

_____

_____

_____

THE FIFTH CHOICE
The Choice to Help Your Life

Check the one area below that best identifies where you are in the healing process now.

Still Struggling ____   Experiencing Success ____

Making Progress ____   Feeling the Healing ____

ACTION

During the next six months, I will make choices that contribute to my healing by:

a. _____

b. _____

c. _____

THE BIG LIE:
"I can figure this out by myself."

Explain why this is a lie.

_____

_____

_____

THE SIXTH CHOICE
The Choice to Embrace Your Life

Check the one area below that best identifies where you are in the healing process now.

Still Struggling ____   Experiencing Success ____

Making Progress ____   Feeling the Healing ____

ACTION

During the next six months, I will embrace and value my life by:

a. _____

b. _____

c. _____

THE BIG LIE:
"If I just act as if there is no problem, it will finally go away."

Explain why this is a lie.

_____

_____

_____

THE SEVENTH CHOICE
The Choice to Forgive

Check the one area below that best identifies where you are in the healing process now.

Still Struggling ____   Experiencing Success ____

Making Progress ____   Feeling the Healing ____

ACTION

During the next six months, I will ask for forgiveness from people I have hurt, and forgive those who have hurt me, by:

a. _____

b. _____

c. _____

THE BIG LIE:
"Forgiveness is only for those who deserve it or earn it."

Explain why this is a lie.

_____

_____

_____

THE EIGHTH CHOICE
The Choice to Risk Your Life

Check the one area below that best identifies where you are in the healing process today.

Still Struggling _____   Experiencing Success _____

Making Progress _____   Feeling the Healing _____

ACTION

During the next six months, I will take these healing risks:

a. _____

b. _____

c. _____

THE BIG LIE:
"I must protect myself from any more pain."

Explain why this is a lie.

_____

_____

_____

THE NINTH CHOICE
The Choice to Serve

Check the one area below that best identifies where you are in the healing process today.

Still Struggling ＿＿＿　　　Experiencing Success ＿＿＿

Making Progress ＿＿＿　　　Feeling the Healing ＿＿＿

ACTION

During the next six months, I will find ways to serve others by:

a. ＿＿＿＿＿＿＿＿＿＿＿＿＿＿＿＿＿＿＿＿＿＿＿＿＿＿＿＿＿＿＿＿＿＿

b. ＿＿＿＿＿＿＿＿＿＿＿＿＿＿＿＿＿＿＿＿＿＿＿＿＿＿＿＿＿＿＿＿＿＿

c. ＿＿＿＿＿＿＿＿＿＿＿＿＿＿＿＿＿＿＿＿＿＿＿＿＿＿＿＿＿＿＿＿＿＿

THE BIG LIE:
"Until I am completely healed and strong, there
is no place for me to serve God."

Explain why this is a lie.

＿＿＿＿＿＿＿＿＿＿＿＿＿＿＿＿＿＿＿＿＿＿＿＿＿＿＿＿＿＿＿＿＿＿＿＿＿

＿＿＿＿＿＿＿＿＿＿＿＿＿＿＿＿＿＿＿＿＿＿＿＿＿＿＿＿＿＿＿＿＿＿＿＿＿

THE TENTH CHOICE
The Choice to Persevere

Check the one area below that best identifies where you are in the healing process today.

Still Struggling ____   Experiencing Success ____

Making Progress ____   Feeling the Healing ____

ACTION

During the next six months, I will commit myself to persevere in my healing efforts by:

_____

_____

_____

THE BIG LIE:
"There is no hope for me."

Explain why this is a lie.

_____

_____

_____

JOURNALING

You have made great progress in your healing journey. You have learned some important truths and gained valuable information from *Healing Is a Choice*. You have also faced some very dangerous lies that can undermine your healing. Now you have the opportunity to look back and measure your growth.

Use your journaling time to summarize your reactions to the book. Note its greatest strengths. List some of the things that you found most helpful. What information from the book will you share with others? Has reading the book changed you in significant ways? If so, how?

How has the Holy Spirit spoken to you during this study? Explain.

_____

_____

_____

_____

_____

_____

_____

PRAYER

God of Grace, Mercy, and Healing, I thank You for giving me this book, Healing Is a Choice. I have been challenged and changed by it. At times it has been hard to face the truth. Some hard choices remain in front of me. Through it all, I thank You for Your constant presence. You have never left me. You have given me reasons to have hope again. I have experienced the constant presence of the Holy Spirit, standing with me in this study. I will be healed, because You have shown me the way. How can I ever thank You? I don't have the words. But I will praise and worship You. You are the God who loves me, and I love You. Bless others, I pray, who have studied this book and learned these truths. Heal them as You are healing me. Forgive my sins and guide me by Your loving hand. Give me strength to persevere. Through Christ, my Rock and Salvation. Amen.

II

Final Thoughts on Healing

AT THIS MOMENT YOU HOLD WITHIN YOUR HAND SOME-
thing that no one can take away from you. Right now you hold
in your hand your future. This very second is the beginning of the
future you choose. You can choose a future that is burdened by an
unresolved past that clouds every day with sickness and confusion.
You can choose to cope with that pain with all of the different,
defective, and deficient ways you have chosen to numb the pain. Or
you can choose a different future right now in this moment. Right
now you can ask God to come into your life in a new way. You can
choose to live to please God and not yourself. You can choose to
live in His promises for healing rather than your history of brokenness. Your future is your choice. No one can take that from you.

There are going to be some difficult times ahead of you. You can
choose to be shocked by those or you can choose right now to accept
difficulty and pain and struggle as a part of life. You can choose to
prepare yourself for those difficult times ahead by healing the difficult times you have experienced in the past. Today is your day, and
you can use it to build the future you always dreamed of. You can
make a difference in this world. You are not the exception. Your
body may not heal, but your soul can. Your mind may always be a
little off center, but your soul can be centered on God's healing grace.

I am begging you as a brother who loves you not to let anything stand in your way of healing. Let no man rob you of your joy. Let no woman take away the peace that is so divine it is difficult to understand. There is no excuse good enough to lead a life less than you were called by God to lead. Heal through God's power. Believe that He loves you and wants to help you out of whatever you have been struggling with. Accept the reality of pain, but invite God to use it to help you and help others. I beg you to make one healing choice today so that someday you will be inviting someone else who is where you are today to walk the path you are walking toward healing. I am asking you to give up your life as you know it so that you can find your life that God has for you. Take hold of your future today and make the choices that will lead to your healing.

A FINAL CHALLENGE

I have challenged you to make ten significant choices in your life, and these choices will reconnect you with God and others in the healing process. Now I am closing out this book with a final challenge to you. This challenge does not replace the other ten, but I believe it will help you in making the most of each one of those choices. If you accept this final challenge, I believe it will change your life forever. It has already changed thousands. I believe it will implant in your heart and soul the words you need to persevere on the path to healing. I believe it can change the way you think about yourself and the way you think about life. It will take less than five minutes a day, but it could change the rest of your day. I am challenging you to read the affirmation, "Today I Choose to Heal," at the end of this book, every day for forty days. Throughout Scripture *forty days* pops up over and over again. It is significant to me that Jesus fasted and prayed for forty days and forty nights. So I am going to ask you to start your day, each day, for forty days by reading the following words out loud in some quiet corner of your world:

OPENING PRAYER

Lord, I am broken and hurting due to the brokenness of others and mistakes of my own. Please use Your powers to heal me and give me courage to make the choices I need to make to allow Your healing in my life. Forgive me for standing in Your way of healing for me. Thank You for allowing my past to end one second ago, and my future to begin right now in this moment with You.

AFFIRMATION:
Today I Choose to Heal

Today I choose to heal.
My healing begins right now, in this moment.
I am no longer bound by my sick past.
There is healing in my future.
For the next twenty-four hours, I choose to live free and heal.
I choose to let go of past hurts that I cannot undo.
I choose to forgive myself for wrong choices in the past.
Today I will dwell on what is good and right, not on the
    darkness I have experienced or on the darkness others
    invite me to live in.

Today I will live beyond myself and live for God.

On this day I will choose to feel my life rather than live in denial.

I will not medicate away my pain, sorrow, or anxiety.

I will allow each negative feeling to lead me to greater depths of healing.

I will not drown out or ignore my negative emotions.

I will work through these feelings and move out of them.

I will not project them onto those around me.

When I am unaware of what choice to make next, I will choose to do the next right thing.

Today I will not hide or run away.

I will connect with those who love me and with those who need my love.

Throughout this day I will stay connected to God and ask Him to guide me and lead me.

Today will be an adventure for me.

I will take a risk and enjoy the unpredictable.

I will not be governed by my fears.

I will choose to do something uncomfortable that might lead me to know the truth about myself or live life to the fullest.

I will not lie to myself today.

I will seek the truth and will ask for help when I need it.

Today I will reestablish some boundaries that will protect me from unhealthy people and unhealthy situations.

I will tear down some walls that are keeping some wonderful people from knowing me and loving me.

If there is some ungrieved loss, I will grieve it as much as I can today and then put it away.

Today I will choose reality and embrace it.

I will accept my life and pick up my life right where it is.

I refuse to wallow in self-pity.

I will not focus on what I do not have or what might have been.

On this day I will not give up.

No matter how difficult the struggle, I choose to persevere.

I will not let any excuse be strong enough to derail my path to healing.

I will never give up or give in to an old life that did not serve me well.

I will allow no one to discourage me.

Today I will heal and rely on God to deliver me through the choices I make.

Today I will allow God to control my life, and each choice I make, I will make with God in mind and love in my heart.

On this day, I choose healing.

I will do what I can do to heal and accept the limitations God has placed before me.

I will see every limitation I encounter as an invitation by God to do for me what I cannot do for myself.

I will accept that healing is sometimes slow and delayed and will grow in character in the meantime.

Today I will step outside of myself and serve others.

I will find a need and fill it.

I will find the hurt of another and help heal it.

I will not become self-absorbed or filled with self-obsession.

I will reach out to someone in need and do what I can to meet that need.

Today I will ask for God's help to live out His purpose.

Today I will live for God and not myself.

Today I choose to live.

Today I choose to love.

Today I choose to heal.

If you take my forty-day challenge, I would like to hear from you.

I would like to hear about your life before you took the challenge, while you were doing it, and afterward. Did it lead you to make healing choices? Let me know with an e-mail to SArterburn@ newlife.com. I may not know you personally, but this will give me a glimpse of your life. Please know that I am loving you and praying for God to bless you with new levels of healing for you and for your relationships.

NOTES

Chapter 2

1. Russ Bynum, "Girl Can't Tell Her Parents Where It Hurts," *The Orange County Register*, Saturday, 6 November 2004, News section, 27.
2. *The American Heritage® Dictionary of the English Language*, Fourth Edition. Copyright © 2000 by Houghton Mifflin Company. Published by Houghton Mifflin Company. All rights reserved.

Chapter 4

1. William Shakespeare, *The Tempest* (Antonio at II, i).

Chapter 5

1. W. W. Norton, *Norton Anthology of English Literature*, 5th Ed., "Devotions Upon Emergent Occasions," Meditation 17, 1962, Vol. 1, 1107.

Chapter 7

1. Jerry Adler and Jordana Lewis, "Forgive and Let Live," *Newsweek,* September 27, 2004, 52.
2. Charlotte van Oyen Wityliet.
3. American Heritage® Dictionary.
4. K. A. Lawler, J. W. Younger, R. L. Piferi, et al. "A Change of Heart: Cardiovascular Correlates of Forgiveness in Response to Cardiovascular Fitness," *Journal of Behavioral Medicine*, October 2003:26(5), 373–93.

Chapter 8

1. L. Frank Baum, *The Wonderful World of Oz* (Chicago: George M. Hill, 1900).

Chapter 9

1. "Healing Hands," *The Orange County Register*, 28 November 2004, Local News, 1.

2. Ruth Bell Graham, *Legacy of a Pack Rat* (Nashville: Thomas Nelson, 1994).
3. Richard Foster, *Celebration of Discipline* (Harper: San Francisco, 1988), 113.
4. Henri Nouwen, *The Wounded Healer* (New York: Random House, 1979).

Chapter 10

1. Thomas E. Dipko, "Believing Against the Odds," *Clergy Journal.*
2. Os Guinness, *In Two Minds* (Downers' Grove, IL: InterVarsity Press, 1976), 39–40.

ABOUT THE AUTHOR

STEPHEN ARTERBURN IS THE HOST OF *NEW LIFE LIVE!*, A radio and television program distributed across the country. He is a best-selling author with more than eight million books in print. He is also the founder of Women of Faith®, a conference attended by more than four million women since its inception. Steve also serves as the teaching pastor of Heartland Church in Indianapolis, Indiana.

If you have a question or a comment for Steve, you can contact him at SArterburn@newlife.com.

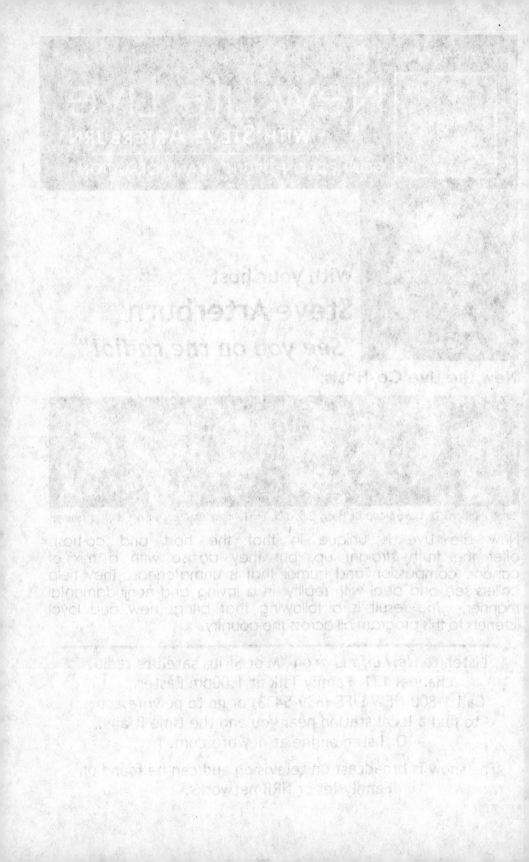

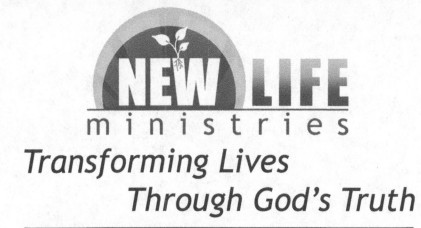

Transforming Lives
Through God's Truth

New Life Ministries is a non profit organization, founded by author and speaker, Stephen Arterburn. Our mission is to identify and compassionately respond to the needs of those seeking healing and restoration through God's truth.

New Life's ministry of healing and transformation includes:

- *A daily call-in radio and TV program, New Life Live!*
- *A nationwide counseling network*
- *Life changing weekend workshops*
    Healing Is a Choice Weekend
    Every Man's Battle
    Lose It for Life Weekend
- *Group Coaching*
- *Treatment for Drug and Alcohol addiction*
- *Books, CDs, Podcasts and others resources*
- *National Call Center manned 365 days a year*

For more information
call 1-800-NEW-LIFE (639-5433) or
visit newlife.com